Lecture Notes in Compute

T0230227

Commenced Publication in 1973
Founding and Former Series Editors:
Gerhard Goos, Juris Hartmanis, and Jan van Leeuwen

Mario Jeckle Ryszard Kowalczyk
Peter Braun (Eds.)

Grid Services Engineering and Management

First International Conference, GSEM 2004
Erfurt, Germany, September 27-30, 2004
Proceedings

Springer

Volume Editors

Mario Jeckle
FH Furtwangen
Robert-Gerwig-Platz 1, 78120 Furtwangen, Germany
E-mail: mario@jeckle.de

Ryszard Kowalczyk
Peter Braun
Swinburne University of Technology
John Street, Hawthorn, Victoria 3122, Australia
E-mail: {r.kowalczyk/pbraun}@it.swin.edu.au

Library of Congress Control Number: 2004112845

CR Subject Classification (1998): H.4, H.3, D.2, H.2, C.2.4, I.2.11

ISSN 0302-9743
ISBN 3-540-23301-6 Springer Berlin Heidelberg New York

Springer is a part of Springer Science+Business Media

springeronline.com

Printed in Germany

Typesetting: Camera-ready by author, data conversion by Olgun Computergrafik
Printed on acid-free paper SPIN: 11322931 06/3142 5 4 3 2 1 0

Preface

This volume consists of the proceedings of the 1st International Conference on Grid Services Engineering and Management (GSEM 2004) that was held in conjunction with the 5th International Conference Net.ObjectDays 2004 (NODE 2004) and the European Conference on Web Services 2004 (ECOWS 2004) in Erfurt, Germany on 27–30 September 2004.

The Grid has emerged as a global platform to support on-demand virtual organizations for coordinated sharing of distributed data, applications and processes. Service orientation of the Grid also makes it a promising platform for seamless and dynamic development, integration and deployment of service-oriented applications. The application components can be discovered, composed and delivered within a Grid of services, which are loosely coupled to create dynamic business processes and agile applications spanning organizations and computing platforms. The technologies contributing to such grids of services include Web services, the semantic Web, grid computing, component software and agent technologies.

The GSEM 2004 conference provided an international forum for presenting the latest theoretical and practical results in technology solutions for engineering and management of Grid services and service-oriented applications. The conference aimed at bringing together researchers and practitioners from diverse fields and interests, including Web services, the semantic Web, Grid infrastructures, software components, workflows, agent technologies and service management, and those looking for new business and research cooperation opportunities in the area of Grid services and service-oriented applications.

These proceedings present the 11 best papers accepted at GSEM 2004 as a result of the thorough peer-review process. More than 21 submissions were reviewed by at least three members of the international program committee and assessed by the conference chairs. The final acceptance decisions were based on the technical merits and quality of the submissions. The papers selected for presentation at the conference represent some of the most interesting latest developments in the areas of architecture, composition, security and management of Grid services.

We would like to take this opportunity to thank all the members of the International Program Committee for their excellent work, effort and support in ensuring the high-quality program and successful outcome of the GSEM 2004 conference. We would also like to thank the organizers of Net.ObjectDays in Erfurt, and especially its chair, Prof. Rainer Unland, for their help and the support provided to GSEM 2004. Finally, our thanks go to Springer for its cooperation and help in putting this volume together.

Mario Jeckle
Ryszard Kowalczyk
Peter Braun

On behalf of the Organizing and Program Committees of the GSEM 2004 conference we would like to dedicate this conference to the memory of its co-chair and our dear colleague Prof. Mario Jeckle, who prematurely died in a tragic car accident before the conference.

September 2004

Ryszard Kowalczyk
Peter Braun

Organization

Conference Chairs

Mario Jeckle	University of Applied Sciences Furtwangen, Germany
Ryszard Kowalczyk	Swinburne University of Technology, Australia

Organizing Committee

Peter Braun	Swinburne University of Technology, Australia
Bogdan Franczyk	Leipzig University, Germany
Holger Krause	tranSIT GmbH, Germany

International Program Committee

S. Ambroszkiewicz (Polish Academy of Sciences, Poland)
P. Braun (Swinburne University of Technology, Australia)
J. de Bruijn (University of Innsbruck, Austria)
B. Burg (HP, USA)
R. Buyya (University of Melbourne, Australia)
F. Casati (HP Labs, USA)
J. Debenham (University of Technology, Sydney, Australia)
F. Dignum (Utrecht University, Netherlands)
D. Fensel (DERI, Austria)
I. Foster (Argonne National Laboratory, USA)
B. Franczyk (Leipzig University, Germany)
M. Grigg (DSTO, Australia)
J. Han (Swinburne University of Technology, Australia)
Y. Han (Chinese Academy of Sciences, China)
M. Himsolt (DaimlerChrysler Research, Germany)
Y. Huang (IBM T.J. Watson Research Center, USA)
M. Jeckle (University of Applied Sciences Furtwangen, Germany)
C. Kesselman (University of Southern California, USA)
R. Kowalczyk (Swinburne University of Technology, Australia)
J.P. Martin-Flatin (CERN, Switzerland)
J. Noll (Telenor, Norway)
A. Polze (HPI, Germany)
C. Preist (HP Labs, UK)
J. Rodriguez-Aguilar (iSOCO Lab, Spain)
M.-C. Shan (HP Labs, USA)
K.M. Sim (Chinese University of Hong Kong, P.R. China)
B. Spencer (NRC, Canada)

S. Staab (University of Karlsruhe, Germany)
M. Stroebel (BMW, Germany)
H. Tianfield (Glasgow Caledonian University, UK)
R. Unland (University of Duisburg-Essen, Germany)
T. van Do (Telenor, Norway)
J. Veijalainen (University of Jyväskylä, Finland)
M. Weske (Hasso-Plattner-Institut/Potsdam University, Germany)
J. Yang (Swinburne University of Technology, Australia)
Y. Yang (Swinburne University of Technology, Australia)
L.J. Zhang (IBM, USA)

Table of Contents

Architecture

Composition

Security

Management

Using Web Services Architecture in a Grid Infrastructure: An Early Implementation of Web Services Actors, Programming a Grid Application to Access Astronomical Databases

Serena Pastore

INAF, National Institute for Astrophysics, Astronomical Observatory of Padova
Vicolo Osservatorio 5, 35122, Padova, Italy
pastore@pd.astro.it

Abstract. The grid paradigm is an useful technique in the astronomical community to enable the information discovery with a very large amount of massive and complex data. Astronomical datasets are essentially structured in catalogs and archives managed by several database management systems. Porting these data in a grid environment has twofold aspects according to put or not the entire management system on grid: this paper presents an approach of a grid application deploy based on web services technology to access an existing astronomical database. The framework hosting the application consists of the grid infrastructure provided by the Italian INFN Institute [1]: this middleware affects both technological choices than current and further develops in order to maintain the compatibility. The document covers the implementation design in this context of all the actors involved in the web service architecture (service requestor, service provider and service broker) and the mapping with their corresponding grid components. This relation gives the interoperability of web services within the existing grid architecture. It is detailed point out the open problem of service discovery in this grid environment: the current implementation of service registry through WS-Inspection documents [2] and/or Universal Description, Discovery and Integration [3] registry could be adopted in a local grid infrastructure, but should be progressively integrated with the main grid information system up to now implemented as Globus Monitoring and Discovery Service (MDS2) [4].

1 Astronomical Data Resources in a Virtual Organization Environment

According to the definition of the grid concept [5], a grid solution is created to allows applications to share data and resources as well to access them across multiple organizations in an efficient way. Each solution can be configured as a physical grid referring to hardware resources shared over a distributed network or as a logical grid referring to software and application sharing. In a research environment such as the astronomical community, one of the key concerns is to find more standard and scalable way to integrate massive and complex data coming from digital survey in a distributed environment.

This data has an exponential growth that causes the problem of information discovery with such amount of data. In this context the grid paradigm is a technique able

M. Jeckle, R. Kowalczyk, and P. Braun (Eds.): GSEM 2004, LNCS 3270, pp. 1–14, 2004.

to share and access the existing data resources (the astronomical datasets) located worldwide representing any kind of astronomical data available such as catalogues, archives, images, spectra, etc. Specifically archives and catalogues must be integrated in grid, since they represent two approaches to store information: archives contain collection of observational data (i.e. images from which data are extracted for further elaboration), while catalogues contain observational results (specific information about objects in the sky). Each dataset has its own set of metadata stored in a custom format and related to the original data in several ways. In general, each data source uses a different database management system paradigm (RDBMS, ODBMS, ORDBMS): querying this aggregation of data sources should be easier if the systems could be accessed through a common standard interface.

In grid view the data are located on several Virtual Organizations [5] in which the distributed researchers could be structured to better share the information. The concept to do "data-intensive" science is do not move data over the net, but bring the compilation to data.

The problem of enabling the porting in grid of astronomical data resources could be view from twofold sides relating to the need to put or not catalogues or archives systems on grid:

- the first solution aims at the porting on the grid of the data source containers: this implies to model the entire database management system and so the engine below as grid resource (such as the other modelled resources of computing and storage);
- the second solution leaves the DBMS outside the grid and aims to develop web services to connect to the database, making a sets of complex queries to data stored on them

The first solution is strictly linked to the entire grid infrastructure and the standards adopted; using some existent project of integrating databases in a grid environment, such as those provided by the GGF DAIS [6] working group is unluckily premature.

This paper reports the work done examining the second approach: programming a grid application able to do queries to a catalogue managed by a database system and located outside the production grid. The queries results to be retrieved could be stored in a grid machine for further elaboration.

The two solutions are yet not exclusive, since they are two different ways to offer shared services to the astronomical virtual organizations.

After a brief description of the grid infrastructure on which the grid application has been developed (section 2), and the relationships between web services model and grid computing (section 3), the document presents an approach to mapping the web services actors - service providers, service requestor and service registry - to their corresponding grid components (section 4) in the context of accessing astronomical databases. The paper finally deals with the open problem of service discovery (section 5): the use of current web service specification of this component (using WS-Inspection documents or UDDI registry) could be necessary integrated with the existent grid information system based on Globus MDS2 [4]. This is the only way with which grid users could discover these data like the other shared resources.

2 Framework of the Grid Application

The design of this grid application aims, as first step, at providing in a grid environment some "query facilities" on existing large catalogues managed by RDBMS. The goal is to create a building block for a more complex application. The overall system is strictly tied to the grid infrastructure in which the application has to be deployed and should be perfectly integrated in future. The running environment consists of the Italian prototypal INFN production grid [1], a testbed that up to now comprises 18 sites connected using the GARR networks [7] and joins 13 different Virtual Organizations gathering collections of individuals and institutions of several research fields sharing resources.

The framework is based upon the INFN-GRID release 2.0.0 [8], a customized software by INFN within the Italian grid project. The infrastructure is built on top of the LHC Common environment (LCG-2) [9] and the European Data Grid (EDG2) middleware [10]. LCG-2 itself is a selection of services derived from Globus [11] and Condor [12] projects and a collections of packages from the European DataTag (EDT) [13] and Virtual Data Toolkit [14] projects.

As far as software implementation is concerned, this middleware uses an "adapted" version of the Globus Toolkit 2.4 provided by VTD; this version of the Globus Toolkit is not based upon grid services and the implementation of an Open Grid Service Architecture (OGSA) [15] model. INFN-GRID by its VOs offers the main grid functionalities ranging from security to data and resource management, information service, monitoring and logging and a collections of grid resources (computation and storage). In the analyzed context, the grid information service is based upon Globus MDS [4] and an information index provided by the Berkely Database Information Index (BDII) [16] to guarantee the dynamic nature of the grid. Both job management through the EDG-WMS (Workload Management System) [17] and data management services through EDG-RMS (Replica Management System) [18] are derived from the EDG project.

The technological choice, according to the constraints originated by this framework, is based on web services architecture. This essentially because web services are one of the most widely adopted and stable architecture for developing distributed applications. Programming plain web services for the application in this environment is mandatory, since the used INFN-GRID infrastructure does not still support grid services: but this solution theoretically maintains the possibility to follow OGSA evolution with the current definition of grid services as an extension for web services specified by OGSI [19] or applying the new WS-Resource framework [20] proposed by Globus and IBM.

3 Integrate Web Services Models and the Grid Computing

Since a web service is a service available over a network as a software system designed to support interoperable machine-to-machine interaction, its technology is suitable to build distributed application such as whose ones running in a grid environment.

The known advantages to choose web services against other technologies are their platform and language independency due to the use of XML based information interchange which gives the interoperability with several systems; on the other hand, overhead and lack of versatility can represent a source of troubles. Generally the key characteristic is that web services are suitable for loosely coupled distributed systems where a client may have no prior knowledge of a web service until it actually invokes it and they could be implemented with several programming languages. The web service shows an interface described in a machine-processable format (specifically the Web Service Description Language (WSDL) [21]) that is network-addressable: the other systems interact with it in a manner shown in its description via standard protocols and data formats with SOAP-messages [22].

The service should be deployed in an runtime environment, such as the application container, that provides a message processing facility and could receive messages from requestors.The web service architecture, specified by W3C consortium as a service oriented ones [23], permits the interaction of three entity:

1. a service provider that offers its web services described in a standard way (such as WSDL).
2. a service requestor that requests a service through SOAP messages (over HTTP/ HTTPS).
3. a service broker that registers and publishes the list of services (through standards like WSIL [2] or UDDI [3]).

The three primary roles of the web service architecture interact using publish, find and bind operations: in a grid infrastructure they should be mapped to their corresponding grid components in order to permit the use of grid application based on this technology.

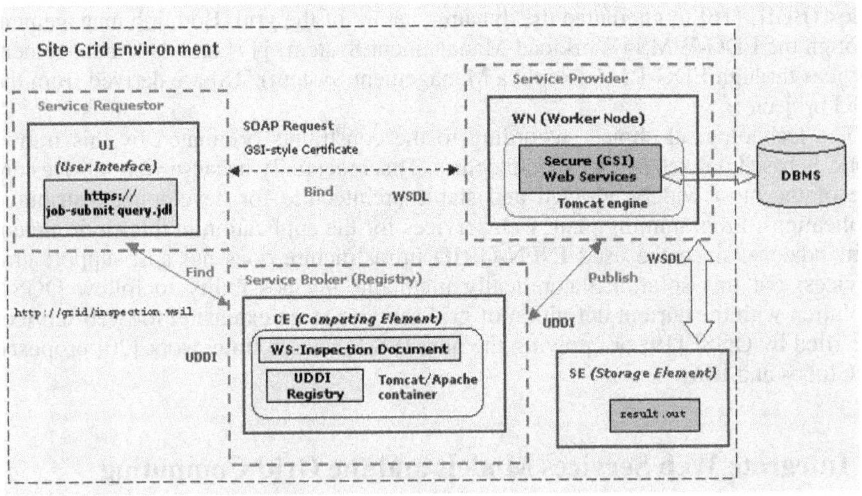

Fig. 1. Web services components and grid actors within a "site grid environment".

Web services and grid actors involved in the integration are described in figure 1: the shown components are the ones representing the minimum set of resources (the so-called "Quantum Grid") required to a site to be attached to the production grid according to its architecture [24].

The building blocks of a typical grid site are four elements: a User Interface (UI), a Computing Element (CE), a Worker Node (WN) and a Storage Element (SE).

Essentially while UI is the access point for a user to the grid, CE and SE are the main site grid resources: CE provides both an interface to an homogeneous farm of computing nodes called WNs as a jobs management and scheduling component, while SE offers an uniform access and services to the storage.

In all these machines the module-specific grid middleware software is installed to guarantee their functionality as grid nodes.

These are the only grid actors with which a grid application developer could directly interact, since they are deployed in the site grid infrastructure of the VO.

All high-level grid services such as the resource broker and the other general components (GSI [25] security, data and resource management and the grid information, monitoring and logging services) are directly provided in a centralized manner and managed by the INFN grid middleware developers. So analyzing the site web services actors, their roles are carry out by UI, WN and CE grid nodes.

The service requestor is essentially a grid client using a UI to access the grid and its resources: the client authenticates itself with a X.509 certificate and it is authorized to use the resources as affiliated to a specified VO.

The service provider is located on the WN, the grid node that actually execute the code, while the service broker is, up to now, located on the CE. The application output could be store on a SE and further replicated (through the Replica Manager System [18]) on other grid nodes to guarantee the reliability.

In this environment the CE together with the SE are the only site components that are visible by the whole grid: even if the web services are actually deployed on one or more WNs, it is the CE that has to execute the client application and knows where to locate the endpoints of the web service.

The binding between UI and WN in this context could be effectively realized, since as far as the WMS is designed, the client query application should be sent as job to the central resource broker: this grid component queries the Information system to find the most suitable CE where to execute the job and the Replica Manager for the management of the input/output file required by the job (as the figure 2 shown).

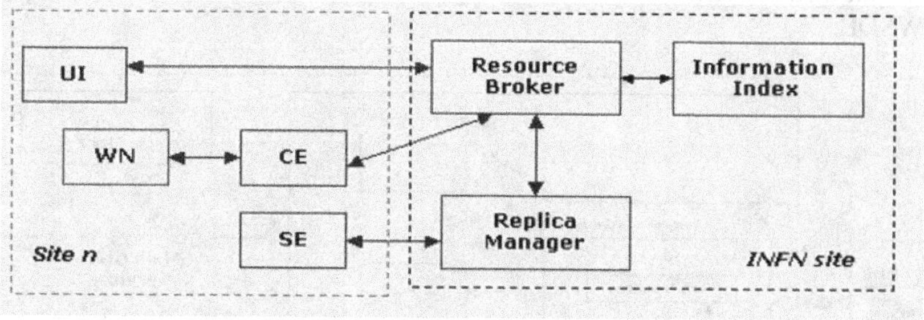

Fig. 2. The main relationships between main grid services provided by INFN site and a specific grid site.

The CE, in turn, dispatches job on the WNs it controls. From a grid client point of view CE is the real service provider. This approach could be overridden using a web browser instead of the command line language to access the application as better explained in section 4.2.

In the same way, the CE should initially be modelled as entry point of web services discovery: the implementation in this node of any type of web service discovery (through WS-Inspection documents or UDDI registry) is mandatory until the main grid information systems will be able to provide such a mechanism for the grid users.

4 Deployment of the Application in the Site Grid Environment

The detailed implementation of the three components of web services model in this site grid environment are explain below. Considering the constraints due to grid middleware and the need to use software packages totally compliant with it to avoid conflicts, the query services have been developed as java web services. It has been used all the available toolkits for develop web service with the java programming language such as those provided by Apache Software Foundation [26].

4.1 The Service Provider: The Web Services Offering "Query Services" Through the Grid

The grid application prototype provides a set of basic services roughly classified as "query services" to the retrieval of data sets from a specific catalogue matching fixed query parameters. The catalogues are stored in MySQL [27] database management system in order to allow the use of available connector drivers to integrate and customize database applications.

The client application should permit the user to select the data source where the information needed is presumably stored, to make a detailed query based on the data source type and to retrieve the results in a format based on XML for further analysis or elaboration. According to the method used by grid client to interact with the web services, the output could be store on a selected storage element.

The web services, as the figure 3 shown, offered by the "service provider" are structured to accept:

- as input a SQL query or the request of the service description as standard WSDL interface;
- as output a file in XML format according to the request or the service description as WSDL.

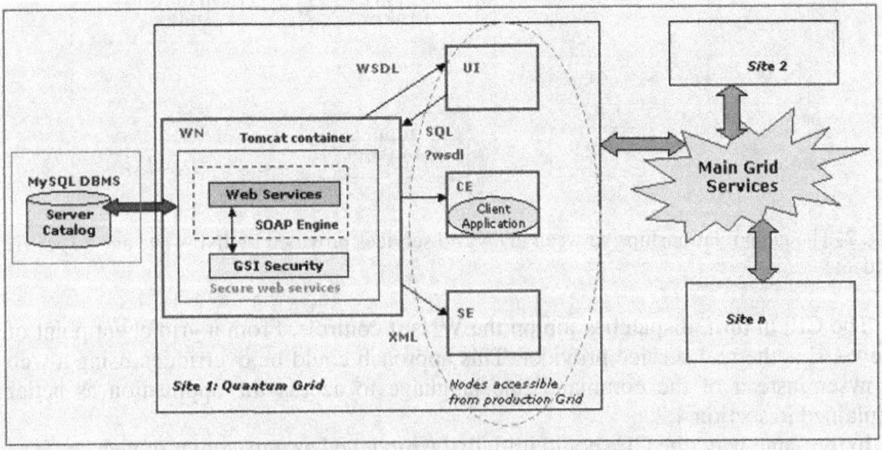

Fig. 3. Input and output of the web services deployed in the WN node and accessed through the other grid components within the main grid.

Since the web service is a software component that performs some functions, it has been deployed within the runtime environment hosted in the WN provided by the Apache Tomcat 4 [28] web application server.

The runtime environment is responsible for executing the code of the web services and for dispatching messages to them: it also provides other quality of services such as security. The connection to the database is provided by the use of MySQL Connector/J driver [29] that is able to convert JDBC (Java Database Connectivity) calls into the network protocol used by MySQL database.

Interacting with a database management system, Tomcat 4 engine guarantees also the efficiency of database connections, by the use of the connection pooling for JDBC provided by the Jakarta-Common DBCP [30]. These components are customized to prevent database connection pool leaks configuring the JNDI DataSource in Tomcat configuration file and in the description file of the web services deployed.

The tools used to develop the java web service available in the INFN-GRID middleware as rpm packages include:

- as deployed environment: Apache Tomcat as the container to provide web services and Apache Axis [31] both as SOAP implementation then as a server which plugs into Tomcat Container.
- as programming tools: Apache Ant [32] to automate all the steps involved in building the executables and packaging them as a Web ARchive file suitable to grid and Axis itself with its tools.

The resultant web application is structured as a WAR file containing files and libraries required to its execution with the SOAP engine embedded. Moreover the web services is secured by means of the EDG security [33] that provides access to these resources only to authorized grid clients. The security process is performed by the authentication of the grid client owning a X.509 certificate, and by the authorization to execute web services through an AXIS handler inserted in the request flow in front of the SOAP endpoint. In this way only VO's authorized users could access these catalogs.

4.2 Service Requestor: Grid Client Accessing to the Web Services

The application client used by a grid user contacts the service provider through a SOAP request addressing the service in two ways:

- from the UI submitting a job to the grid: to run an application on grid resources in INFN production grid, a user has to use the `edg-job-submit` command with, as argument, a simple text files written in JDL (Job Description Language) format [34] a language based on Condor ClassAds library [35]. This file contains the name of the executable, all input/output parameters and the requirements needed by the job to be executed.
- from a client web browser by an HTTP connection over SSL/TLS: the user requests directly the services (knowing its location) making a secure connection to the nodes hosting the services or interacts with a service registry (a WSIL document or UDDI registry) hosted in a web server on the CE.

In both cases the request flow is intercepted by the grid security mechanism that verifies user's credentials and, if the user is authorized, allows for the connection to the database management system to retrieve query results. The grid client owns a GSI-style (X.509) certificate: the true authentication process is performed by the web browser on which the client has installed its certificate or by the `grid-proxy-init` command launched from the UI. By both these methods, the user receives a proxy certificate, derived from its identity certificate, with which it could work.

In the first access method, the job is send to the resource broker in order to select the CE where the client application able to contact the web service is stored: the CE in turn dispatches it to the WN for the true computation, while the output is normally stored on a SE in a custom format (XML-like).

In the second method the user accesses the catalog through JSP pages specifically written to use the application by a web browser or makes a direct connection to the implemented service registry. A screenshot of the prototypal implementation of the JSP pages is shown in figure 4: from a web form the user can specify authorization parameters and can submit its specific query to the database.

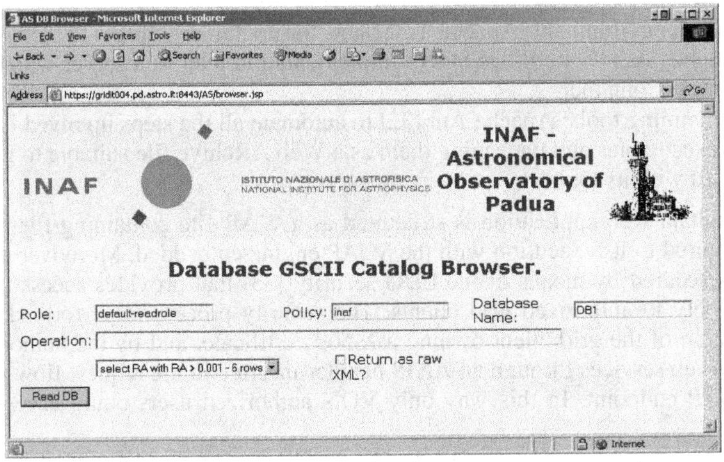

Fig. 4. Screenshot of the online access to the catalog trough JSP pages.

4.3 Service Broker: Deployment in the Site Grid Environment

The service broker is a fundamental part of web service architecture, since it facilitates the process of performing discovery between the requestor and the provider. Up to now, according to W3C definition, there are three leading viewpoints on how to discovery service should be conceived [23]:

- as a registry in an authoritative, centrally controlled store of information;
- as an index with a simple compilation or guide to show there the information exists;
- as peer-to-peer (P2P) discovery without centralized registries, letting the web services to discover each other dynamically.

At the present time the implemented solution are a UDDI Registry and a WS-Inspection (WSIL) document. Since similar in scope they are complementary means rather than competitive model of service discovery and so they could be integrated themselves. WSIL and UDDI assist in the publishing and discovery of services with two distinctly different models: UDDI uses a centralized model of one or more repositories containing information on entities and the services they provide, WSIL uses a decentralized approach where service description information can be distributed to any location using a simple XML document format relying on other description mechanism.

It may be advantageous to use both the methods since they could be integrated to offer better service discovery (as shown in figure 5). The WSIL solution, suitable for small-scale integration, has been adopted as a first step at site level; then it is on a test phase the implementation of a UDDI registry in order to permits the scalability of the solution, the compatibility with the middleware and the possible integration with the main grid information services.

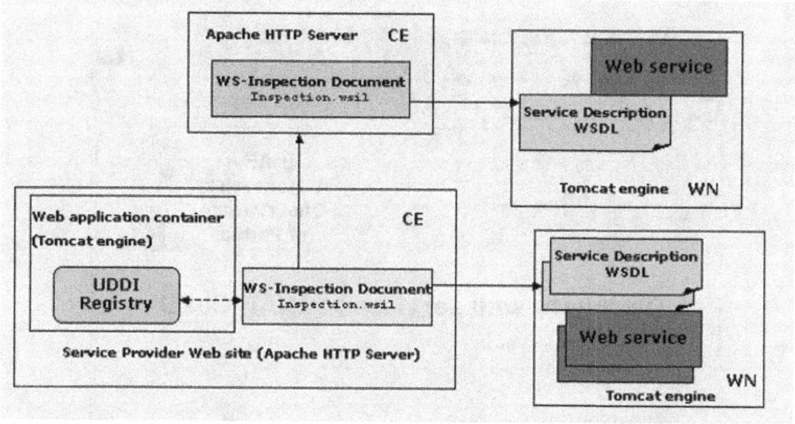

Fig. 5. Integration of the two implementation of service discovery specification

4.3.1 The WSIL Solution

The WSIL (web service inspection language) offers an XML document format for the discovery and aggregation of web services descriptions in a simple and extensible fashion.

It allows publisher to advertise their services defining how a service requestor can discover an XML web service description on a web server. WSIL documents are located using simple conventions over the web infrastructure: the document which has a fixed name tagged as `inspection.wsil`, will contain the web services corresponding HTTP accessible WSDL document which describes their interface. It should be placed at common entry points for a web site (such as http://gridit001.pd.astro.it/inspection.wsil). However this is a top level document, and the WSIL documents can be linked in order to allow service providers to organize their services listing in a hierarchical manner.

To implement such a solution, the WS-inspection file contained the requested information is stored in the CE web server through the Apache HTTP web server.

The service discovery could be provided using an Apache WSIL project called WSIL4J (web service inspection language for Java API) [36]. This consists in a java class library that provides an API to locate and process WS-Inspection documents.

The library can be used both to read and parse WS-Inspection document as generate new ones. It requires some libraries (such as JAXP compliant XML parser, WSDL for Java API (WSDL4J) included in the Apache Axis libraries and UDDI for Java API (UDDI4J [37]). The latter library is required only if WSIL document is used in conjunction with a UDDI registry: it generates and parses messages sent to and received from a UDDI server. A java program is on develop using all these libraries to reference WSIL4J and discovery the documents.

4.3.2 The UDDI Solution

The UDDI is the most widely used mechanism: there are different implementation of this standard on study phase such as the Apache jUDDI [38] or the project UDDIe [39] an extension of UDDI developed by the School of Computer Science at Cardiff University.

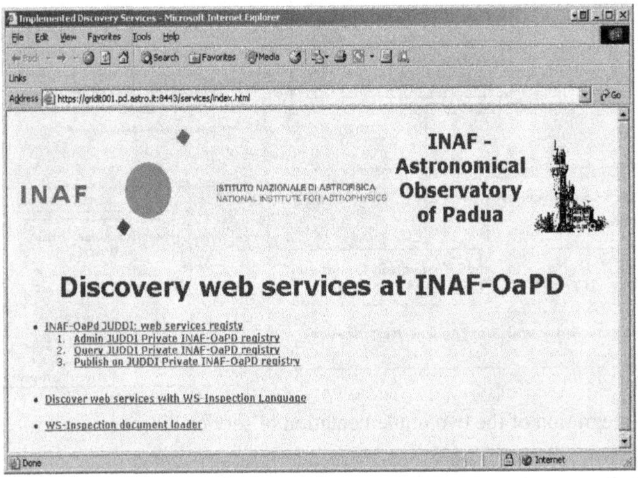

Fig. 6. An example of a web page listing the available discovery methods.

jUDDI is an open source Java implementation of UDDI specification on development. It comes as a web application to be deployed in the Apache Tomcat container and uses MySQL server to registry the information, so it should be complaint with the Italian grid infrastructure. Also UDDIe comes as web application deployed in the Tomcat container and uses relational databases such as the recommended Oracle Server to store data.

This solution permits to develop a private UDDI registry in a CE in order to be view by the whole grid environment: the likely adoption of a such implementation in the grid infrastructure is strictly tied to the future development of the information services provided by the Italian production grid. Up to now the developed grid application is used by grid clients connecting directly to a web page containing a reference to all of the described discovery methods as shown in figure 6.

The integration of these methods in the main grid information system is related to its structure.

5 Integration with the Information Services of the Production Grid

The Information system of the INFN production grid [40], as seen in figure 7, is based on Globus MDS 2.x [4] and the BDII information index.

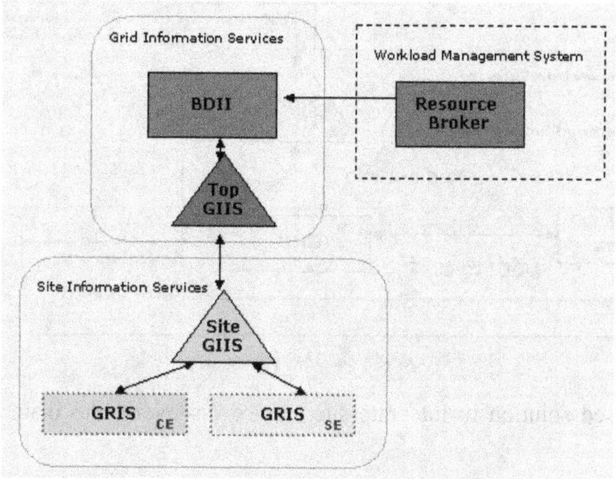

Fig. 7. The INFN production grid information hierarchical system.

MDS provides a single standard interface and schema for the information services used within a VO. It uses the LDAP protocol (implemented as OpenLDAP [41]) and a defined schema (the Glue schema [42]) as uniform means of querying system information offering a directory service infrastructure for computational grid.

MDS defines an hierarchical approach presented to users through three types of servers: Grid Information Index Server (GIIS), Grid Resource Information Server (GRIS) and Information Providers (IPs).

The default configuration of MDS in INFN shows a local GRIS running on each functional node (CE, SE) at the different sites reporting on the characteristics and status of the services and a single-site GIIS running by default on the CE combining the various GRISes.

At each site a GIIS collects information about all resources in a site. The BDII (Berkeley Database Information Index), a specialized GIIS, interacts not only with the information system, but also with the WMS components and in particular with the Resource Broker (RB). The BDII collects all information coming from the site GIISes and stores them in a permanent database: the GIISes themselves register to the BDII. Up to now a single Resource Broker is implemented in the INFN testbed and a unique central BDII is configured to get publish information from resources in all sites.

In this environment is on study phase how and where to implement a UDDI registry: the possibility to use a different version of MDS and its directory server (such as the MDS 3 knows as Index Service [43]) could give a chance to move the service registry to a higher level, but this is for now premature.

The proposed solution is oriented, as figure 8 shown, to integrate the service broker implemented as a UDDI registry into a site GRIS server in order that it could register to the GIIS and then to the central BDII.

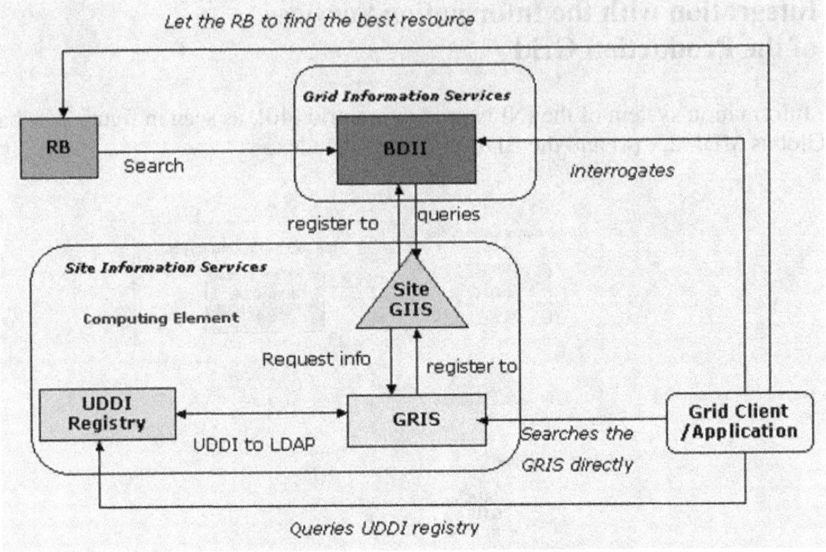

Fig. 8. The proposed solution to integrate site service discovery into main grid information system.

In this schema the grid client or the grid application could use several ways to get the needed information using the main grid components or directly the UDDI registry.

This could guarantee the discovery of a specific application by the main grid information system and so by the Resource broker, but necessary means the integration of UDDI specification into an LDAP schema. The feasibility of this mapping in on study phase.

6 Conclusions

The first test of these java web services has shown the robustness of the technology adopted and their compatibility with the overall production grid. Knowing the location of the services directly or through WS-Inspection documents, a grid user could query the database searching the data both through UI as the a web browser.

It's on study the feasibility to adopt the private UDDI registry in this environment as automatic web services discover mechanism at site level eventually linked with the WSIL solution. But the open problem remains the implementation of a "web services broker" at the high-level of the grid information services in order to let grid users and particular astronomical VO users, to automatically discover and use the services in the framework of the production grid.

Also the work regarding the web services programming is on progress with further developments such as the eventually transformation of our web services in grid services to advantage of their enhancements. This is yet heavily influenced both of the needs of do not loosing compatibility with the Italian production grid, as by the future directions of OGSA since it's not be clear if its specification will be towards WS-Framework rather than OGSI [44].

References

1. The INFN Production Grid for Scientific Applications, http://grid-it.cnaf.infn.it
2. WS-Inspection: Web Service Inspection Language (WSIL), http://cvs.apache.org/viewcvs/*checkout*/ws-wsil/java/docs/WSInspectionOverview.htm
3. UDDI, Universal Description, Discovery and Integration of Web Services, http://www.uddi.org
4. MDS The Monitoring and Discovery Service version 2, http://www.globus.org/mds/mds2/
5. Foster I., Kesselman C., Tuecke "S. The Anatomy of the Grid: Enabling Scalable Virtual Organizations", 2001
6. GGF DAIS-WG (Database Access and Integration Services), http://www.gridforum.org/6_DATA/dais.htm
7. GARR Italian Scientific research and University Network, http://www.garr.it
8. INFN-GRID release, http://grid-it.cnaf.infn.it/index.php?packages&type=1
9. LHC Computing Grid (LGC), http://cern.ch/lcg
10. EDG – European Data Grid, http://www.eu-datagrid.org/
11. The Globus Toolkit, http://www-unix.globus.org/toolkit/
12. The Condor project, http://www.cs.wisc.edu/condor
13. The European Data Tag project (EDT), http://datatag.web.cern.ch/datatag
14. The Virtual Data Toolkit (VDT), http://www.lsc-group.phys.uwm.edu/vdt/
15. I. Foster, C. Kesselman, J. Nick and S. Tuecke, The Physiology of the Grid: An Open Services Architecture for Distributed System Integration", 2001, http://www.globus.org/research/papers/ogsa.pdf
16. Berkeley Database Information Index, http://www-it.desy.de/physics/projects/grid/testbed/EDG/BDII.html
17. EDG Workload Management Software (WMS), http://server11.infn.it/workload-grid/
18. EDG Replica Management System (RMS), http://edg-wp2.web.cern.ch/edg-wp2/replication/index.html
19. Open Grid Service Infrastructure (OGSI), http://www.ggf.org/ogsi-wg
20. The WS-Resource Framework, http://www.globus.org/wsrf/
21. WSDL, Web Services Description Language (WSDL) 1.1, W3C Note 15 March 2001, http://www.w3.org/TR/2001/NOTE-wsdl-20010315
22. SOAP, Simple Object Access Protocol, W3C recommendation, http://www.w3.org/TR/2003/REC-soap12-part0-20030624/
23. Web Services Architecture, W3C Working Group Note 11 February 2004, http://www.w3.org/TR/2004/NOTE-ws-arch-20040211/
24. "Software architecture models", DataGrid-12-Note-0.6
25. GSI – Grid security Infrastructure: an overview, http://www.globus.org/security/overview.html
26. The Apache Software Foundation projects, http://www.apache.org
27. MySQL database server, http://www.mysql.com
28. Apache Tomcat 4, the servlet container used in the implementation of Java servlet and JSP technologies, http://jakarta.apache.org/tomcat/tomcat-4.1-doc/index.html
29. MySQL Connector/J a native Java driver, http://www.mysql.com/products/connector/j/
30. DBCP (database connection pool): JNDI datasource howto, http://jakarta.apache.org/tomcat/tomcat-4.1-doc/jndi-datasource-examples-howto.html
31. Apache Axis, a SOAP engine http://ws.apache.org/axis/
32. Apache Ant a Java-based build tool, http://ant.apache.org/
33. EDG Security and Transparent Access, http://edg-wp2.web.cern.ch/edg-wp2/security/index.html
34. The JDL (Job description language) tutorial, http://grid-it.cnaf.infn.it/fileadmin/users/job-submission/job_submission.html

35. Condor ClassAds library: classified advertisement home page, http://www.cs.wisc.edu/condor/classad
36. Apache WSIL4J Web Services Inspection Language for Java API, http://cvs.apache.org/viewcvs/*checkout*/ws-wsil/java/README.htm
37. UDDI4J (http://www-124.ibm.com/developerworks/oss/uddi4j/) the java class library that provides an API to interact with a UDDI registry.
38. jUDDI – an open source java implementation of the UDDI specification for web services, http://ws.apache.org/juddi/
39. The UDDIe, Universal Description, Discovery and Integration Extension project http://www.wesc.ac.uk/projects/uddie/uddie/index.htm
40. F. Donno, L. Gaido, A. Ghiselli, F. Prelz, M. Sgaravatto, DataGrid Prototype 1, EU-DataGrid Collaboration
41. LDAP, Lightweight Directory Access Protocol and its implementation OpenLDAP software, http://www.openldap.org/
42. GLUE Schema Official documents, http://www.cnaf.infn.it/~sergio/datatag/glue
43. MDS/Index Service, http://www-unix.globus.org/toolkit/docs/3.2/infosvcs/
44. Czajkowski K. Ferguson D., Foster I., Graham S., Maguire T., Snelling D., Tuecke S.: From Open Grid Services Infrastructure to WS-Resource Framework: Refactoring & Evolution, 3/05/2004

A Scalable Entry-Level Architecture for Computational Grids Based on Web Services

Mario Jeckle, Ingo Melzer, and Jens Peter

University of Applied Sciences Furtwangen
Robert-Gerwig-Platz 1, D-78120 Furtwangen, Germany
mario@jeckle.de, paper@ingo-melzer.de, info@jens-peter.com
http://www.jeckle.de/
http://www.ingo-melzer.de/

Abstract. Grid computing has recently become very popular and this development deserves to be called a hype. To benefit from the techniques of Grid computing, it is not necessary to invest a lot in software for smaller solutions. Simple Grids sized at entry-level can be implemented using some ideas of service-oriented architectures. Especially when building such a new system, it is interesting to know, how the result will most likely perform and how big the benefits will be.
This paper gives an approach to implement such an entry-level Grid solution for computational tasks and introduces a computational model to estimate the performance of these solutions.

1 Introduction

At the latest, since the Grid project *SETI@home* [7] became well known, Grid computing can be called a hype and many software companies try to benefit from this development. However, for smaller system a Grid solution can easily be implemented from scratch, and platform independent solutions can be applied in most system environments. Based on the idea of service-oriented architectures, a simple and flexible approach is presented in this paper for implementing computational Grids. Also a computational model is introduced to estimate the performance of Grid solutions.

The remainder of this paper is structured as follows. First, the young history of Grid applications is explored and different instances of Grids are sketched. Based on this, the paradigm of Service-oriented architectures which is increasingly confluent with Grid-based techniques is introduced. Additionally, interpreted programming languages with platform independent execution environments are discussed since these languages seem to be well suited for implementing Grid contributing nodes.

Based on this, section three introduces a new computational model which allows the estimation of expected performance for Grid applications relying on the techniques introduced before. The computational model refactors proven heuristics well-known in the field of parallel processing. As a foundation of our proposed formula two prototypical Grid implementations sketching edge cases are discussed.

M. Jeckle, R. Kowalczyk, and P. Braun (Eds.): GSEM 2004, LNCS 3270, pp. 15–29, 2004.

2 Technologies Involved

2.1 Grid Computing

The Grid – A Brief History. Historically, the name *Grid* was chosen by virture of the analogy to the power grid, which distributes electrical power to each citizens power outlet, without knowledge where the electricity came from. Likewise, the vision of applying the grid idea to computing is that computing power (i.e., the ability to store or process data) will be available also through an outlet. When aranging the evolution of Grid into generations, the focus can be set on the standardization of the technology involved.

The pre-history of applying the grid idea to computing is based on technologies for distributed computing like the COMMON OBJECT REQUEST BROKER ARCHITECTURE (CORBA), which is standardized by the OBJECT MANAGEMENT GROUP [8]. Also techniques like REMOTE METHOD INVOCATION (RMI) and JINI [9] from Sun were launched to provide a software infrastructure for distributed computing. And also DCE and DCOM are proposed as solutions for Grid-computing.

All these technical approaches share the characteristc of beeing a *point solution* to the issues to be addressed when stiving a solution for interconnecting various resources. The term point solution (which was initially coined by [5]) here referes to techniques which may contribute to solve certain aspects of the main problem but which fail in addressing all issues at one time.

In the early 1990s some research projects focused on distributed computing were founded. The publication of early results to the I-WAY [5] project which were presented at the 1995 Super Computer conference represent the first true Grid and thus mark the first generation of such approaches. The I-WAY implementation connected 17 high-end computers over high-performance networks to one *metacomputer*, which runs 60 different applications. The success of this demonstration led the DARPA fund a new research project titled GLOBUS [4] under the lead of FOSTER and KESSELMANN.

Another project which fits in the first generation of Grid computing is FACTORING VIA NETWORK-ENABLED RECURSION (FAFNER for short) [6], which was launched in context of the *RSA Factoring Challenge*. FAFNER creates a metacomputer which was deployed to attack content that is cryptographically secured by using the RSA algorithm. In detail FAFNER strives to attack the basic idea of the RSA algorithm, which is the usage of large composite numbers for securing arbitrary content. Since fast factorization or large composite numbers is a challenge which still lacks an efficient mathematical algorithm, attacks require enormous amounts CPU time. Technically speaking, FAFNER provides a Web interface for a factoring method which is well suited for parallel and distributed execution, the *number field sieve* [19]. The project implemented a software daemon which is based on the PERL scripting language which are accessed through the Common Gateway Interface protocol. The daemon handles the retrieval of input values to the local system and the submission of results via HTTP's well-known GET and POST methods. This approach proved to be successful and paved the way of other Web-based projects. Other, mostly scientific based projects, like SETI@HOME [7], GENOME@HOME, or FIGHTAIDS@HOME were launched. Also some mathematic based problems gained help from concentrated computing power like the GREAT INTERNET MERSENNE PRIME SEARCH or the GENERALIZED FERMAT PRIME SEARCH. The still increasing number of computers connected to the internet via its access to the World Wide Web widens the amount of potential contributors to these projects.

With the current, i.e. the second, generation of the Grid, three main issues have to be focused. These were heterogeneity, scalability and adaptability. In this context answers to the following questions have to be found:

- **Identity and Authentication:** How should machines which are authorized to participate within the Grid be uniquely identified and authenticated?
- **Authorization and Policy:** How is decentralized authorization handled and how are certain policies (like Quality of Service) guaranteed?
- **Resource Discovery:** How are resources which are offered by the Grid discovered?
- **Resource Allocation:** How is handling of exclusive or shared resource allocation handled?
- **Resource Management and Security:** How are the distributed resources managed in an uniform way, esp. how can a certain level of security be provided for all nodes participating within the Grid?

Today there are enormous efforts of companies like IBM, Sun, and HP to advance the Grid idea to a next evolutionary step. The main focus here is the service-oriented architecture approach on which the next generation of Grids will be based. In essence the idea of distributed processing and data storage underlying the Grid idea is increasingly merged with the technical infrastructure summarized as WEB SERVICE. By doing so the level of standardization reached by virtue of widely accepted Grid infrastructures such as the GLOBUS toolkit is leveraged by the ubiquitous technical infrastrucutre of Web-based services.

Data Grid vs. Computational Grid. The current state of applying the Grid idea is summarized by [4] as:

> "Grid computing enables virtual organizations to share geographically distributed resources as they pursue common goals, assuming the absence of central location, central control, omniscience, and existing trust relationship"

The absence of such a central control means, that there is no centralized instance acting like an operating system which is in power to manage execution characteristics (e.g. scheduling, memory management, interrupt handling). But, for ease of management purposes some Grid implementations of major software vendors deploy a centralized control in terms of a dedicated node offering the tasks to be computed to the participating Grid nodes.

The abstract notion of *Grid* is differentiated further by companies providing software and hardware infrastructure for Grids like IBM and Sun. In detail Sun refers to *CampusGrid* while IBM chooses the term *IntraGrid* when addressing Grids which are deployed company internal only. Consequentially, company-spanning Grids are termed *ExtraGrids* and Grid-based solutions relying on the Internet's technology are named *InterGrids.* Since the latter ones are potentially distributed globally Sun introduced the additional term *GlobalGrid* [11].

Further, often Grids are distinguished from an operational point of view. Here two major directions have emerged. First, data-centric Grids which focus on the transparent access to data distributed geographically. In essence these "Grids should provide transparent, secure, high-performance access to federated data sets across administrative domains and organizations" [10].

An example for a data Grid is the *European DataGrid Initiative* [12], a project under the lead of the European nuclear research center. CERN's data Grid initiative which also involves IBM should manage and provide access from any location worldwide to the unpresented torrent of data, billions of gigabyte a year, that CERN's *Large Hadron Collider* is expected to produce when it goes online in 2007 [13]. The second mainstream of Grid computing is the computational Grid. In this approach, the idle time of network detached machines is shared and used by other Grid-enabled applications. A computational Grid can be based on an *IntraGrid*, which uses the spare CPU-time of desktop computers for compute intensive tasks. Such a systems is used by the swiss company NOVARTIS for solving problems in the medical research. The systems uses 2700 desktop computers to provide a computing power from about 5 terra FLOPS [14].

In this paper we describe an architecture which combines the technical aspects (i.e., the deployment of Web-based service-oriented technology) of Inter-Grids with the application area of IntraGrids. In detail this means benefiting from the transfer of techniques typically found in InterGrids to closed organizations which deploy IntraGrids to Grids which are deployed accross organizational boundaries. The advantage by doing so lies in lowered costs of infrastructure and an increased amount of standardized components. Additionally, our approach takes this further and establishes the notion of an entry-level Grid which adds ease of deployment and operation.

2.2 Service-Oriented Architectures

Some of the latest Internet-related developments share the idea of utilizing different functionalities over the net without the requirement of using a browser. The most general and to some degree visionary version is termed SERVICE-ORIENTED ARCHITECTURE, or for short SOA.

The basic idea of a SOA is quite simple. A developer implements a service, which can be any functionality made available to others, and registers his service in some global registry like some yellow pages for services. A user, which is most often some other service, is thereafter able to find the registered service, retrieve all information about invoking the just found service, and call the service. In the end, all this should happen without human involvement. This last step is called *loosely coupled*, because the connection or coupling is made at run-time when needed, in other words just in time.

2.3 Web Services

Today, the most advanced instance of a SOA is called Web services. The technical basis of the Web service philosophy is grounded on the idea of enabling various systems to exchange structured information in a decentralized, distributed environment dynamically forming a extremely loosely coupled system. In essence this lead to the definition of lightweight platform-independent protocols for synchronous remote procedure calls as well as asynchronous document exchange using XML encoding via well-known Internet protocols such as HTTP.

After some introductory approaches which were popularized under the name XML-RPC [22] the SOAP[1] protocol which has been standardized by the World Wide Web Consortium [1, 2] establishes a transport-protocol agnostic framework for Web services that can be extended by users on the basis of XML techniques.

The SOAP protocol consists of two integral parts: A messaging framework defining how to encode and send messages. And an extensibility model for extending this framework by its user. Firstly, a brief introduction of the messaging framework is given before showing value of the extensibility mechanisms to accomplish the goals defined above. Technically speaking, SOAP resides in the protocol stack above a physical wire protocol such as HTTP, FTP, or TCP. Although the specification does not limit SOAP to HTTP-based transfers, this protocol binding is currently the most prominent one and is widely used for Web service access. But it should be noted that the approach introduced by this paper is designed to operate completely independent of the chosen transport protocol and resides solely on the SOAP layer.

All application data intended to be sent over a network using the SOAP protocol must be transferred into an XML representation. To accomplish this, SOAP defines two message encoding styles. Therefore, the specification introduces rules for encoding arbitrary graphs into XML. Most prominent specialization of this approach is the *RPC style* introduced by the specification itself which allows the exchange of messages that map conveniently to definitions and invocations of method and procedure calls in commonly used programming languages. As introduced before SOAP is by nature protocol agnostic and can be deployed for message exchange using a variety of underlying protocols. Therefore a formal set of rules for carrying a SOAP message within or on top of another protocol needs to be defined for every respective transport protocol. This is done by the official SOAP specification for HTTP as well as SMTP.

Inside the SOAP protocol, the classical pattern of a message body carrying the payload and an encapsulating envelope containing some descriptive data and metainformation is retained. Additionally, SOAP allows the extension of

[1] At the time of its definition the acronym stood for *Simple Object Access Protocol*. In the standardized version SOAP is no longer an acronym.

the header content by the use of XML elements not defined by the SOAP specification itself. For distinguishing these elements from those predefined by the specification the user has to take care that they are located in a different XML namespace. The example below shows a complete SOAP message accompanied with the transport protocol specific data necessary when using the HTTP binding. Additionally a user defined header residing in a non-W3C and thus non normative namespace is shown as part of the SOAP `Header` element.

```
POST /axis/theService/ HTTP/1.1 Content-Type: text/xml;
charset=utf-8 Accept: application/soap+xml
Host: 10.0.0.1:8080
Content-Length: nnn

<?xml version="1.0" ?>
<env:Envelope xmlns:env="http://www.w3.org/2003/05/soap-envelope">
 <env:Header>
    <ns1:DeliveryNotification env:mustUnderstand="true"
    env:role="http://www.w3.org/2003/05/soap-envelope/role/ultimateReceiver"
       xmlns:ns1="urn:xmlns:daimlerchrysler.com:research">
       <ns1:SendTo URI="MailTo:john.doe@daimlerchrysler.com"/>
    </n1:DeliveryNotification>
 </env:Header>
 <env:Body>
    <ns2:CalcParams>
       <ns2:ID>7492653</ns2:ID> <ns2:x>42</ns2:x> <ns2:y>3.14</ns2:y>
       <!-- more details omitted for brevity ... -->
    </ns2:CalcParams>
 </env:Body>
</env:Envelope>
```

In contrast to the payload which is intended to be sent to the receiver of the SOAP message clearly identified by HTTP's `Host` header, SOAP headers may or may not be created for processing by the ultimate receiver. Specifically, they are only processed by machines identified by the predefined `role` attribute. By doing so, the extension framework offers the possibility of partly processing a message along its path from the sender to the ultimate receiver. These intermediate processing steps could fulfill arbitrary task ranging from problem oriented ones like reformatting, preprocessing, or even fulfilling parts of the requests to more infrastructural services such as filtering, caching, or transaction handling. In all cases the presence of a node capable of (specification compliant) processing of a SOAP message is prescribed. This is especially true since an intermediary addressed by the `role` attribute is required to remove the processed header after executing the requested task. Additionally, the specification distinguishes between headers optionally to be processed (e. g. caching) and those which are interspersed to trigger necessary message behavior. The latter ones must additionally be equipped with the attribute `mustUnderstand`. If a header addressed to an intermediary flagged by this attribute cannot be processed, the SOAP node is forced to raise an exception and resubmit the message to the sender. Thus it is ensured that all headers mandatory to be processed are consumed by the respective addressees and removed afterwards.

Loosely Coupled: An important property of a SOA and Web services it the fact that they are loosely coupled. This means that they are not statically liked and binding does not happen at compile time. During its execution, a service can search for some other services, which might at this moment in time still be unknown, retrieve information about the search results, and invoke one of the just found services. This allows to move services to different machines and simple change the information in one of the registries. No other service has to be changed or re-compiled. A promising starting point for a highly flexible infrastructure.

WS-Notification: Later specifications such as WS-NOTIFICATION [24] allow the implementation of the publish/subscribe pattern. This allows to automatically trigger certain action as soon as certain criteria have been met. WS-Notification allows the implementation of Grid infrastructures and Grid based applications. The OPEN GRID SERVICES ARCHITECTURE, short OGSA, moves very close to the Web services world and the latest version is based on Web services standards. If this development continues, it will soon be very difficult or even impossible to tell Web services and Grid services apart. This development became obvious one year ago in the OPEN GRID SERVICES INFRASTRUCTURE, short OGSI, definition 1.0 which has been released in April 2003. It states in this context "a Grid service is a Web service that conforms to a set of conventions (interfaces and behaviors) that define how a client interacts with a Grid service".

There are a number of alternatives to WS-Notification. Some features can be implemented using WS-Eventing [23] and part 2 of WSDL 2.0 offers a message exchange pattern, too.

2.4 Interpreted Languages

One of the main challenges for Grid application frameworks such as the OGSA-OGSI approach is multi-platform support. That is for avoiding prescriptions concerning platform details such as the deployed operating system running machines participating the Grid. Also the infrastructure should not set out limits regarding the programming language chosen for implementing machine's code locally executed but contributing to the Grid. In general, these challenges can be tackled by providing portable implementations as well as by specifying solely interfaces whose description do not reveal details of the programing language specific manifestation. Classically, the required interfaces descriptions are provided by using standardized paradigm neutral approaches such as CORBA's Interface Definition Language (IDL) or WSDL, the in some sense comparable approach introduced by Web service technology.

Unfortunately, description mechanisms which concentrate solely on callable interface do specifiy wire representations of the data to be exchanged between communicating nodes. Therefore typically extra agreements have to be settled. In CORBA's case this is the Common Data Representation resp. the XML for Web service deployment.

Besides this the internal implementation of nodes participating the Grid may vary vastly. In general this is rather a blessing than a cure. But, especially for entry level Grids the costly creation or even adaptation of code to deploy on single nodes should be as lightweight as possible. Likewise, the potential requirement to port applications to other platforms curbs the amount of specialities of the respective language platform which can be used to an absolute minimum. Therefore the reliance on the lowest common denominator, i.e. basic functionality known to be supported by various plattforms is an archetypical design decision to ensure widest possible portability.

Our approach for supporting entry-level Grids therefore introduces the usage of a portable implementation and execution plattform as third cornerstone (besides basic Grid ideas and reliance on standardized Web service technology) of the proposed architecture. It should be emphasized that this does not tie the approach to a single specific platform. But it has not escapted our notice thas this founds a clear preference for interpreted or at least hybrid (i.e. approaches which incorporate a compile cycle which produces a result which is interpreted at runtime) languages such as formed by the JAVA or Microsoft .NET platform.

As a result of this architectural constraint we are able to interconect various physical platforms on short notice to a metacomputer. The computational nodes constituting the metacomputer will be able to offer current programing paradigms such as object orientation and concurrency without additional adaptation effors. Additionally, basing Grid applications on current programming approaches bears twofolded benefits for both, the Grid and the deployed software execution environment. On the one hand deployment of Grid-based technology is leveraged by the level of additional standardization. On the the other hand the installation basis of the respective language environments is additionally widened.

3 Performance Estimation

3.1 Computation Model

The architecture presented in this paper is based on a Web service enabled server using the standardized SOAP communication protocol. The server hosts the main controlling service and a Web service toolkit. Due to the usage of standards it is technically feasible to add additional Grid nodes on short notice. These nodes share their local resources for processing by using the same software implementation available for different platforms and operating systems.

The main advantage of such an architecture is that the creation of a Grid is a lightweight process. In essence it simply requires the distribution of the software and its install on the participating machines. At runtime these machines will act as clients requesting computational tasks fromt he node acting as server. At development time the application implementing the problem to be solved has to be transfered in an Grid-enabled application, so it is necessary to identify the code needed to build a *job list* which contains the amounts of work which should be distributed to the clients. Technically, one Grid node provide a *job queue* as a central service. The next step is to wrap a Web service around the processing code of the application and deploy the service, which is an Web service RPC, on the server. To add new nodes to the Grid, solely the Web service has to be deployed to a network attached computer. Additionally, the new node has to be announced to the queue holding serving. This could be done by simply adding its network address to a configuration file or online by sending a predefined message.

This Grid is build up as a logical star topology, a single computer, the controller, coordinates the available resources. This controller has to fulfill different tasks in the Grid, for example he has to build the list of jobs, what means that the original task the Grid-enabled application has to process must be split in smaller pieces, the jobs, for parallel execution. The controller has to distribute these jobs to the available nodes, the computers which share their computing resources to the Grid and receive the processed results from the nodes. Communication with the participating nodes is operated in an asynchronous mode. Thus either asynchronous Web service calls have to be used or asynchronous communication has to be emulated on-top of synchronous communication. One way to achieve the latter ist to deploy multithreading within the controller.

On the node, there is also a Web service deployed which receives and process a job. The controller and the nodes are connected through a network, no matter if it is a local departemental network or the internet.

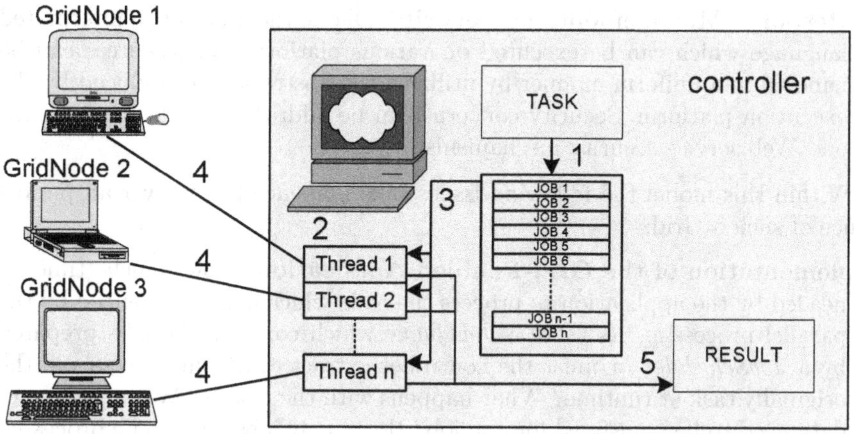

Fig. 1. Architecture

Fig. 1 is a schematically presentation of the architecture including the emulation of asynchronous communication by multithreaded synchronous communication.

1. The primary task is split into a number of single jobs by the *JobScheduler*.
2. The controller invoke for every active node an own *ServiceThread*.
3. Every thread grabs a jobs from the *JobQueue*.
4. The job is send to the nodes for processing and the *ServiceThread* wait for the result. When an error occurs, for example the Grid node is temporarily not available, the job is republished to the *JobQueue* and the *ServiceThread* will wait for an estimated time to send a new job to the node.

5. After the successful processing of a job, the node sends back the result to his *ServiceThread* and it is stored by the controller.

Based on that architecture, the following answers for the basic questions in Chapter 2.1 can be presented:

- **Identity and Authentication:** Solely the controller initiates connections to the nodes. The participating nodes can register themselves actively to take part within a computation task. For authenticating nodes the initiating SOAP requests can be signed digitally.
- **Authorization and Policy:** Based on a validated digital signature nodes are authorized to receive data for fulfilling the computation tasks. Policies concerning aspects of Quality of Service are ensured by the controller. If a node does not send back its computed result in a certain amount of time the node is marked inactive and the data is distributed to another node.
- **Resource Allocation:** Grid nodes can determine the share of processing time they devote to the computation of received tasks independent from the controller. In case of high node utilization the nodes are also allowed to withdraw from the Grid without requiring them to signal this to the controller.
- **Resource Management and Security:** Due to the usage of an interpreted language which can be executed on various platforms all resources can be handled in a uniform manner by utilizing the abstraction introduced by the execution platform. Security concerns can be addressed by deploying XML and Web service security mechanisms.

Within this model the following issues take influence to the over all performance of such a Grid:

Implementation of the Grid-Enabled Application: How much time is needed by the application to process the code which is not influenced by the parallel processing? Is there a *JobQueue* which contains the jobs prepared by a *JobScheduler* or must the controller extract every single job from the originally task at runtime? What happens with the results? What amount of data need to be transfered for one job? How many jobs need to be processed in a second?

Performance of the Controller Computer: Because the controller has to coordinate every job and result, the performance of the controller can be a key indicator for the performance of the whole Grid. How many jobs per second can be transfered? Is there a local database the results where stored in? Must the controller host other applications than the Grid?

Networkperformance: With what type of network are the nodes connected to the controller? What is the maximal bandwidth of the network? Is every node in the same subnet? What is about the other traffic on the network?

Processingroutines on the Grid Node: How much time need a node to process a job?

It is very interesting to forecast the performance benefit before transferring an application in a Grid-enabled application. There were some efforts to forecast the speedup of an application when running it on a parallel processor system. One of the formulas to forecast the speedup is the GUSTAFSON-BARSIS (1) approach:

$$SpeedUp = \#CPU + (1 - \#CPU) * P_{seq} \tag{1}$$

But this could not easy be transfered to a Grid where the parallel processors are connected via a network and the application and not the operating system need to handle the distribution of the processes to the additional computing power. In this case, not only the sequential (code which could not processed parallel) part of the application is an indicator for the speedup. Other parameters are the network latency, the time need to transmit the application parameters to process to the nodes, and the overhead the application produce to prepare sending and receiving of the parameters. By now, there is no approach to forecast such a speed up for Grid services.

In consideration of this issues the following formula (2) can give a forecast on the speedup of an entry-level Grid:

$$SpeedUp = \#CPU - \#CPU * (P_{seq} + NL) - \underbrace{(\#CPU * P_{over})}_{\text{GridFactor}} \tag{2}$$

The maximal speedup must be less than the number of processors so there are some other parameter we have to look at. The factor P_{seq} represents the sequential part of the application and will influence the maximum speedup because this factor will rise when the over all time the application need to process will decrease when it is processed by more computers. The network latency, or NL, is not static, it represents a range between 0 and 1 and has to be explored by a statistical review based on network performance tests.

A significant factor is P_{over}, the overhead of performance of the application. This overhead and the number of used CPUs or Grid nodes is the so called *GridFactor*. This *GridFactor* is a key performance indicator for the Grid. Some problems can be easy adapted for parallel processing but there is an immense overhead when there are more processing units involved. For example the processing time for a job is under 1 ms but the time needed to prepare the parameter for this job is about 100 times higher, there is no sense to process this kind of problem in a parallel way. With every additional Grid node the performance will go from bad to worse and with such a bad *GridFactor* there will be no speedup at all. The value of P_{over} has also be explored by statistical review based on tests with a prototype of the Grid-enabled application.

3.2 Validation

The results with a huge P_{over} and therefrom a high *GridFactor* can be shown with the Grid-enabled example application for matrices multiplication. The results of the time measurement tests with this application shows, that the processing time is stable, no matter if we have one node or ten nodes connected to the Grid. One handicap was that this application has had no *JobScheduler* to prepare the jobs and the other handicap was that the processing time on a nodes was approximate zero. The missing *JobScheduler* results in that the controller must prepare every job at runtime. And it take more time to prepare a job for a node than the node need to process it (about 1 nanosecond). The *GridFactor* for this kind of application is to high that there is no speedup at all.

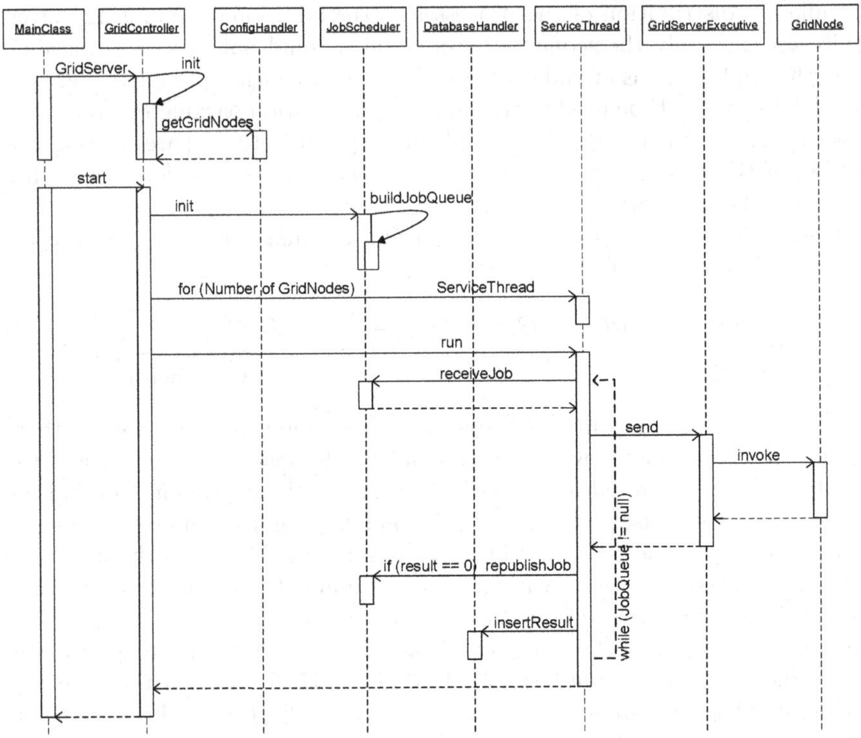

Fig. 2. Sequence Diagram

The second application was implemented based on a thesis at the Fraunhofer Institute for Manufacturing Engineering and Automation IPA in Stuttgart [16]. It is a tool for analyzing networks, in this case specially to identify the leaks in the waver transport network of a computerchip fab. To enable the stand alone application for the Grid, the processing unit with the algorithms was extracted and the *JobScheduler* was modified. A Web service with the processing routine was deployed on the nodes and the amount of data was about 4kB for each job. Fig. 2 shows a sequence diagram of that application.

Fig. 3 shows the speedup reached with this application. Two different scenarios were tested with the application. The test were based on a sample network model with 31 nodes and 72 edges. Two different analyses were run on the model. The first test scenario was to analyze the network with one component to

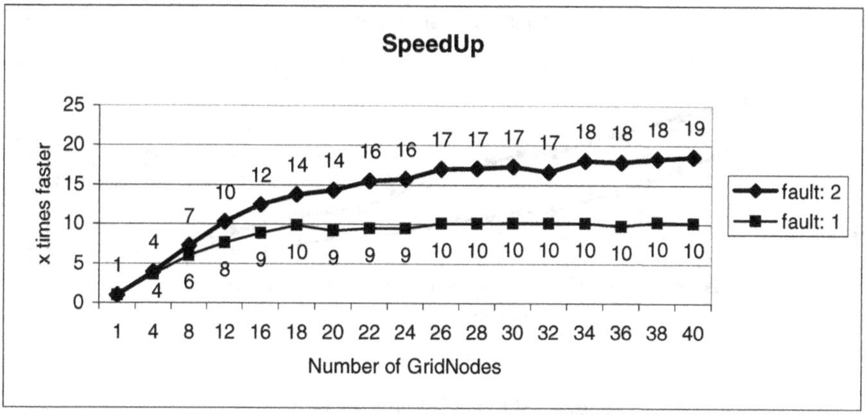

Fig. 3. SpeedUp

fail(*fault:1-test*). For this simulation 103 calculations have to be done. The second analyze simulates two defect components(*fault:2-test*) what results in 5253 calculations. The different speedups of the tests caused on the different P_{seq} and NL parts. In the *fault:1-test*, the ratio of P_{seq} and NL to the application time over all was higher. And the processing time on the clients a bit lower because the need to calculate only with one parameter. The *fault:2-test* shows a much better speed up. Within this test the ratio of P_{seq} and NL to the application time over all was lower, the time the nodes need to process a little bit higher.

With the Grid-enabled version of this software the time needed to analyze this small network with about 103 components shrink from over 80 minutes with a single slave to 6 minutes with 20 slaves. With the distributed computing it is now possible to analyze a network in a manageable timeframe. The tests were executed on computers with a Athlon© 1100 MHz processor connected with a switched 100Mbit Ethernet. The Grid was based on a Tomcat server and the Web service framework Axis, both from the Apache Software Foundation [18].

The *GridFactor* for this application was better because the speedup is rising with the number of nodes. In Fig. 3 is shown that the speedup is rising slower with additional Grid nodes which is a result of the rising *GridFactor*. The tested application caused a processing time on the Grid nodes between 700 and 1100 milliseconds, so there was a average load from one call for every Grid node per second. Fig. 4 shows that there can be about 60 to 100 calls per second with a payload of 4kByte so NL is small and probably has not influenced the speedup stagnation happend by about 20 nodes.

The maximum number of calls depending to the size of data (Fig. 4) was measured with the *SOAPing-Tool* [17], which can be used for testing the answer/reply behavior for a SOAP call in the tradition of the *ICMP Echo* service, better known as *PING*. The role of the controller fulfill a computer with a Pentium©-III Mobile processor with 1100 MHz and there was a computersystem based on an Athlon© XP 3000+ as a Grid node. The measured data is the average value from about 50000 *SOAPings* for each payload.

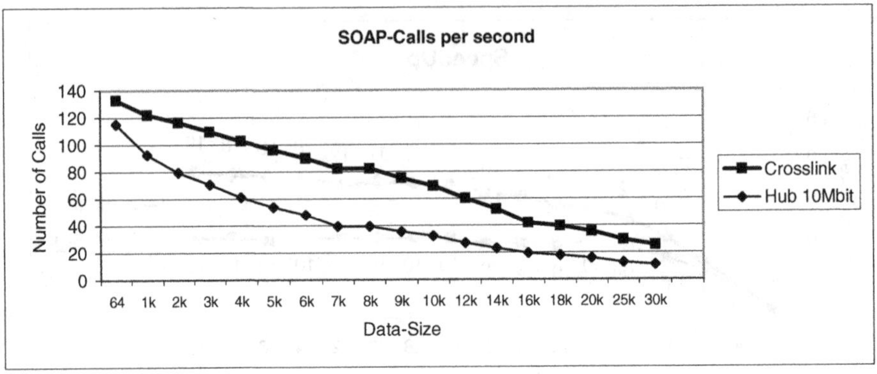

Fig. 4. SOAP-Calls per second

4 Related Work

Confluence of Web service technology and Grid applications are currently part of the next release of the OGSA/OGSI toolkit. It is expected by virtue of publications available from the GLOBAL GRID FORUM that in future all nodes participating in a Grid (regardless is speaking of data or computational Grids) will be accessible by using Web service interfaces. As a consequence the seminal standards WSDL and SOAP will widen its position as ubiquitous infrastructure based on the Web's base technology such as HTTP.

Concerning performance estimation of computational Grids only heuristics [20] and models with limited applicability [21] have been published so far. Both approaches addtionally lack consideration of entry-level technology such as interpreted languages and Web services.

5 Summary

It is not very difficult to implement platform independent solutions for computational Grids from scratch as it has been done for this paper. However, it is interesting to know how such solutions scale given the specific problem to be calculated. For this purpose, this paper has introduced a simple model including two formulas to estimate the performance of a computational Grid solution. This allows judge the potential benefit of an implementation before starting the real implementation and also helps to evaluate scenarios which might be used for Grid computing.

References

1. M. Gudgin, M. Hadley, J.-J. Moreau, H. F, Nielsen: W3C Candidate Recommendation: SOAP 1.2 Part 1: Messaging Framework, 20 December 2002 `http://www.w3.org/TR/soap12-part1/`

2. M. Gudgin, M. Hadley, J.-J. Moreau, H. F. Nielsen: W3C Candidate Recommendation: SOAP 1.2 Part 2: Adjuncts, 20 December 2002 http://www.w3.org/TR/soap12-part2/
3. R. Fielding, et al: Hypertext Transfer Protocol – HTTP/1.1, RFC2616, June 1999 http://www.ietf.org/rfc/rfc2616.txt
4. Globus http://www.globus.org
5. T. DeFanti, I. Foster, M. Papka, R. Stevens, T. Kuhfuss: *Overview of the I-Way.* International Journal of Supercomputer Applications, 10(2):123-130, 1996. http://www.globus.org/research/papers.html
6. FAFNER http://www.npac.syr.edu/factoring.html
7. SETI@home http://setiathome.ssl.berkeley.edu/
8. OMG http://www.omg.org
9. JINI http://www.jini.org/
10. A. Grimshaw: Data Grids in *Ahmar Abbas, Grid Computing: A Practical Guide to Technology and Applications*, 2004 Charles River Media, Hingham
11. A. Abbas: Grid Computing Technology – An Overview in *Ahmar Abbas, Grid Computing: A Practical Guide to Technology and Applications*, 2004 Charles River Media, Hingham
12. The DataGrid Project http://eu-datagrid.web.cern.ch
13. D. De Roure et al: The evolution of the Grid in *Fran Berman, Geoffrey C. Fox, Anthony J. G. Hey: Grid Computing*, 2003 John Wiley and Sons, West Sussex
14. Schlafende PC mutieren zum Supercomputer, Neue Zürcher Zeitung, 7.11.2003 http://www.nzz.ch/netzstoff/2003/2003.11.07-em-article97JEJ.html
15. A Future e-Science Infrastructure http://www.nesc.ac.uk/technical_papers/DavidDeRoure.etal.SemanticGrid.pdf
16. T. Geldner, *Graphenbasierte Layoutplanung von Transportnetzwerken in Halbleiterfabriken*, Konstanz/Stuttgart 2004
17. SOAPing http://www.jeckle.de/freeStuff/soaping/index.html
18. The Apache Software Foundation http://www.apache.org/
19. A. K. Lenstra, H. W. Lenstra, Jr., M. S. Manasse, J. M. Pollard: The Number Field Sieve, ACM Symposium on Theory of Computing, 1990.
20. S. Sodhi: Automatically Constructing Performance Skeletons for use in Grid Resource Selection and Performance Estimation Frameworks, Proceedings of the 15th ACM/IEEE Supercomputing Conference, 2003.
21. C. Lee, J. Stephanek: On Future Global Grid Communication Performance, Global Grid Forum, 1999.
22. D. Winer: XML-RPC Specification, available electronically, 1999. http://www.xmlrpc.com/spec
23. L. F. Cabrera, C. Critchley, G. Kakivaya et al.: WS-Eventing, available electronically, 2004. http://ftpna2.bea.com/pub/downloads/WS-Eventing.pdf
24. S. Graham, P. Niblett, D. Chappell et al.: Web Service Base Notification, 2004. ftp://www6.software.ibm.com/software/developer/library/ws-notification/WS-BaseN.pdf
25. M. Gudgin, A. Lewis, J. Schlimmer (eds.): Web Services Description Language (WSDL) Version 2.0 Part 2: Message Exchange Patterns, W3C Working Draft, World Wide Web Consortium, available electronically, 2004. http://www.w3.org/TR/2004/WD-wsdl20-patterns-20040326

Enhancing Java Grid Computing Security with Resource Control

Jarle Hulaas[1], Walter Binder[1], and Giovanna Di Marzo Serugendo[2]

[1] School of Computer and Communication Sciences
Swiss Federal Institute of Technology Lausanne (EPFL)
CH-1015 Lausanne, Switzerland
{jarle.hulaas,walter.binder}@epfl.ch

[2] Computer Science Department, University of Geneva
CH-1211 Geneva 4, Switzerland
Giovanna.Dimarzo@cui.unige.ch

Abstract. This paper outlines an original Computational Grid deployment protocol which is entirely based on Java, leveraging the portability of this language for distributing customized computations throughout large-scale heterogeneous networks. It describes practical solutions to the current weaknesses of Java in the fields of security and resource control. In particular, it shows how resource control can be put to work not only as basis for load balancing, but also to increase the security and general attractiveness of the underlying economic model[1].

Keywords: Grid Computing, Resource Control, Mobile Code.

1 Introduction

Grid computing enables worldwide distributed computations involving multi-site collaboration, in order to benefit from the combined computing and storage power offered by large-scale networks. The way an application shall be distributed on a set of computers connected by a network depends on several factors.

First, it depends on the *application* itself, which may be not naturally distributed or on the contrary may have been engineered for Grid computing. A single run of the application may require a lot of computing power. The application is intended to run several times on different input *data*, or few times, but an a huge amount of data. The application has at its disposal computational, storage and network *resources*. They form a dynamic set of CPUs of different computing power, of memory stores (RAM and disks) of different sizes, and of bandwidths of different capacities. In addition, the basic characteristics of the available CPUs, memory stores and bandwidth are not granted during the whole computation (a disk with an initial capacity of 512MBytes when empty, cannot be considered having this capacity when it is half full). Code and data may be stored at different *locations*, and may be distributed across several databases.

[1] This work was partly financed by the Swiss National Science Foundation.

M. Jeckle, R. Kowalczyk, and P. Braun (Eds.): GSEM 2004, LNCS 3270, pp. 30–47, 2004.

Computation itself may occur at one or more locations. Results of the computation have to be collected and combined into a coherent output, before being delivered to the client, who may wait for it at still another location. The network *topology* has also an influence on the feasibility of the distribution. Centralized topologies offer data consistency and coherence by centralizing the data at one place, security is more easily achieved since one host needs to be protected. However, these systems are exposed to lack of extensibility and fault-tolerance, due to the concentration of data and code to one location. On the contrary, a fully decentralized system will be easily extensible and fault-tolerant, but security and data coherence will be more difficult to achieve. A hybrid approach combining a set of servers, centralizing each several peers, but organized themselves in a decentralized network, provides the advantages of both topologies. Finally, *policies* have to be taken into account. They include clients and donators (providers) requirements, access control, accounting, and resource reservations.

Mobile agents constitute an appealing concept for deploying computations, since the responsibility for dispatching the program or for managing run-time tasks may be more efficiently performed by a mobile entity that rapidly places itself at strategic locations. However, relying completely on mobile agents for realizing the distribution complicates security tasks, and may incur additional network traffic.

This paper proposes a theoretical model combining the use of a trusted, stationary operator with mobile agents, running inside a secure Java-based kernel. The operator is responsible for centralizing client requests for customized computations, as well as security and billing tasks, and for dispatching the code on the Grid. We exploit the portability and networking capabilities of Java for providing simple mobile software packets, which are composed of a set of bytecode packages along with a configurable and serializable data object. We thus propose to use what is sometimes called $single-hop\ mobile\ agents$, which, compared to fully-fledged mobile agents, do not require heavy run-time support. These agents prevent the operator from becoming a bottleneck, by forwarding input code and data to computation locations and performing some management tasks. They start the different parts of the computations, ensure the management and monitoring of the distributed computations, and eventually collect and combine intermediate and final results.

The objective of this model is to propose a realistic deployment scenario, both from an economic and technical point of view, since we describe a setting where providers of computing resources (individuals or enterprises) may receive rewards in proportion to their service, and where issues like performance and security are addressed extensively, relying on actual tools and environments. While we put emphasis on being able to support *embarassingly parallel* computations, the model is sufficiently general to enable the distribution of many other kinds of applications.

Section 2 reviews distributed computations, Section 3 presents the model, Section 4 advocates the application of Java in Grid computing, whereas Section 5 describes the design and implementation of a secure execution environment, which constitutes a first necessary step towards the full realization of the model. Finally, Section 6 summarizes some related approaches, before concluding.

2 Distributed Computations

Worldwide distributed computations range from parallelization of applications to more general Grid distributions.

2.1 Parallelization

Distribution of computing across multiple environments shares similarities with the parallelization of code on a multi-processor computer. We distinguish two cases, the first one corresponds to single instruction, multiple data (SIMD), while the second one corresponds to multiple instruction, multiple data (MIMD). Figure 1 shows both cases.

In case (a), the client's host ships the same code, but with a different accompanying data to multiple locations. After computation, the different results are sent back to the client's host. The final result is simply the collection of the different results. This kind of distribution is appropriate for intensive computing on a huge amount of the same type of data. It corresponds to the distribution realized by the SETI@home[2] experiment that uses Internet connected computers in the Search for Extraterrestrial Intelligence (SETI). Donators first download a free program. The execution of the program then downloads and analyzes radio telescope data. Note that in this case, the downloaded data may come from a different source.

In case (b), code and data are split into several parts, then pairs of code and data are sent to several locations. The result is obtained by a combination (some function) of the different results.

Such a distribution is suitable for applications that can be divided into several pieces. This scheme fits the case of Parabon[3]. The client defines jobs to be performed. Transparently, the API divides the job into several tasks, on the client side; a task is made of a code, data, and some control messages. Tasks are sent to the Parabon server, which then forwards each task to a donator, using the donator's CPU idle time for computing the task. Once the task is achieved, the server sends back the result to the client, where the API then combines all results together, before presenting them to the client.

As a particular case of the MIMD example, code and data may be divided into several sequential parts. Computation would occur then in a pipeline-like style, where the next piece of code runs on the result of the previous computation.

These examples all exploit idle CPU time of the computer participating in the computations. The execution of the code on the data will ideally occur inside a secure "envelope", which ensures, on one hand, that the donator cannot exploit the code, the data and the results of the client; on the other hand, that the client

[2] http://setiathome.ssl.berkeley.edu/

[3] http://www.parabon.com

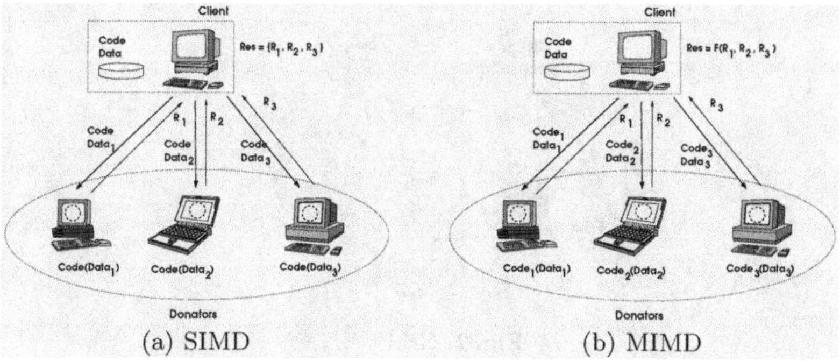

Fig. 1. Parallelisation

does not execute malicious code in the donator's host. This is however not the case in practice, since current environments cannot provide such guarantees. The model proposed here at least partly addresses this issue (see Section 4).

2.2 Grid

The more general case of distributed computing is provided by the Grid computing concept which enables collaborative multi-site computation [11]. Grid computing goes beyond traditional examples of peer-to-peer computing, since there is a concern of proposing a shared infrastructure for direct access to storage and computing resources.

Figure 2 shows a generic Grid computation, encompassing the different classes of Grid applications [10]. The client, requesting the computation, the software to run, the data, and the results may be located at different sites. The data is even distributed across two databases. In this example, the code and the two pieces of data are moved to the donator's location, where the computation takes place. The result is then shipped to the client.

The CERN DataGrid [7] provides an example where physicists are geographically dispersed, and the huge amount of data they want to analyze are located worldwide.

3 Proposed Model

In this section we give an overview of our overall architecture, we outline our business model, and describe the different roles of participants in our Grid computing infrastructure, as well as their interactions.

3.1 Participating Parties in the Grid Computing Model

Our model involves 3 distinct parties: the *operator* of the Grid, *resource donators*, and *clients*. The operator is in charge of maintaining the Grid. With the aid of

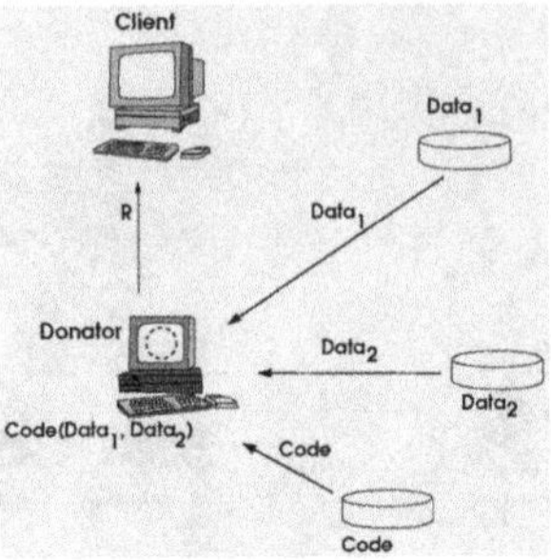

Fig. 2. Grid

a mobile *deployment agent*, he coordinates the distribution of applications and of input data, as well as the collection and integration of computed results. The operator downloads the applications, and distributes them to resource donators that perform the actual computation.

Clients wishing to exploit the Grid for their applications have to register at a server of the operator before they are allowed to start computations. During the registration step, the necessary information for billing is transmitted to the operator. Afterwards the client is able to send a *deployment descriptor* to the operator.

The deployment descriptor comprises the necessary information allowing the operator to download the application, to prepare it for billing and accounting, and to distribute the application and its streams of input data to different active resource donators, taking into consideration their current load. The mobile deployment agent, which is created by the operator based on the contents of the client's deployment descriptor and coordinates the distributed client application, is not bound to a server of the operator; the client may specify the server to host the deployment agent, or decide to let the agent roam the Grid according to its own parameters. This approach improves scalability and ensures that the operator does not become a bottleneck, because the operator is able to offload deployment agents from his own computers.

Resource donators are users connected to the same network as the operator (e.g., the Internet) who offer their idle computing resources for the execution of parts of large-scale scientific applications. They may receive small payments for the utilization of their systems, or they may donate resources to certain kinds of applications (e.g., applications that are beneficial for the general public). Resource donators register at the Grid operator, too. They receive a dedicated execution environment to host uploaded applications. Portability, high performance, and security are key requirements for this execution platform. Section 4 gives detailed information on our platform, which is completely based on the Java language. The operator dispatches downloaded applications to active resource donators. The deployment agent is in charge of supervising the flows of initial and intermediate data to and from the resource donators, as well as the final results, which are passed back to the destination designated by the client.

Allowing the deployment agent to be moved to any machine on the Grid improves efficiency, as the deployment agent may locally access the required data there. As explained later, the deployment agent, or its clones, is also responsible for minimizing the flows of Grid management data between the donators and the operator.

3.2 Business Model

In our model the operator of the Grid acts as a trusted party, since he is responsible of all billing tasks[4]. On the one hand, clients pay the operator for the distributed execution of their application. On the other hand, the operator pays the resource donators for offering their idle computing resources.

The client buys *execution tickets* (special tokens) from the operator, which the deployment agent passes to the resource donators for their services. The resource donators redeem the received execution tickets at the operator. The execution tickets resemble a sort of currency valid only within the Grid, where the operator is the exclusive currency issuer. They enable micro-payments for the consumption of computing resources. There are 3 types of execution tickets: tickets for CPU utilization, for memory allocation, and for data transfer over the network. The coordinating deployment agent has to pass execution tickets of all types to a resource donator for exploiting his computing resources.

Execution tickets have to be protected from faking, e.g., by cryptographic means, and from duplication, as the operator keeps track of all tickets actually issued. Execution tickets can be distributed at a fine granularity. Hence, the loss of a single execution ticket (e.g., due to the crash of a resource donator) is not a significant problem. In case the deployment agent does not receive the desired service from a resource donator for a given execution ticket, it will report to the operator. If it turns out that a resource donator collects tickets without delivering the appropriate service, the operator may decide to remove him from the Grid. The detection of such malicious donators is possible by correlating the amount of requested tickets with the work actually performed, which is measured by CPU monitoring inside the dedicated execution environment.

3.3 Deployment of Applications

In order to start an application, the client transmits a deployment descriptor to the operator, who will retrieve and dispatch the application to different resource donators and also create a deployment agent for the coordination of the distributed execution of the application.

The deployment descriptor, sent by the client, consists of the following elements:

- A description of the application's code location and structure. The client informs the operator of the application he wants to run. The operator will

[4] The operator may also be responsible for guaranteeing that only applications corresponding to the legal or moral standards fixed by the donators are deployed.

then download the application, and prepare it for resource control, before dispatching it to the donators. The application's structure establishes cut points and defines the different parts of the application that can run concurrently, as well as possible computational sequences. The client may specify himself the composition of computations, which reflects the calculus he desires to achieve (SIMD, MIMD, other). However, he does not customize the part of the description related to cut points, since it is tightly dependent on the application;
- A description of the source for input data. Usually, scientific applications have to process large streams of input data, which can be accessed e.g. from a web service provided by the client. The interface of this service is predefined by the operator and may support various communication protocols (e.g., RMI, CORBA, SOAP, etc.);
- A descriptor of the destination for output results. Again, this element designates the location of an appropriate service that can receive the results;
- Quality-of-service (QoS) parameters. The client may indicate the priority of the application, the desired execution rate, the number of redundant computations for each element of input data (to ensure the correctness of results), whether results have to be collected in-order or may be forwarded out-of-order to the client, etc. The QoS parameters allow the client to select an appropriate tradeoff between execution performance, costs, and reliability. The QoS parameters are essential to select the algorithms to be used by the deployment agent. For instance, if the client wishes in-order results, the deployment agent may have to buffer result data, in order to ensure the correct order.

In the following we summarize the various steps required to deploy a client application in the Grid. Figure 3 illustrates some of them.

1. Prospective resource donators and clients download and install the mobile code environment employed by the chosen operator, in order to be able to run the computations and/or to allow the execution of deployment agents.
2. Donators register with the operator and periodically renew their registration by telling how much they are willing to give in the immediate future; a calibration phase is initially run at each donator site to determine the local configuration (processor speed, available memory and disk space, quality and quantity of network access, etc.).
3. A client registers with the operator and sends the deployment descriptor (steps 1 and 2 of Figure 3).
4. The operator reads the deployment descriptor and:
   (a) Chooses an appropriate set of donators according to the required service level and to actually available resources; a micro-payment scheme is initiated, where fictive money is generated by the operator and will serve as authorization tokens for the client to ask donators for resources; a first wave of credit is transferred to the donator set, thus signifying that the corresponding amount of resources are reserved.

   (b) Creates a mobile agent, the deployment agent, for coordinating the distribution, execution and termination of the client application (step 3); this deployment agent will shift the corresponding load from the operator to the place designated by the client, or to a donator chosen according to load balancing principles; the deployment agent may clone itself or move to the appropriate places for ensuring that input and output data is transferred optimally, thus avoiding useless bottlenecks at central places like the operator server.
   (c) Downloads the client application (step 4) and rewrites it (reification of resources, step 5); the resulting code is signed to prevent tampering with it, and deployed directly from the operator's server (step 6).
   (d) Dispatches the deployment agent to the appropriate initial place for execution (step 7).
5. The deployment agent launches the distributed computation by indicating (step 8) to each donator-side task where to locate its respective share of input data (step 9), and starts monitoring the computation.
6. The deployment agent acts as a relay between the operator and the donators. The agent receives regular status reports from the various locations of the resource-reified application (step 10); this enables him to monitor the progress of the computations, and to detect problems like crashes and to assist in the recovery (e.g., by preparing a fresh copy of the appropriate input data, or by finding a new donator to take over the corresponding task); the status reports are filtered and forwarded to the operator (step 11) in order to help maintaining a reasonably good view of the global situation (the operator might decide to schedule a second application on under-utilized donators); when necessary, the operator will ask the client for more credit (step 12), who will then buy more authorization tokens from the operator (step 13). The deployment agent then passes the execution tickets to the donators (steps 14 and 15)
7. When results have to be collected, the deployment agent may clone or migrate to the destination (step 16) and coordinate the incoming flows of data (step 17). He may perform a last filtering and integrity control of data before it is definitely stored.

We favored this model over a completely decentralized peer-to-peer setting, since it simplifies the implementation of a global strategy for load balancing and ensures that some trusted party – the operator – can control the computations as they progress. In this approach, the operator also is in a natural position for managing all operations related to the validation of client-side payments and corresponding authorizations. Using mobile code for the deployment agent ensures that the server of the operator does not become a bottleneck and a single point of failure. In the current model, the application code has to be transferred to the operator's computer, since it needs to be checked for security purposes (e.g., by code inspection), to be prepared for billing and accounting (using resource reification), and to be partitioned according to the deployment descriptor.

Currently, in order to simplify the deployment of the dedicated execution environment, resource reification is performed at the operator's site. However, this might also occur at the donator sites, at the expense of possibly transforming the same application in the same way on n sites, hence a waste of resources. Another disadvantage is that the donators would be in direct contact with the end-client: this hampers the transparency of our current proposal, and might have practical inconveniences by short-circuiting the trusted third-party that the operator implements (e.g., the application could no longer be verified and digitally signed by the operator, which has a recognized certificate).

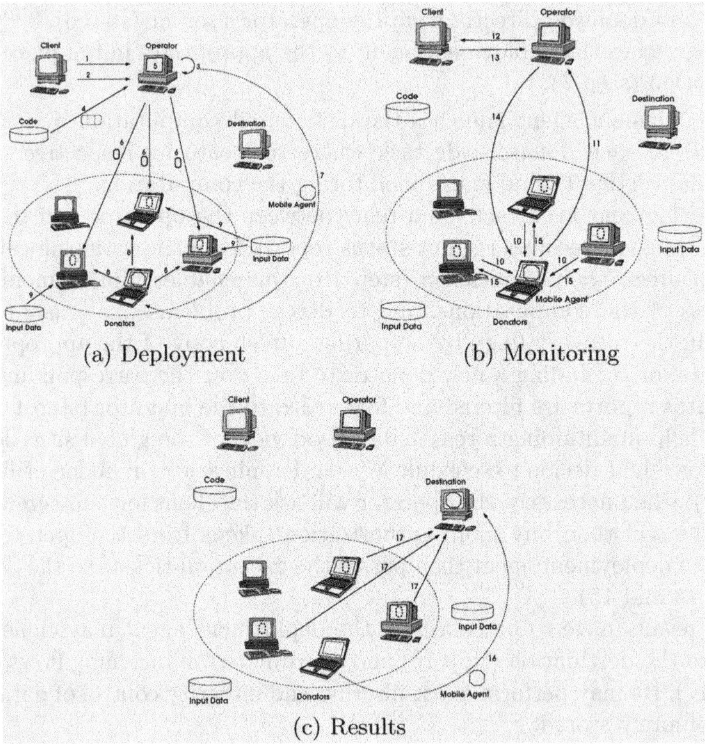

Fig. 3. Application Distribution

4 Using Java for the Distribution of Computations

Here we motivate the use of Java for the implementation of distributed computations and their distribution within a network. In our model we use Java-based mobile agents for the distribution of deployment agents (to a server specified by the client) and of computational tasks (to resource donators). A secure Java-based kernel, the JavaGridKernel, serves as execution platform for deployed components in both cases. In that way, we leverage the benefits of Java and of mobile code, while at the same time offering enhanced security to protect hosts from faulty applications.

4.1 Why Java?

Recently, platforms for Grid computing have emerged that are implemented in Java. For instance, Parabon offers an infrastructure for Grid computing which is based completely on Java. In fact, the Java language offers several features that ease the development and deployment of a software environment for Grid computing. Its network-centric approach and its built-in support for mobile code enable the distribution of computational tasks to different computer platforms.

Java runtime systems are available for most hardware platforms and operating systems. Because of the heterogeneity of the hardware and of operating systems employed by Internet users, it is crucial that a platform for large-scale Grid computing be available for a large variety of different computer systems. Consequently, a Java-based platform potentially allows every computer in the Internet to be exploited for distributed, large-scale computations, while at the same time the maintenance costs for the platform are minimal ("write once, run everywhere").

Apart from its portability and compatibility, language safety and a sophisticated security model with flexible access control are further frequently cited advantages of Java. As security is of paramount importance for the acceptance of a platform for Grid computing, the security and safety features of Java are highly appreciated in this context.

4.2 Performance Issues

Java has its origins in the development of portable Internet applications. The first implementations of Java runtime systems were interpreters that inefficiently executed Java Virtual Machine (JVM) bytecode [16] on client machines. Also, several features of the Java programming language impact performance: the fact that it is a type safe, object-oriented, general-purpose programming language, with automatic memory management, and that its implementation does not directly support arrays of rank greater than one, means that its execution may be less efficient compared to more primitive or specialized languages like C and Fortran.

However, optimizations performed by current state-of-the-art Java runtime systems include the removal of array bounds checking, efficient runtime type checking, method inlining, improved register allocation, and the removal of unnecessary synchronization code. See [15] for a survey of current compilation and optimization techniques that may boost the performance of Java runtime systems for scientific computing. In [17] the authors report that some Java applications already achieve 90% of the performance of equivalent compiled Fortran programs.

Considering the advantages of Java for the development and deployment of platforms for Grid computing, we think that a minor loss of performance can be accepted. Furthermore, the availability of more nodes where distributed computations can be carried out may often outweigh minor performance losses on each node. Ultimately, we are confident that maturing Java runtime systems will offer continuous performance improvements in the future.

4.3 Security Considerations

A high level of security is crucial for the acceptance of a platform for Grid computing. At first glance, Java runtime systems seem to offer comprehensive security features that meet the requirements of an execution environment for Grid computing: language safety, classloader namespaces, and access control based on dynamic stack introspection. Despite these advantages, current Java runtime systems are not able to protect the host from faulty (i.e., malicious or simply bugged) applications.

In the following we point out serious deficiencies of Java that may be exploited by malicious code to compromise the security and integrity of the platform (for further details, see [6]). Above all, Java is lacking a *task model* that could be used to completely isolate software components (applications and system services) from each other. A related problem is that, unfortunately, thread termination in Java is an inherently unsafe operation, which may e.g. leave shared objects, such as certain internals of the JVM, in an inconsistent state. Also related to the lack of task model is the absence of *accounting and control of resource consumption* (including but not limited to memory, CPU, threads, and network bandwidth). Concerning the implementation of current standard Java implementations, an issue is that several bytecode verifiers sometimes accept bytecode that does not represent a valid Java program: the result of the execution of such bytecode is undefined, and it may even compromise the integrity of the Java runtime system. Finally, while the security model of Java offers great flexibility in terms of implementing access control, it lacks central control: security checks are scattered throughout the classes, and it is next to impossible to determine with certainty whether a given application actually enforces a particular security policy.

All these shortcomings have to be considered in the design and implementation of Java-based platforms for Grid computing. Therefore, massive re-engineering efforts are needed to create sufficiently secure and reliable platforms.

5 The JavaGridKernel for the Secure Execution of Mobile Code

We have designed JavaGridKernel, a Java-based middleware that provides solutions to the security problems mentioned before and, hence, represents a state-of-the-art platform for the creation of secure environments for Grid computing. Several researchers have stressed the importance of multi-tasking features for Java-based middleware [2]. An abstraction similar to the *process* concept in operating systems is necessary in order to create secure execution environments for mobile code. However, many proposed solutions were either incomplete or required modifications of the Java runtime system.

In contrast, the JavaGridKernel has been designed to ensure important security guarantees without requiring any native code or modifications of the underlying Java implementation. The JavaGridKernel builds on the recent Java Isolation API [13], which offers the abstraction of *Isolates*, which fulfill a similar purpose as processes in operating systems and can be used to strongly protect Java components from each other, even within the same JVM. The Isolation API ensures that there is no sharing between different Isolates. Even static variables and class locks of system classes are not shared between Isolates in order to prevent unwanted side effects. Isolates cannot directly communicate object references by calling methods in each other, but have to resort to special communication links which allow to pass objects by deep copy. An Isolate can be terminated in a safe way, releasing all its resources without hampering any other isolate in the system. The Java Isolation API is supposed to be supported by future versions of the JDK. For the moment, it is necessary to resort to research JVMs that already provide the Isolation API, such as the MVM [8].

One crucial feature missing in Java is resource management, i.e., accounting and limiting the resource consumption (e.g., CPU and memory) of Java components. In the context of the JavaGridKernel, resource management is needed to prevent malicious or erroneous code from overusing the resources of the host where it has been deployed (e.g., denial-of-service attacks). Moreover, it enables the charging of clients for the consumption of their deployed applications. To address these issues, we have developed J-RAF2[5], The Java Resource Accounting Framework, Second Edition, which enables fully portable resource management in standard Java environments [5]. J-RAF2 transforms application classes and libraries, including the Java Development Kit, in order to expose details concerning their resource consumption during execution. J-RAF2 rewrites the bytecode of Java classes before they are loaded by the JVM. Currently, J-RAF2 addresses CPU, memory and network bandwidth control. For memory control, object allocations are intercepted in order to verify that no memory limit is exceeded. For CPU control, the number of executed bytecode instructions are counted and periodically the system checks whether a running thread exceeds its granted CPU quota. This implements a rate-based control policy; an additional upper hard limit on the total CPU consumed by any given computation can also be set and an associated overuse handler would then send an appropriate message to the deployment agent, to displace the task and hopefully prevent the loss of intermediate results. Control of network bandwidth is achieved by wrapping the standard input-output libraries of the JDK inside our own classes. J-RAF2 has been successfully tested in standard J2SE, J2ME, and J2EE environments. Due to special implementation techniques, execution time overhead for resource management is reasonably small, about 20–30%.

The Java Isolation API and J-RAF2 together provide the basis for the JavaGridKernel, which offers operating system-like features: Protection of compo-

[5] http://www.jraf2.org/

nents, safe communication, safe termination of components, and resource management. The JavaGridKernel extends these features with mechanisms to dynamically deploy, install, and monitor Java components. It should be noted that these mechanisms apply to the Java Virtual Machine and the associated executable bytecode representation: this approach is therefore in reality not restricted to programs written in the Java source language, but extends to all languages implemented on the JVM.

In the past we used the J-SEAL2 mobile object kernel [4] to implement an infrastructure for Grid computing. J-SEAL2 severely restricted the programming model of Java in order to enforce protection, safe communication, and termination of components. As the Java Isolation API provides these features in a standardized way without restricting the programming model, it is better suited for a Grid environment where also components designed without these J-SEAL2 specific restrictions in mind should be deployed.

The JavaGridKernel is perfectly suited for the development of platforms for Grid computing: It is small in size (only a few additional classes are required at run-time) and compatible with the Java 2 platform (but requires the Java Isolation API). Therefore, the distribution and installation of the kernel itself incurs only minimal overhead. The JavaGridKernel supports mobile code, which enables the distribution and remote maintenance of scientific applications. Finally, whereas scientific applications make heavy use of CPU and memory resources, the resource control features provided by J-RAF2 ensure a fair distribution of computational resources among multiple applications and prohibit an overloading of host machines. As explained below, resource control also provides additional security by thwarting dishonest behaviours on the donator side, thus making the model more attractive from an economic perspective.

The JavaGridKernel provides five special components: A mediator component to control the execution of uploaded applications, a network service to receive application code (Net-App service), a second network service allowing applications to receive input data and to transmit their results (Net-Data service), a system monitor to prevent an overloading of the machine, as well as a monitor window that displays information regarding the running applications, the elapsed time, etc. to the resource donator. In the following we give an overview of these components:

- The *mediator* is responsible for the installation and termination of applications, as well as for access and resource control. It utilizes the Net-App service to receive control messages from the deployment agents that coordinate the distributed applications. It receives application archives, which contain the application code as well as a deployment descriptor. The deployment descriptor comprises a unique identifier of the application, as well as information concerning the resource limits and the priority of the application. The unique application identifier is needed for dispatching messages to the appropriate application. Requests to terminate an application are also received from the Net-App service. The mediator component ensures that applications employ only the Net-Data service and guarantees that an ap-

plication only receives its own input data and that its output data is tagged by the application identifier. The mediator uses the system monitor in order to detect when the machine is busy; in this case, applications are suspended until the system monitor reports idle resources.
- The *Net-App service* is responsible for exchanging system messages with the coordinating deployment agent. When the platform is started, the Net-App service contacts the operator's server, which may transfer application archives to the platform. Optionally, a *persistency service* can be used to cache the code of applications that shall be executed for a longer period of time. The Net-App service also receives requests to terminate applications that are not needed anymore.
- The *Net-Data service* enables applications to receive input data and to deliver the results of their computation to the coordinating server. Messages are always tagged by an application identifier in order to associate them with an application. Access to the Net-Data service is verified by the mediator component. Frequently, continuous streams of data have to be processed by applications. The Net-Data service supports (limited) buffering of data to ensure that enough input data is available to running applications.
- The *system monitor* has to detect whether the machine is busy or idle. If the computer is busy, applications shall be suspended in order to avoid an overloading of the machine. If the computer is idle, applications shall be started or resumed. An implementation of the system monitor may employ information provided by the underlying operating system. However, such an approach compromises the full portability of all other components, since it relies on system-dependent information. Therefore, we follow a different approach: J-RAF2 enables the reification of the CPU consumption of applications [5], which allows to monitor the progress of applications. If the number of executed instructions is low (compared to the capacity of the hosting computer), even though applications are ready to run, the system monitor assumes that the computer is busy. Therefore, it contacts the mediator component in order to suspend computations. If, on the other hand, at the same time, requests for tickets originate from the same donator, it may be interpreted as malicious behaviour. Periodically, the system monitor resumes its activity in order to notice idle computing resources. When the computer becomes idle, all applications are resumed.
- The *monitoring window* presents information about the past and current work load of the system to the resource donator. It shows detailed status information of the running applications, the time elapsed for the computations, the estimated time until completion, if available, as well as some general information regarding the purpose of the computation. As the resource donator is in control of his system, it is important to show him detailed information of the utilization of his machine.

The mobile code execution environment for the deployment agents is based on the JavaGridKernel as well. But as the deployment agents stems from the operator, a trusted party, the security settings are relaxed. There are a few mandatory services needed by the deployment agent: access to the client web services that provide the input data and consume the output results, as well as network access for the communication with resource donators and the operator. Communication with the resource donators is necessary for the transmission of the application data, while communication with the operator is essential for the implementation of a global strategy for load balancing and for payment issues.

Regarding mobile code security, let us recall that the research community has not yet found a complete and general solution to the problem of malicious (donator) hosts, thus low-level tampering with Java bytecode (even cryptographically signed) or with the JVM is always possible if the attacker is sufficiently motivated, e.g., if a donator wants to steal results belonging to the client, or to hack the resource consumption mechanism in order to artificially increase his income. Our portable resource control mechanisms can nevertheless be exploited in several ways to detect such behaviours. First, if it is possible to determine statically the amount of resources required to achieve the given task, this detection will be trivial even across heterogenous machines, since J-RAF2 expresses CPU resource quantities in a portable unit of measurement (the bytecode). Second, it will always be possible to compare total consumptions at various donator machines and to correlate them with the size of the requested computations. The malicious host problem is however present in grid computing in general, not only with the mobile code approach proposed here.

6 Related Work

The primary purpose of mobile code is to distribute applications and services on heterogeneous networks. Many authors relate mobile code, and more often mobile agents as a practical technology for implementing load-balancing in wide-area networks like the Internet. Load-balancing can be either static (with single-hop agents, in the sense that once a task is assigned to a host, it does not move anymore) or dynamic (with multi-hop mobile agents enabling process migration). A survey of load-balancing systems with mobile agents is presented in [12]. Security and efficiency have immediately been recognized as crucial by the research community, but it was necessary to wait for technology to mature. Resource monitoring and control is needed for implementing load-balancing, and more generally for realizing secure and efficient systems, but is unavailable in standard Java, and particularly difficult to implement in a portable way. For instance, Sumatra [1] is a distributed resource monitoring system based on a modified JVM called Komodo. See [5] for a further study on the portability of resource monitoring and control systems in Java.

According to [20], almost all Grid resource allocation and scheduling research follows one of two paradigms: centralized omnipotent resource control – which is not a scalable solution – or localized application control, which can lead to unstable resource assignments as "Grid-aware" applications adapt to compete for resources. Our primary goal is however not to pursue research on *G-Commerce* [20], even though we sketch an economical model based on virtual currency. For these reasons, our approach is hybrid. We relax the conservative, centralized resource control model by proposing an intermediary level with our deployment agents, designed to make the architecture more scalable. We have identified a similar notion of mobile coordination agent in [9], with the difference that our agents do not only implement application-level coordination (synchronization, collection of intermediate results), but also management-level activities (local collection and filtering of load-balancing data), following the general approach we exposed in [19]. As described in [18], control data generated by distributed resource control systems may be huge – and even higher in G-commerce systems, because of bidding and auctioning messages – and mobile agents may thus profitably be dispatched at the worker nodes for filtering the data flows at their source. We propose a further level of filtering to be accomplished by the deployment agents; this is even more necessary as we intend to control all three resources (CPU, memory and network). CPU is widely regarded as the most important factor. In [14] the authors propose to place worker agents within a Grid according not only to CPU load, but also to network bandwidth requirements; they relate a speed improvement of up to 40%, but the measurements were made in local-area clusters instead of dynamic sets of Internet hosts. Finally, memory control is usually ignored, but we contend that it has to be implemented in order to support typical scientific Grid computations, since they often imply storing and processing huge amounts of data.

Among the approaches that are not agent-based, the Globus initiative provides a complete toolkit addressing, among others, issues such as security, information discovery, resource management and portability. The Globus toolkit is being adopted as a standard by most multi-organisational Grids [10, 11]. The latest major version, Globus Toolkit 3, allows for the execution of Java code; it has a resource management facility, which is partly based on native code, and is thus not entirely portable. Resource management in Globus is not designed to be as accurate as provided by J-RAF2, and more specifically, resource accounting is not provided, which prohibits our fine-grained monitoring and incentive of usage-based payment for offered computing resources. As several aspects in Globus 3, the protection between jobs is biased towards the availability of the Unix kind of processes; this provides for good security, but is more expensive in memory space than Java isolates, which are designed for security without compromising the possibility of sharing Java bytecode between protection domains. Finally, the basic job deployment and coordination mechanisms of Globus are not as flexible as the one permitted by the presently proposed mobile-agent based approach. These are a few aspects where we can propose some enhancements, but one should not be mistaken about the fact that Globus is an accomplished framework, whereas this paper essentially represents a theoretical work, based on a set of concrete building blocks.

Compared to a previous workshop position paper of ours [3] the model presented here relies on concepts and tools that are more mature and provide better guarantees of security and portability, while enabling a much more natural programming model than the one imposed by the J-SEAL2 mobile agent platform [4].

7 Conclusion

Our goal is to customize computations on open Internet Grids. To this end, we believe that a Grid environment should provide high-level primitives enabling the reuse and combination of existing programs and distributed collections of data, without forcing the client to dive into low-level programming details; the Unix scripting approach is our model, and this translates into our abstract *deployment descriptor* proposal. From the implementation point of view, this translates into a mobile *deployment agent*, which synthesizes and enhances the benefits of several previous approaches: the deployment agent optimizes its own placement on the Grid, and consequently it reduces the overall load by minimizing the communications needed for application-level as well as management-level coordination. There are of course still some open questions. The first pertains to the actual efficiency of the proposed model, which cannot be entirely determined before the complete implementation of the distributed control mechanisms. We have however tried to address the performance issue both at the host level, by proposing a solution which tries to minimize the management overhead, and at the global level, with a mobile agent-based approach which makes the whole system more scalable. The second concerns human factors such as validating the economical model (will it be attractive enough to generate real revenues?), or enabling the donator to decide on the lawfulness or ethics of computations submitted to him. This paper however concentrates on technological aspects, and claims that the comprehensive combination of a *pure Java* implementation enhanced with a secure, resource controlled execution platform is a unique asset for the portability, security and efficiency required for the success of Internet-based Grid computing.

References

1. A. Acharya, M. Ranganathan, and J. Saltz. Sumatra: A language for Resource-Aware mobile programs. In J. Vitek and C. Tschudin, editors, *Mobile Object Systems: Towards the Programmable Internet, Second International Workshop*, volume 1222 of *LNCS*. Springer, July 1996.
2. G. Back and W. Hsieh. Drawing the red line in Java. In *Seventh IEEE Workshop on Hot Topics in Operating Systems*, Rio Rico, AZ, USA, March 1999.
3. W. Binder, G. Di Marzo Serugendo, and J. Hulaas. Towards a Secure and Efficient Model for Grid Computing using Mobile Code. In *8th ECOOP Workshop on Mobile Object Systems, Malaga, Spain, June 10*, 2002.
4. Walter Binder. Design and implementation of the J-SEAL2 mobile agent kernel. In *The 2001 Symposium on Applications and the Internet (SAINT-2001)*, San Diego, CA, USA, January 2001.
5. Walter Binder, Jarle Hulaas, Alex Villazón, and Rory Vidal. Portable resource control in Java: The J-SEAL2 approach. In *ACM Conference on Object-Oriented Programming, Systems, Languages, and Applications (OOPSLA-2001)*, Tampa Bay, Florida, USA, October 2001.

6. Walter Binder and Volker Roth. Secure mobile agent systems using Java: Where are we heading? In *Seventeenth ACM Symposium on Applied Computing (SAC-2002)*, Madrid, Spain, March 2002.
7. P. Cerello and al. Grid Activities in Alice. In *International Conference on Computing in High Energy Physics 2001 (CHEP'01)*, 2001.
8. Grzegorz Czajkowski and Laurent Daynes. Multitasking without compromise: A virtual machine evolution. In *ACM Conference on Object-Oriented Programming, Systems, Languages, and Applications (OOPSLA'01)*, USA, October 2001.
9. P. Evripidou, C. Panayiotou, G. Samaras, and E. Pitoura. The pacman metacomputer: Parallel computing with java mobile agents. *Future Generation Computer Systems Journal, Special Issue on Java in High Performance Computing*, 18(2):265–280, October 2001.
10. I. Foster and C. Kesselman. Computational Grids. In *The Grid: Blueprint for a Future Computing Infrastructure*, chapter 2. Morgan Kaufmann, 1999.
11. I. Foster, C. Kesselman, and S. Tuecke. The Anatomy of the Grid – Enabling Scalable Virtual Organizations. *International Journal of Supercomputer Applications*, 15(3), 2001.
12. J. Gomoluch and M. Schroeder. Information agents on the move: A survey on load-balancing with mobile agents. *Software Focus*, 2(2), 2001.
13. Java Community Process. JSR 121 – Application Isolation API Specification. Web pages at http://jcp.org/jsr/detail/121.jsp.
14. A. Keren and A. Barak. Adaptive placement of parallel java agents in a scalable computer cluster. In *Workshop on Java for High-Performance Network Computing*, Stanford University, Palo Alto, CA, USA, February 1998. ACM Press.
15. Andreas Krall and Philipp Tomsich. Java for large-scale scientific computations? In *Third International Conference on Large-Scale Scientific Computations (SCICOM-2001)*, Sozopol, Bulgaria, June 2001.
16. Tim Lindholm and Frank Yellin. *The Java Virtual Machine Specification.* Addison-Wesley, Reading, MA, USA, second edition, 1999.
17. J. E. Moreira, S. P. Midkoff, M. Gupta, P. V. Artigas, M. Snir, and R. D. Lawrence. Java programming for high-performance numerical computing. *IBM Systems Journal*, 39(1):21–56, 2000.
18. O. Tomarchio, L. Vita, and A. Puliafito. Active monitoring in grid environments using mobile agent technology. In *2nd Workshop on Active Middleware Services (AMS'00) in HPDC-9*, August 2000.
19. A. Villazón and J. Hulaas. Active network service management based on meta-level architectures. In *Reflection and Software Engineering*, volume 1826 of *LNCS*, June 2000.
20. R. Wolski, S. Plank, T. Bryan, and J. Brevik. Analyzing Market-based Resource Allocation Strategies for the Computational Grid. *International Journal of High Performance Computing Applications*, 15(3), 2001.

An Approach to Flexible Application Composition in a Diverse Software Landscape

Roy Oberhauser

Corporate Technology, Siemens AG
Otto-Hahn-Ring 6, 81730 Munich, Germany
roy.oberhauser@siemens.com

Abstract. With the escalating complexity, aggregation, and integration of software in enterprise, mobile, and pervasive arenas, it becomes increasingly difficult to compose, deploy, and operate applications that span a distributed and diverse software landscape. Furthermore, the increasing aggregation of software artifacts, including platforms, frameworks, components, services, and tools, lack a standard metadata description capability that hinders rapid and flexible distribution, deployment, and operation. This paper presents a general approach, realized with the FAST Framework, to improving the development, deployment, and operation of distributed applications that consist of diverse software artifacts. Application specification and composition is based on configuration queries that flexibly combine modules and a container that non-intrusively manages module lifecycles. The results show benefits with regard to simplified configurability, enhanced reuse via XML-based description propagation, improved distributed-application-provisioning intervals vs. local configurations, as well as applicability to Grid, Web Services, and MDA.

1 Introduction

As a trend, the complexity of software applications is escalating, where complexity is a function of the types and number of relationships among the software elements. This escalation is especially true of distributed applications in areas such as enterprise and pervasive infrastructures and applications. Increasing software integration as well as the aggregation of software artifacts, e.g. as shown in the tendency to utilize standardized platforms and API providers (e.g. J2EE, .NET), open source software frameworks, etc., contribute to the overall underlying complexity of an application.

Simultaneously, competitive pressures compel developers to more rapidly produce software that is parameterized to fit various predefined and hard-to-predict post-defined operational contexts and configurations. As these pressures in turn cause developers and maintainers to handle multiple projects simultaneously, when considered in conjunction with geographically distributed teams, the rapid reuse and propagation of deployment configurations will become a growing necessity.

Conversely, software operators (a set that includes developers) are faced with a daunting set of amassed choices with regard to both the parameterization and (reproducible) configuration of aggregated, distributed, and legacy software. This is exac-

M. Jeckle, R. Kowalczyk, and P. Braun (Eds.): GSEM 2004, LNCS 3270, pp. 48–62, 2004.

erbated by the inherent variability of software, as in versioning of any of the constituent parts of a distributed application. This has given rise to the adage "Never touch a running system," and the problems in this area are described with case studies in [1]. While a myriad of configuration and deployment mechanisms exists, no unifying, widely adopted, practical, and economic solution in this diverse, heterogeneous software landscape is available.

Considering these aforementioned challenges, the primary objective is to support distributed application configurations (especially with regard to composability, flexibility, manageability, and reuse) by means of a non-intrusive infrastructure with minimal requirements for describing and provisioning the involved software artifacts. An artifact can be a piece of software or anything associated with it (e.g., tools, documentation). A solution that comprehensively addresses all possible software configurations and artifacts is beyond scope; rather, the contribution of this paper is a practical and economic approach that deals with various basic issues in the current gap in distribution, deployment, and operation, thereby drawing attention to this area.

The paper is organized as follows: Section 2 reviews related work to elucidate the current gap. In Section 3, the solution approach and constraints are presented. This is followed in Section 4 by a description of the solution realization, referred to in this paper as the FAST Framework. At the core of the framework is a container that manages modules and configurations and communicates with other containers. Section 5 discusses the results, and in Section 6, a conclusion is drawn.

2 Related Work

Because the focus of this paper touches such a universal aspect of software, it can easily be related in some way to a range of other efforts and work. Since not all related work and aspects can necessarily be addressed, only primary and/or key comparable work will be mentioned.

In the area of composition and integration, the VCF [2] approach to component composition relies on a Java API and requires component model plugins. Its focus is limited to components, and thus cannot provide a unifying approach that includes preexisting and non-component-oriented artifacts. FUJABA [3], a meta-model approach to tool integration, requires plug-ins and does not address distributed applications. [4] provides a survey of various composition environments, all of which cannot provide a unifying approach due to constraints, platform-dependencies, or a composition focus at the more intrusive communication or interaction level, resulting in development phase dependencies or runtime impacts. As to composability in Web Services (e.g., BPEL4WS, WSCI), its focus is the interaction abstraction level, leaving the infrastructural aspects of aggregation, configurability, distribution, provisioning, deployment, and manageability for a diverse software environment unaddressed.

As to platform-specific provisioning frameworks, SmartFrog [5] is a flexible, object-oriented framework for the deployment and configuration of remote Java objects. It has a security concept and its own declarative non-XML language includes parameterized and inheritable templates. However, its component model requires inheritance from Java objects - thus requiring a Java wrapper class for each external software artifact it manages, and the more flexible concept of queries for application composition does not appear to be supported. Jini's Rio [6] provides dynamic provisioning capabilities, policies, and telemetry using an agent-based Dynamic Container. Service components are described using XML-based metadata (an OperationalString). A component model (Jini Service Beans) is provided and, for managing external services, Service Control Adapters must be written. Its model is platform-dependent and its reliance on Jini's RMI mechanism makes infrastructural interoperability in diverse landscapes problematic.

Common configuration management tools, such as HP's OpenView, IBM's Tivoli, etc., address various enterprise deployment and operation issues, yet they do not necessarily scale down for small projects, devices, or budgets, and various other tools are often tied to operating systems. Management standards activities, such as the Open Management Interface and OASIS Web Services Distributed Managmement Technical Committee, address management interfaces for Web Services (WS), but will likely not be able to manage all related and legacy artifacts. Platform-specific management initiatives, such as Java Management Extensions (JMX), will necessarily be limited to their platform, and have typically neglected the aspect of metadata.

Metadata initiatives, such as the WS-MetadataExchange, may allow WS to exchange metadata with one another, but first the WS must be operational, and no metadata standard exists for describing basic operational aspects of software artifacts. Platform-specific metadata such as contained in Java JAR files, in .NET, and in JSR 175 "A Metadata Facility for the Java Programming Language," are not easily accessible or modifiable by operators, especially for diverse environments. Where tooling creates the metadata, it tends to become so complex and all encompassing that manual creation for incorporation of other artifacts is avoided.

Model-Driven Architecture (MDA) [7] is primarily a development-centric paradigm and depends on the existence of models for the involved artifacts. While [8][9][10] describe the combination of Model-Integrated Computing (MIC) with middleware, the approach to distributed configuration and parameterization appears to be application synthesis, close integration with the CCM container CIAO, and in the future advanced meta-programming with reflection [11] and AOP [12]. How these distributed applications and each (non-modeled-)artifact are managed and configured in each operational environment variant over their lifetime, in conjunction with potential overlapping integration that occurs in SOA environments, is not detailed. While beyond the scope of this paper, in a model-centric environment a unifying approach for artifact metadata could conceptually, via XML Metadata Interchange (XMI) and the Meta-Object Facility (MOF), be integrated into such a tool chain to address various deployment, configuration, and parameterization aspects for artifacts at development-, initialization-, and run-time.

While viewpoints differ, Grid initiatives such as the Globus Alliance are primarily focused on resource sharing, security, performance, QoS, and the larger provisioning problem [13] with runtime interoperability protocols and toolkit APIs in view. Many (legacy) software artifacts are and will remain outside of this scope, yet the Grid resources being shared, e.g. via WSRF [14], may well be dependent on these hidden artifacts and their proper distributed configuration, management, and parameterization. A unified and cost efficient approach to these challenges is needed.

3 Solution Approach

To discuss the solution approach, it is helpful to work with an example that also illustrates the various challenges when different inter-related and inter-dependent software components, services, applications, frameworks, and infrastructures are combined. Although this illustration was realized for test purposes, the intent of this illustration is not to show an ideal distributed application, but rather to bring to the forefront the issues diverse artifacts and infrastructures can create.

As to solution constraints, no interference in the interfaces, installation, communication, and interactions between or within a module should necessarily occur, nor should changes be required to a module. Thus, encapsulation is not to be enforced, but rather a mechanism for developers to manually supply the relevant and missing metadata is provided, which may be partial but sufficient for the operational tasks. The relative simplicity and ubiquity of XML is a desirable quality to further adoption and standardization efforts, supports the rapid creation of missing module descriptions, and avoids coupling to the artifact itself (in contrast to JMX). Reuse of specified configurations and module descriptions as well as a lifecycle management mechanism shall be supported. Emphasis should be given to enhanced support for an operational view, benefiting operators, developers, and testers. Due to a lack of implementations and tools to realize this approach, a framework is necessary to interpret the configuration and module descriptions and manage the modules.

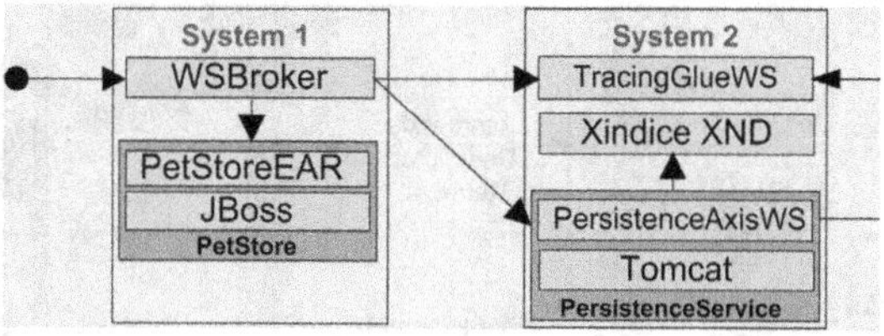

Fig. 1. Problem view showing sample distributed application interactions using diverse software artifacts

In Fig. 1 the problem view is presented using an illustration. Given a JBoss-ported reference J2EE PetStore enterprise application (PetStoreEAR) that is dependent on a J2EE application server JBossto become operational, this grouping of software artifacts can be considered a configuration PetStore. Another grouping, called the PersistenceService, consists of an XML persistence Web Service (PersistenceAxisWS) that abstracts XML Native Database (XND) differences, is based on the Apache Axis WS framework, is deployed as a web application (WAR) within a web server (Apache Tomcat), and uses Apache Xindice as an XND. Now hypothetically, without modifying either of these configurations, a PetStoreSupplier distributed application configuration would like to intercept all placed orders to the PetStore configuration, e.g. via an HTTP Proxy with interception capability (called WSBroker), persist these orders as XML via the PersistenceService configuration, and provide tracing data to a tracing Web Service implemented with the webmethods GLUE WS toolkit (TracingGlueWS). Note that the problem space could involve non-Java software.

To converge on a solution, the problem domain was partitioned into three separate areas:

1. The first area dealt with module description: what are the common attributes of software artifacts or modules that should typically be described, how should they be described, and what strategies can be used to reduce redundancy, manage change, and keep the involved effort and maintenance low?
2. The second area dealt with configuration description: how should modules best be flexibly aggregated into a grouping, how can redundancy be reduced, and how can the reuse or propagation of configurations be supported?
3. The third area consisted of the distributed software infrastructure necessary for supporting the lifecycle of modules and configurations with minimal intrusion and constraints in a diverse software landscape.

As a starting point, the FAST Framework will provide the overall structure necessary for lifecycle management, configuration support, and any common and shared modules and tools, shown in Fig. 2 using the problem example from Fig. 1. Discussion of modules, configurations, and containers follows.

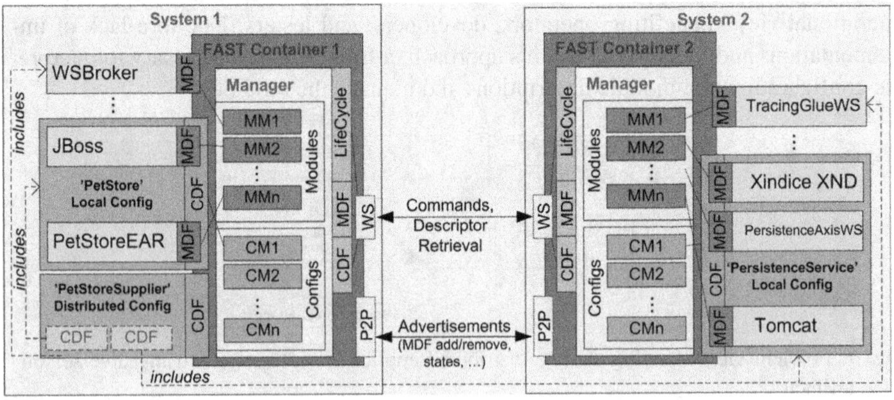

Fig. 2. Sample distributed application with the FAST Framework, showing containners, modules, configurations, and sub-configurations

3.1 Modules

As modularity plays a key role in dealing with complexity, for this paper, a module is an abstraction for the partitioning of a (semi-)independent unit of software (software artifact) required by an application, at any desired abstraction level, and can include frameworks, services, components, packaged applications, web and application servers, documentation, etc. For reuse, extensibility, and flexibility, a module is described via an XML-based Module Descriptor File (MDF), as seen in Fig. 2. This MDF supplies the necessary and desired metadata, typically the information required for its lifecycle management along with any additional information, as shown in the example in Listing 1. Note that an XML Schema definition specifies the allowable values, and is not shown due to space constraints.

Listing 1. Module Descriptor File (MDF) example

```
<module name="PersistenceAxisWS" uid="1422756542">
  <description>
    <category>soa.ws.persistence</category>
    <author>John Doe</author>
    <timestamp> 27-Apr-04 9:12:14.06 GMT</timestamp>
    <version>1.0</version>
...
  </description>
  <dependencies>
    <query id="1" type="module">
      <name>Xindice</name>
    </query>
    <query id="2" type="module">
      <name>Tomcat</name>
      <version min="4.1" max="5.0.19"/>
    </query>
    <query id="3" type="module">
      <name>Axis</name>
    </query>
  </dependencies>
  <management>
    <instances min="0" max="1">
      <instance nbr="1">
        <port>9876</port>
      </instance>
    </instances>
    <lifecycle>
...
      <task type="uninstall">
        <cmd type="ant">
          undeploy/tomcat_undeploywar.xml</cmd>
      </task>
    </lifecycle>
    <templates>
      <template name="axis_webservice" version="1.0">
        <settings>
          <setting name="ws_uri" value="http://${env.ip}:
            ${instance.port}/axis/PersistenceAxisWS"/>
        </settings>
      </template>
    </templates>
  </management>
  <tools>
    <query id="3" type="module">
      <name>Axis TCP Monitor</name>
    </query>
  </tools>
  <documentation>
    <query id="4" type="module">
      <name>Command-Line</name>
```

```
      <parameters>
        <parameter>-DCMD</parameter>
        <parameter>docs/PWS-UserGuide.pdf</parameter>
      </parameters>
    </query>
  </documentation>
</module>
```

Each module is given a name and a uid attribute that allows the unique identification of an MDF. Various options can be used to generate the uid, such as tools or the use of a central uid provider. Digital signatures could be included to permit creator verification and detect content tampering. Under description, information about the MDF itself is included. The element dependencies specifies modules necessary for this module to function properly. Hereby dependencies use query, which allow constraints to be specified (name, version, location, etc.) and are resolved at runtime to find a matching candidate, e.g., the best, a range, or exactly one required candidate of the available modules known to the Container.

Under management, the number of instances of this module that can be started as well as any instance-specific parameters can be specified. The module lifecycle transitions can be associated with actions to be performed, and are specified under lifecycle with task (see Fig. 3). Because all module types should be supportable and creating multiple processes is not always desirable for resource-constrained contexts, different external process (e.g. Apache Ant) and internal process (e.g., same Java Virtual Machine) cmd (command) types, including parameters, are supported for lifecycle management. One feature (not shown) is the ability to specify a pattern for lifecycle progress and error checking in the output files of external modules.

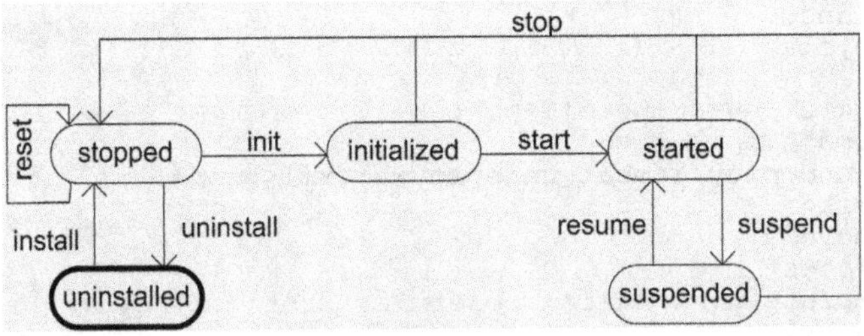

Fig. 3. Module and configuration typical lifecycle state diagram (additional states supported)

A template, defined in an XML Schema definition (not shown), allows the inclusion of pre-specified XML, and is a contract in the sense that a module that incorporates template indicates that it fulfills its requirements, e.g. requirements for interfaces or protocols that must be supported, pre-configuration of parameters, valid parameter ranges, etc. Templates are analogous in some ways to a class; they can be instantiated with parameters and support inheritance, thus hierarchies of templates are possible as well as overriding of default settings. The template contract in a module can be validated against the template's XML Schema definition. In this case, the axis_webservice template schema (not shown) includes the AXIS template schema (not shown) which specifies the HTTP, SOAP, and WSDL versions that are supported, and specifies the `ws_uri` value. Note that `setting` is used to set parameters for a software artifact; for artifact configuration settings in text files, scripts (e.g. sed, python) are supported, for XML files XSLT, and JMX is used for runtime (re-)configuration support. While templates are optional, for maximum reuse effectiveness, they should be specified and propagated, e.g. via a central repository. This specification could be done in both general and domain-specific areas via standards bodies, consisting of software vendors, research institutes, etc.

Under `tools`, any tools associated with this module can be included, while `documentation` provides the queries (e.g. commands) or links to retrieve the documentation associated with this module.

MDFs allow the information for a module to be described and associated once, and then reused in many different configurations.

3.2 Configurations

Configurations are a hierarchical composition of modules or sub-configurations and described in a Configuration Descriptor File (CDF), as seen in Fig. 2. A set of queries is used to allow maximum flexibility in specifying and resolving the actual modules or configurations, while minimizing redundant information. Sub-configurations allow a hierarchical reuse in the specification of configurations, e.g. in Fig. 2 both the PersistenceService and the PetStore are sub-configurations of the PetstoreSupplier configuration.

Listing 2. Configuration Descriptor File (CDF) example

```
<configuration name="PetStoreSupplier" uid="4968365039">
  <description>
    <category>application.demo</category>
    <author>John Doe</author>
    <timestamp> 27-Apr-04 9:51:14.06 GMT</timestamp>
    <version>1.0</version>
...
  </description>
  <dependencies>
    <query id="1" type="module">
      <name>TracingGlueWS</name>
    </query>
    <query id="2" type="module" startuporder="1"
        location="localhost">
      <name>WSBroker</name>
    </query>
    <query id="3" type="config" startuporder="1, 4"
        location="strategy_best">
      <name>PetStore</name>
    </query>
    <query id="4" type="config" startuporder="1"
        location="192.168.3.100">
      <name>PersistenceService</name>
    </query>
  </dependencies>
  <management>
```

```
    <instances min="0" max="1"/>
    <lifecycle/>
  </management>
  <tools/>
  <documentation/>
</configuration>
```

An example of a CDF is shown in Listing 2. The `name` and `uid` attribute are equivalent to that described for MDFs, as are the `description`, `dependencies`, `management`, etc. The number of instances allowed of this configuration among a set of containers may be specified by `instances` if it does not conflict with the sum of the underlying MDFs and CDFs constraints.

As to startup ordering, by default parallel or independent lifecycles are assumed unless the `startuporder` attribute is included as an attribute specifying a sequential list of one or more queries that must first be successfully started. Different strategies for the distribution of a configuration can be used. The `location` attribute in a query is optional, and allows either an IP address to be specified, the name of a strategy, e.g. `strategy_best`, or a DNS hostname. If no location is specified, then the Container will decide based on its default strategy. For distributed configurations with unspecified location attributes, the master or hosting Container (the first to start the "init" transition) annotates the location information before distributing the configuration, thus ensuring that other Containers can determine their responsibilities.

The lifecycle of configurations are equivalent to those of modules (see Fig. 3).

3.3 Containers

A Container non-intrusively manages the lifecycle its software modules or configurations. As a form of bootstrapping, its CDF specifies its own core modules. It also supplies its own MDF, as shown in Fig. 2, to describe its capabilities and states. Any extensions to the Container are done as modules via MDFs, providing a plug-in capability. At a minimum (equivalent to an empty Container CDF), the Container contains the software for parsing MDF/CDFs and lifecycle management, allowing it to be lightweight for resource-constrained contexts. Containers can optionally interact via the Container Discovery and related modules to support the distribution of metadata and the discovery of remote configurations and modules. Any inter-Container interaction is done via XML-based protocols to better support interoperability with heterogeneous Container implementations.

4 Solution Realization

While the reference implementation is Java-based, the solution approach can be implemented for a wide variety of platforms and languages while supporting interoperability, due to the reliance on XML for metadata (MDFs and CDFs) and inter-Container protocols (SOAP and JXTA [15]). The following provides insight into the realization while elaborating the potential of this approach. The inclusion of various modules listed below supports basic to enhanced framework configurations depending on the requirements.

4.1 Container

For each module that the Container manages, a Module Manager is allocated, shown as MMn in Fig. 2. Likewise, for each configuration being managed, a Configuration Manager (CCn in Fig. 2) is allocated. DOM4J was used to parse the needed MDF and CDF information into Java objects. Dependencies are resolved to determine lifecycle sequencing. Support for Apache Ant was integrated as a task type. A Container shell allows command control of the container.

4.2 Modules

Over 50 module descriptions for various software artifacts were created in the current FAST distribution, verifying that it can support many different types of modules. Below are some examples of infrastructural modules, which can be viewed as a Container extensibility mechanism:

- **Container Discovery Module.** Responsible for advertising the existence or change of its modules and configurations to other Containers and detecting other Containers and their state changes. Currently JXTA advertisements are used, however other discovery mechanisms, including registries, can be supported.
- **Container Management Web Service Module.** This optional module supports remote management via SOAP, providing module and configuration descriptor retrieval.
- **Deployer Service Module.** This module supports the deployment of software as a container-independent, distributed, transactional, discoverable deployment service with adapters for various containers (JBoss, OSGi Oscar, Java VM, etc.). A GUI, as shown in Fig. 4, provides operators insight into the location and dependencies within deployment units.
- **Web Services Broker (WSBroker) Module.** An optional module that contains an HTTP Proxy combined with an interception framework that includes the Apache Bean Scripting Framework, allowing Java- or script-based interceptors that provide a variation point for technically trained operators to perform routing, logging, or other functions.
- **Web Services Registry (WSRegistry) Module.** This optional module contains a UDDI-protocol-compliant mechanism to access Web Services.
- **Tracing Web Service (TWS) Module.** This optional module enables the monitoring of operational interactions between modules via built-in or interception (e.g., WSBroker) mechanisms, and made available to tooling for the operational view.
- **Persistence Web Service Module**. This optional module provides a generic Web Service interface to persist data in different XML storage mechanisms.

5 Solution Results

While many possible criteria could be used to evaluate the solution, tests were chosen that would answer the following questions regarding practical suitability: Does dis-

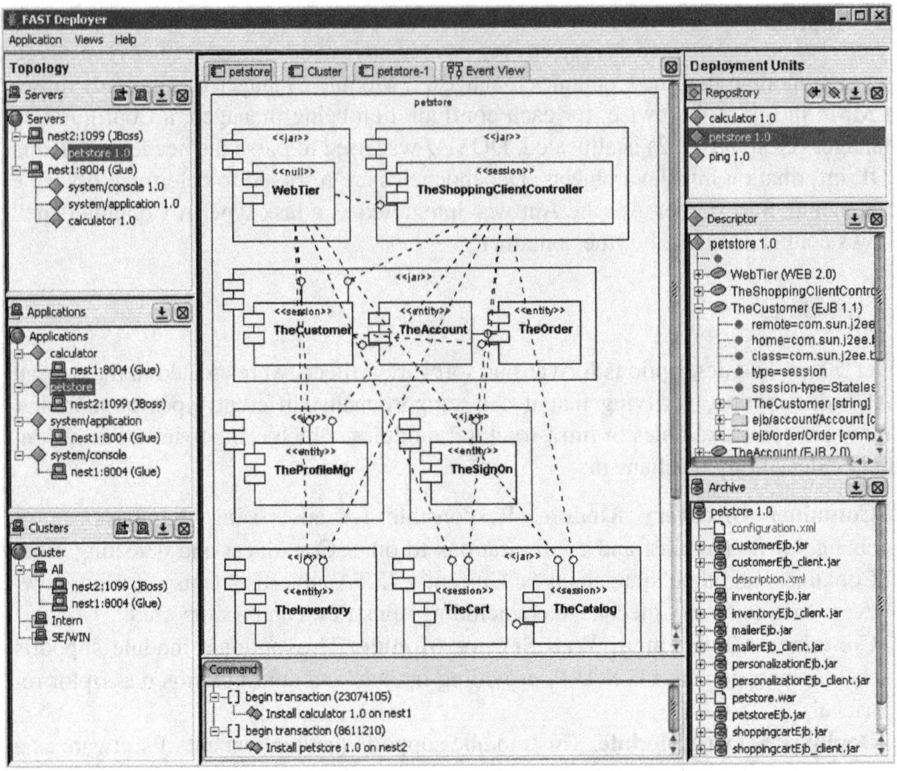

Fig. 4. Screenshot of the FAST Deployer GUI

tributed provisioning show significant performance advantages over local provisioning? How does the amount of time for software (re-)deployment (transfer) compare to any potential gain via distribution? How fast does the infrastructure react to faults? What is the memory footprint and scalability profile? How usable was the solution in practice?

The hardware consisted of two Fujitsu Siemens Scenic W600, i8656 (model MTR-D1567) PCs with dual 3GHz CPUs connected by a 100MBit Ethernet LAN and a hub. PC100 had 512MB and PC101 768MB RAM. The software configuration was Windows XP SP1, JXTA 2.2, WebMethods Glue 4.1.2, and Java JDK 1.4.2. Note that no performance or memory tuning was done to the implementation, and for resource-constrained scenarios another XML-based discovery mechanism could be used.

The Distributed Application Provisioning Test (Table 1) used 13 modules in a Configuration as shown in Table 1, first measuring their local startup times and then the time when the configuration was distributed across both machines, showing nearly a factor 2 improvement for the application to become ready. By making the distribution of module locations easy, performance gains for startup and shutdown can be reached (due to parallelism). This could improve development cycle efficiencies and application testing realism.

Table 1. Distributed Application Provisioning Test module startup times in milliseconds for a diverse software configuration locally and distributed across 2 PCs.

Module name (time in msec)	Local PC100	Local PC101	Distributed (PC100 except *=on PC101)
Demo Supplier Config. (start)	0	0	0
Jini 1.2.1 HttpServer	1234	2750	1594
Jini 1.2.1 RMIDaemon	1359	4391	1782
Jini 1.2.1 LookupServer	1390	5657	2063
Jini 1.2.1 TransactionManager	1468	6000	2328
James 2.1 Email Server*	4015	4641	5360
TracingWebService	6515	7391	5907
Jini 1.2.1 JavaSpaces	6687	7438	6282
ScriptService	12515	11047	11360
Apache Xindice XML DB 1.0	13234	8250	8750
SupplierOrderWebService	11734	12344	11938
WebServiceBroker*	6671	5797	5516
Jakarta Tomcat 5.0.16	25359	23625	18719
JBoss 3.2.1*	41156	35782	18938
Configuration ready	41656	35782	19375

Table 2. Maximum heap space used by the Container under various conditions.

Container Condition (WS=ContainerWebService)	Max Heap Used
A: No modules loaded; WS and JXTA disabled	1MB
B: 50 modules loaded; WS and JXTA disabled	1.2MB
C: No modules loaded; WS enabled; JXTA disabled	2.2MB
D: No modules loaded; WS and JXTA enabled	7MB
E: No modules loaded; WS and JXTA enabled; Peer advertisement of 50 module states received from 2nd Container	7.5MB

The Deployment Unit Transfer Test determines the amount of time needed to transfer a file by the FAST Deployer into a remote EJB container. The time to remotely deploy from PC100 to PC101 a new 1236KB petstore.ear (modified to run on JBoss) was measured to be 3.4 seconds. While this shows a need for improvement, it does not invalidate the case for distributed provisioning when compared to the shown performance gains for typical software artifacts.

The Failure Reconfiguration Test shows the reaction time of the infrastructure to a module failure in a distributed configuration. The James Email Server process was killed on PC100. The reaction time was 200ms from detection of a state change on PC100 through sending of a state-changed advertisement, to receipt on PC101 to the point where it begins to start its local James Email Server module. Thus the infrastructure reaction time would not typically be the primary factor, but rather module startup time.

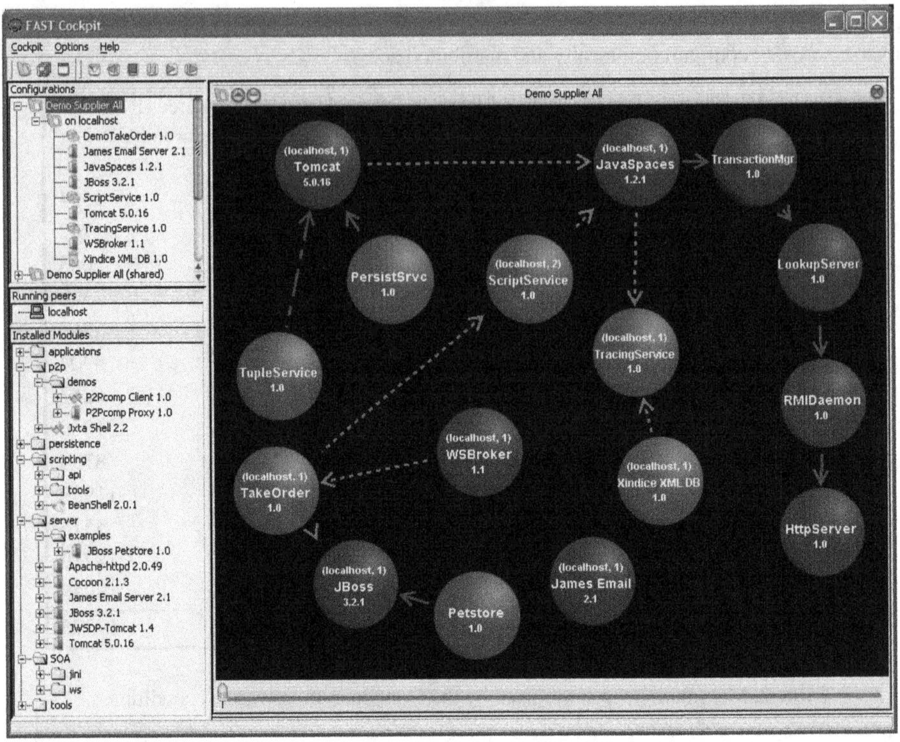

Fig. 5. The FAST Cockpit showing a graphical representation of a configuration of modules (as spheres) with directed lines of interactions and dependencies

In the Memory Footprint Test (Table 2), the heap space of the Container on PC100 was measured under various circumstances as shown in Table 2. The difference between condition B and A shows that under most expected scenarios, managing even a large number of modules does not affect the memory footprint significantly. Thus the solution could potentially be applied to resource-constrained contexts.

Other criteria include the experience with usage of the solution realization within the organization. A GUI tool, the FAST Cockpit (see Fig. 5), was developed to demonstrate the operator-friendly possibilities once MDFs, CDFs, and Containers are available. Configurations with their associated modules are listed in the top-left box and can be created by drag-and-drop of installed modules - categorized both in the bottom-left and with sphere colors. Animated tracing with playback is operated with buttons on the top menu and the event slider at the bottom of the configuration. The status of modules is represented with colored fonts and icons and module outputs are available in separate windows.

An internal distribution among colleagues in the organization has enabled the operation of complex configurations of distributed applications without the operator necessarily being aware of the infrastructural issues and dependencies involved. Based on feedback, a significant improvement in the time required to specify, compose, and instantiate distributed applications has been observed as well as comprehension benefits. Note that the amount of time needed to create an MDF depends on the person's skills and the familiarity with the software being described and MDF concepts, but times of less than 15 minutes have been measured. The time to create a CDF using the Cockpit is a matter of drag-and-drop of modules and any startup sequence dependency specification. Thus, the investment in the one-time MDF creation typically pays off quickly, analogous to the investment in a makefile.

The feasibility, suitability, and advantages of this approach were hereby validated, and future work will continue to improve these results.

6 Conclusion

Despite the growing marketplace competitiveness and pressure for faster software delivery schedules, the challenges with regard to composing, configuring, deploying, and operating distributed applications in a diverse software landscape have not received adequate attention. There remains no unifying, widely adopted, practical, and economic solution.

While the current FAST realization has shown good results, ongoing and future work includes determining to what degree the security, policies, QoS and Service-Level-Agreements can be addressed without annulling the current simplicity and interoperability; correctness; concurrent configuration conflict checking; addressing any single-points-of-failure; performance and memory tuning; a repository for MDF and CDF propagation; a wizard for MDF creation; evaluating the issue of semantics in MDFs and CDFs; and efforts towards more prevalent, standard, or unified software artifact metadata.

FAST presents a practical solution to the current gap with regard to both the goal of distributed application composition in this diverse landscape and given constraints such as effort, cost, and others. A comprehensive solution could be realized by universal software standardization efforts for flexible-granularity and flexible-aspect (e.g. operational) software metadata, in combination with platform, development environment, and tool vendor support for utilizing this metadata.

Acknowledgements

The author would like to thank the following individuals for their efforts with regard to various aspects of FAST: Ulrich Dinger, Emmanuel Gabbud, Christoph Huter, Klaus Jank, Josef Pichler, Christian Reichel, and Martin Saler.

References

1. Anderson, P., Beckett, G., Kavoussanakis, K., Mecheneau, G., Toft, P.: Experiences and Challenges of Large-Scale System Configuration. (2003) http://www.epcc.ed.ac.uk/gridweaver/

2. Oberleitner, J., Gschwind, T., Jazayeri, M.: The Vienna Component Framework: Enabling Composition Across Component Models. Proceedings of the 25th International Conference on Software Engineering (ICSE). IEEE Press (2003)
3. Burmester, S., Giese, H., Niere, J., Tichy, M., Wadsack, J., Wagner, R., Wendehals, L., Zuendorf, A.: Tool Integration at the Meta-Model Level within the FUJABA Tool Suite. In Proc. of the Workshop on Tool-Integration in System Development (TIS), ESEC/FSE 2003 Workshop 3. Helsinki, Finland (2003)
4. Lüer, C., van der Hoek, A.: Composition Environments for Deployable Software Components. Technical Report 02-18. Department of Information and Computer Science, University of California, Irvine (2002)
5. Goldsack, P., Guijarro, J., Lain, A., Mecheneau, G., Murray, P., Toft, P.: SmartFrog: Configuration and Automatic Ignition of Distributed Applications. HP OVUA (2003)
6. Jini Rio: http://rio.jini.org/
7. Object Management Group: Model-Driven Architecture (MDA) - A Technical Perspective, ormsc/2001-07-01 edition (2001)
8. Gokhale, A., Schmidt, D., Natarajan, B., Wang, N.: Applying Model-Integrated Computing to Component Middleware and Enterprise Applications. Special issue of Communications of ACM on Enterprise Components, Services, and Business Rules, Vol 45, No 10, Oct (2002)
9. Wang, N., Natarajan, B., Schmidt, D., Gokhale, A.: Using Model-Integrated Computing to Compose Web Services for Distributed Real-time and Embedded Applications. www.cs.wustl.edu/~schmidt/PDF/webservices.pdf
10. Gokhale, A., Natarjan, B., Schmidt, D., Wang, N., Neema, S., Bapty, T., Parsons, J., Gray, J., Nechypurenko, A.: CoSMIC: An MDA Generative Tool for Distributed Real-time and Embdedded Component Middleware and Applications. In Proceedings of the OOPSLA 2002 Workshop on Generative Techniques in the Context of Model Driven Architecture. ACM, Nov. (2002)
11. Kon, F., Roman, M., Liu, P., Mao, J., Yamane, T., Magalhaes, L., Campbell, R.: Monitoring, Security, and Dynamic Configuration with the dynamicTAO Reflective ORB. In Proceedings of the Middleware 2000 Conference. ACM/IFIP, Apr. (2000)
12. Kiczales, G., Lamping, J., Mendhekar, A., Maeda, C., Lopes, C., Loingtier, J., Irwin, J.: Aspect-Oriented Programming. In Proceedings of the 11th European Conference on Object-Oriented Programming, June (1997)
13. Foster, I., Kesselman, C., Tuecke, S.: The Anatomy of the Grid: Enabling Scalable Virtual Organizations. International Journal of Supercomputer Applications and High Performance Computing, 15(3) (2001)
14. WS-Resource Framework (WSRF) http://www.globus.org/wsrf/
15. JXTA: http://www.jxta.org

An Ontology-Based Framework for Semantic Grid Service Composition

Claus Pahl

Dublin City University, School of Computing
Dublin 9, Ireland
Claus.Pahl@dcu.ie

Abstract. The Semantic Grid aims at enhancing Grid architectures by knowledge engineering techniques. The service notion is central in this approach. Service-level agreements, called contracts, are formed to define the service usage conditions. Ontology technology can form the framework to capture semantical conditions for contracts. Often, applications of Grid services involve a combination of several services. We present an ontology-based framework for service composition for the Semantic Grid. We take a process-oriented view of services, achieving an intrinsic representation of services and their composition in an ontology.

Keywords: Semantic Grid, Service composition, Ontology, Service processes.

1 Introduction

Knowledge is expected to become more central in Grid architectures [1, 2]. The Semantic Grid aims at enhancing Grid architectures by knowledge engineering techniques. Semantic Web ontologies can support this endeavour [3, 4].

The service notion is central in this approach. We view Grid architectures as sets of services [1, 5–7]. Services are provided to Grid users. Service-level agreements, called contracts, define the service usage conditions. Ontology technology can form a marketplace framework to capture semantical conditions for contracts in a common, shared format. Grid service applications are often complex. Services need to be composed to achieve a complex goal. Two aspects characterise our approach. Firstly, services shall be considered as processes – services can be viewed from an external perspective as interacting agents in a distributed Grid environment [8]. Secondly, a composition language based on this process view can enable service interoperability for the Grid.

Our aim here is to develop a Semantic Web-based Grid service ontology that acts as service composition framework. An ontology framework can enable knowledge representation for the Grid, for instance for the representation of service contract agreements between provider and user of services. We will introduce a composition language integrated with a knowledge representation framework.

Reasoning about service descriptions and service matching to identify suitable services in marketplace and to define consistent service compositions is an

M. Jeckle, R. Kowalczyk, and P. Braun (Eds.): GSEM 2004, LNCS 3270, pp. 63–77, 2004.

important activity. We will present here a services development ontology that provides matching support [9]. Ontologies are knowledge representation frameworks defining concepts of a domain and their properties; they provide the vocabulary and facilities to reason about these. Ontologies provide a shared and agreed knowledge infrastructure. Two types of ontologies are important for the Grid services context. Application domain ontologies describe the domain of the grid software under development. Software ontologies describe the service entities and aspects of the development and deployment life cycle.

Formality in the Semantic Web framework facilitates machine understanding and automated reasoning – automation is essential for the future Grid. The ontology language OWL is equivalent to a very expressive description logic [10], which provides well-defined semantics and reasoning systems. It has already been applied to Grids [2].

The need to create a shared understanding for an application domain is long recognised. Client, user, and developer of a software system need to agree on concepts for the domain and their properties. However, with the emergence of distributed software development such as Grids and service-oriented architectures also the need to create a shared understanding of software entities and development processes arises.

We introduce the background including Grid architectures, services, and ontologies in Section 2. In Section 3, we define a simple ontology language for Semantic Grid service description. The description of composed services is subsect of Section 4. In Section 5, we address matching of service processes. We discuss the wider context of semantic services for the Grid and related work in Section 6. We end with some conclusions.

2 Semantic Grid Services and Architectures

2.1 Grid Architectures

Grid technology aims at supporting sharing and coordinated use of resources in dynamic, distributed virtual organisations [5]. In the *Open Grid Service Architecture* [5], a Grid service is defined as a Web service that provides a set of well-defined interfaces and that follows specific conventions. Aspects that are Grid-specific in the Web services context are:

- *statefulness* – services often encapsulate a hidden state,
- *dynamic assembly* and *transient character*,
- *upgradeability* – due to the dynamic nature, change management is essential.

Grids can be described as *layered architectures* with three conceptual layers [1]:

- *Data and computation*: This layer deals with the allocation, scheduling, and execution of computational resources.
- *Information*: This layer deals with representation, storage, access, sharing, and maintenance of information, i.e. data associated with its semantics.

- *Knowledge*: This layer deals with the acquisition, usage, retrieval, publication, and maintenance of knowledge, i.e. information capturing goals, problems, and decisions.

We will demonstrate that ontologies not only support the information and knowledge layer, but that ontologies can also help to integrate the computational aspects of the lower data and computation layer.

It is important to note that our ontological framework is not specific to any of the layers or specific services. We will introduce an abstract framework suitable for the composition of any services – no matter on which layer.

2.2 A Basic Services Model and Service-Related Activities

The composition of Grid services to address complex goals and to form higher-level applications requires a service model that captures the essential characteristics of services for this context. Descriptions, contracts, and compositions determine the requirements for such a service model [11]:

- *Explicit export and import interfaces.* In particular explicit and formal import interfaces make services more context independent. Only the properties of required and provided services are specified.
- *Contractual (semantic) description of services.* In addition to syntactical information such as service signatures, the abstract specification of behaviour (a contract) is a necessity for reusable services.
- *Service protocol.* An interaction protocol describes the ordering of service activations that a user of a service has to follow in order to use the service in a meaningful and consistent way.

Our aim is to capture composition in form of *processes* – expressions that describe *business processes* and *workflows* through ordering dependencies and invocations of services. The consistency of a process would depend on individual service descriptions based on the service model.

Three *development activities* are essential in this context – which we will address in the subsequent three sections:

- *Description.* An ontology language will allow us to describe individual services in a Semantic Web-compatible framework.
- *Composition.* An extension of the ontology will allow composition of services to higher-level services to be expressed.
- *Matching.* Inference capabilities of the ontological framework will be used to reason about matching between provided and required service processes.

The activities are essential parts of the *lifecyle* of a Grid service [1].

2.3 Ontology Technology

Ontologies are means of knowledge representation, defining so-called shared conceptualisations. Ontologies are frameworks for terminological definitions that can

```
Service DocumentStorageServer
    provided services
        crtDoc(id:ID)
        rtrDoc(id:ID):Doc
        updDoc(id:ID,upd:Doc)
        delDoc(id:ID)
    contract information
        updDoc(id:ID,upd:Doc)
            preCond  wellFormed(upd)
            postCond rtrDoc(id)=upd ∧ wellFormed(upd)
    service interaction protocol
        crtDoc;!(rtrDoc+updDoc);delDoc
```

Fig. 1. A Sample Application: a Document Storage Service.

be used to organise and classify concepts in a domain. Combined with a symbolic logic, we obtain a framework for specification, classification, and reasoning in an application domain. Terminological logics such as description logics [10] are an example of symbolic logics.

The Semantic Web is an initiative for the Web that builts up on ontology technology [3]. XML is the syntactical format. RDF – the Resource Description Framework – is a triple-based formalism (subject, property, object) to describe entities. OWL – the Web Ontology Language – provides additional logic-based reasoning based on RDF.

We will use Semantic Web-based ontology concepts to formalise and axiomatise Grid service processes, i.e. to make statements about services and to reason about them. We will base our ontology on Description logic [10]. Description logic, which is used to define OWL, is based on concept and role descriptions. *Concepts* represent classes of objects; *roles* represent relationships between concepts; and *individuals* are named objects. Concept descriptions are based on primitive logical combinators (negation, conjunction) and hyprid combinators (universal and existential quantification). Expressions of a description logic are interpreted through sets (concepts) and relations (roles).

Description logic is particularly interesting for the software development context due to a correspondence between description logics and modal logic [12, 13]. This will allows us to embed modal reasoning about processes in a description logic context – achieving an intrinsic specification of processes.

2.4 An Example

An example shall illustrate our service ontology – see Fig. 1. It describes a *document storage and access service*. The service is an example for a *data and computational layer Grid service*. The `DocumentStorageServer` service allows users to create, retrieve, update, and delete documents.

- An empty document can be created using `crtDoc`. The service `rtrDoc` retrieves a document, but does not change the state of the server component, whereas the update service `updDoc` updates a stored document without returning a value. Documents can also be deleted.
- We have illustrated contract-related information by specifying one of the operations by pre- and postcondition. If documents are XML-documents, these can be well-formed (correct tag nesting) or valid (well-formed and conform to a schema definition).
- The interaction protocol defines an ordering constraint that has to be obeyed if the service is to be used.

A service user might need the following services to assemble a higher-level service:

`create(id:ID)`,`retrieve(id:ID):Doc`, and `update(id:ID,upd:Doc)`

The user might require `create;!(retrieve+update)` to implement a goal or business process. The `create` service is expected to be executed first, followed by a repeated invocation of either `retrieve` or `update`.

3 Description of Semantic Grid Services

Dynamic assembly and management of Grid services rely on a high degree of automation. Semantical information about services can support automation. Semantics equally support upgradeability. Backward compatibility is required for Grid Service architectures. A semantical framework can capture explicit constraints to maintain integrity during change management.

3.1 An Ontology for Service Description

The starting point in defining an ontology is to decide what the basic ontology elements – concepts and roles – represent. An intuitive idea would be to represent services as concepts. Our key idea, however, is that the ontology formalises a software system and its specification, see Fig. 2.

- Concepts – circles in the diagram – shall represent static Grid system descriptions such as invariants and/or other syntactical and semantical aspects. Importantly, systems are dynamic, i.e. the descriptions of properties are inherently based on an underlying notion of state and state change.
- Roles – rectangles in the diagram – shall represent two different kinds of relations. *Transitional roles* represent accessibility relations, i.e. they represent processes resulting in state changes. *Descriptional roles* represent properties in a given state, i.e. static relations.

A language based on these constructs introduces a general terminological framework. Central here is the notion of states that capture properties of a system and a service. We will focus on functional properties here; non-functional aspects could be integrated as invariant (*inv*, see Fig. 2) properties[1].

[1] Ontological frameworks for semantic Web services such as OWL-S [9] provide this type of support.

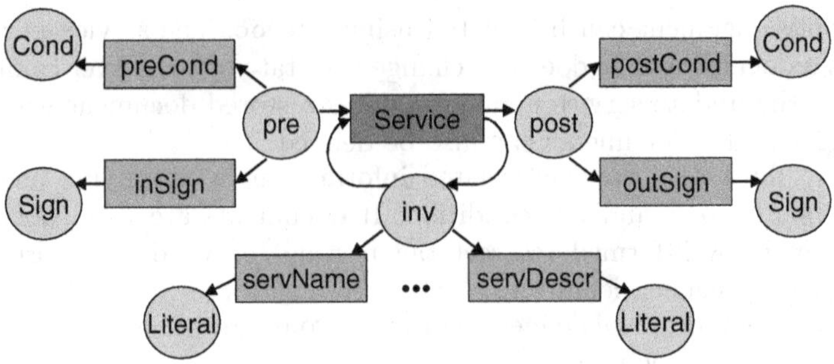

Fig. 2. Semantic Grid Services Ontology.

3.2 A Basic Ontology Language – Syntax

We develop a description logic to define our service description, composition, and matching ontology. A description logic consists of three types of entities. Individuals can be thought of as constants, concepts as unary predicates, and roles as binary predicates.

Concepts are the central entities. They can represent anything from concrete objects of the real world to abstract ideas. Constructors are part of ontology languages that allow more complex concepts (and roles) to be constructed. Classical constructors include conjunction and negation. Hybrid constructors are based on a concept and a role – we present these in a description logic notation.

- **Concepts** are collections or classes of objects with the same properties. Concepts are interpreted by sets of objects.
- **Roles** are relations between concepts.
- **Individuals** are named objects.
- **Concept descriptions** are formed according to the following rules: A is an atomic concept, and if C and D are concepts, then so are $\neg C$ and $C \sqcap D$. Combinators such as $C \sqcup D$ or $C \rightarrow D$ are defined as usual.

Roles allow us to describe a concept through its relationship to other concepts. Two basic forms of role applications are important for our context. These will be made available in form of concept descriptions. Value restriction and existential quantification extend the set of concept descriptions.

- A **value restriction** $\forall R.C$ restricts the value of role R to elements that satisfy concept C.
- An **existential quantification** $\exists R.C$ requires the existence of a role value.

Quantified roles can be composed. Since $\forall R_2.C$ is a concept description, the expression $\forall R_1.\forall R_2.C$ is also a concept description.

The constructor $\forall R.C$ is interpreted as either an accessibility relation R to a new state C for transitional roles such as `update`, or as a property R satisfying a constraint C for descriptional roles such as `postCond`.

3.3 A Basic Ontology Language – Interpretation

We interpret concepts and roles in Kripke transition systems [13]. Kripke transition systems are semantical structures used to interpret modal logics that are also suitable to interpret description logics [10]. A **Kripke transition system** (KTS) $M = (\mathcal{S}, \mathcal{L}, \mathcal{T}, I)$ consists of a set of states $\mathcal{S}$, a set of role labels $\mathcal{L}$, a transition relation $\mathcal{T} \subseteq \mathcal{S} \times \mathcal{L} \times \mathcal{S}$, and an interpretation I.

We use Kripke transition systems to facilitate the transitional character of service-based Grid systems. Concepts are interpreted as states. Transitional roles are interpreted as accessibility relations. The set $\mathcal{S}$ interprets the state domains *pre*, *post*, and *inv* – see Fig. 2. We can extend the set $\mathcal{S}$ of states by several auxiliary domains such as *Cond*, *Sign* or *Literal* or other aspects that capture contract-specific properties. *Cond* represents conditions or formulas, *Sign* denotes a domain of service signatures and *Literal* denotes string literals.

For a given Kripke transition system M with interpretation I, we define the model-based **semantics of concept descriptions**[2]:

$$\begin{array}{ll} (\neg A)^I & = \mathcal{S} \backslash A^I \\ (C \sqcap D)^I & = C^I \cap D^I \\ (\forall R.C)^I & = \{a \in S | \forall b.(a,b) \in R^I \rightarrow b \in C^I\} \\ (\exists R.C)^I & = \{a \in S | \exists b.(a,b) \in R^I \wedge b \in C^I\} \end{array}$$

Expressive role constructs are essential for our application. We distinguish

- **transitional roles** $R_{\mathcal{T}}$ that represent component services: $(R_{\mathcal{T}})^I \subseteq \mathcal{S} \times \mathcal{S}$. They are interpreted as accessibility relations on states.
- **descriptional roles** $R_{\mathcal{D}}$ that are used to describe properties of services dependant on the state: $(R_{\mathcal{D}})^I \subseteq \mathcal{S} \times \mathcal{D}$ for some auxiliary domain $\mathcal{D}$. These are interpreted as relations between states and property domains.

Some predefined roles, e.g. the identity role *id* interpreted as $\{(x,x) | x \in \mathcal{S}\}$, shall be introduced. The predefined descriptional roles are defined as follows:

$$\begin{array}{llll} preCond^I & \subseteq pre^I \times Cond^I & postCond^I & \subseteq post^I \times Cond^I \\ inSign^I & \subseteq pre^I \times Sign^I & outSign^I & \subseteq post^I \times Sign^I \\ servName^I & \subseteq inv^I \times Literal^I & servDescr^I & \subseteq inv^I \times Literal^I \end{array}$$

Note, that these descriptional roles are part of the wider ontology framework – for the remainder of the paper, we will concentrate on transitional roles.

4 Composition of Grid Services

Composition of services to *higher-level services* becomes a central activity in distributed computational environments, if reuse and sharing is an objective [14]. We introduce a notion of *service processes* for two reasons:

[2] The semantics of description logics is usually given by interpretation in models. However, it can also be defined by translation into first-order logic [10]. Concepts C can be thought of as unary predicates $C(x)$. Roles R can be thought of as binary relations $R(x,y)$. Then, $\forall R.C$ corresponds to $\forall x.R(y,x) \rightarrow C(x)$.

- *Provider side*: Services are sets of operations. An ordering of these operations, specified through an *interaction protocol*, is often necessary to guarantee a coherent usage of the service. Grid services are often stateful. Lifecycle constraints do often apply, e.g. a *create*-operation might need to be invoked before any other functionality can be used.
- *Client side*: Service usage is not restricted to request-response interactions. Service usage can be based on a composition of individual services or service operations to complex *higher-level processes* to satisfy user needs. Grid service architectures are often based on a factory service that might create multiple service instances and combine these to a higher-level service. A process-style description can define higher-level services.

Providing a framework that represents these service processes is required.

4.1 Service Process Expressions

An ontology supporting service composition requires an extension of basic description logics by *composite roles* that can represent *service processes* [10]. These are necessary to express *interaction protocols* for a single service and to define composed *higher-level services.*

The following **role constructors** shall be introduced for **service process composition**:

- $Q\,;R$ **sequential composition** with $(Q\,;R)^I = \{(a,c) \in S^I \times S^I | \exists b.(a,b) \in Q^I \wedge (b,c) \in R^I\}$; often we use $\circ$ instead of ; for functional composition
- $!R$ **iteration** with $!R^I = \bigcup_{i \geq 1} (R^I)^i$, i.e. the transitive closure of R^I
- $Q + R$ **non-deterministic choice** with $(Q + R)^I = Q^I \cup R^I$

Each service process is assumed to be sequential; concurrently executed services are, however, possible. This language, which defines role expressions, is a regular language. This property might be useful if finite state machine or automata-based approaches for analysis are used. Two additional constructs:

- Often, we want to express the sequential composition of functional roles. A **role chain** $R_1 \circ \ldots \circ R_n$ is a sequential composition of functional roles (roles that are interpreted by functions).
- $A(R_1, \ldots, R_n)$ is an **abstraction** refering to a composite role A based on the roles $R_1, \ldots, R_n$.

Expressions constructed from role names and role constructors are **composite roles**. For example, the value restriction

$\forall$ `create;!(retrieve+update) . postState`

is based on the composite role `create;!(retrieve+update)`.

Axioms in this description logic allow us to reason about service behaviour. Questions concerning the consistency and role composition with respect to behaviour protocols can be addressed. For instance [13]

$$\forall R\,;S.C \Leftrightarrow \forall R.\forall S.C \quad \text{and} \quad \forall R + S.C \Leftrightarrow \forall R.C \sqcup \forall S.C$$

are two axioms that describe logical properties of the two role combinators sequence (;) and choice (+). The equivalence

$$\forall R.C \sqcap D \Leftrightarrow \forall R.C \sqcap \forall R.D$$

is a pure logical axiom that describes a property of the $\sqcap$-combinator.

A special form of a role constructor are quantified constructors:

- The role expression $\exists(u_1, \ldots, u_n).P$ is an **existential predicate restriction**, if P is an n-ary predicate of a concrete domain – concepts can only be unary – and $u_1, \ldots, u_n$ are role chains.
- Analogously, we define a **universal predicate restriction** $\forall(u_1, \ldots, u_n).P$.

For example, $\exists(x, y).equal$ expresses that there are role values (sometimes called role fillers) for the two roles x and y that are equal. The expression $\forall(x, y).equal$ requires all role values to be equal.

4.2 Names and Parameterisation

The ontology language that we have defined by introducing role constructors for service composition is not yet complete. We can formulate process expressions in terms of service names, but we cannot refer to *data* and we cannot express *service parameters*, cf. Section 2.1.

In ontology languages, individuals are introduced in form of assertions. For instance, `Doc(D)` says that individual `D` is a document `Doc` and `length(D,100)` says that the length of `D` is 100.

- An **individual** x with $C(x)$ is interpreted by $x^I \in \mathcal{S}$ with $x^I \in C^I \subseteq \mathcal{S}$.
- The **set constructor**, written $\{a_1, \ldots, a_n\}$ introduces the individual names $a_1, \ldots, a_n$.
- The **role filler** $R : a$ is defined by $(R : a)^I = \{b \in \mathcal{S} | (b, a^I) \in R^I\}$, i.e. the set of objects that have a as a filler for R.

This allows us to introduce individuals on the level of concepts and roles. The fills constructor $R : a$ for a role stands for all objects that have a as a filler of role R.

The essential difference between classical description logic and our variant here is that we need names to occur in role and concept descriptions. A description logic expression $\forall$`create.valid` usually means that `valid` is a concept, or predicate, that can be applied to some individual object; it can be thought of as $\forall$`create(x).valid(x)` for an individual `x`. If roles are services, then `x` should not represent a concrete individual, but rather a name or a variable. For instance the creation service `create` has a parameter `id`. Our objective is to introduce names into the description language. We extend the language defined earlier on by *parameterised roles*.

- We denote a **name** n by a role $\underline{n}_N$, defined by $\underline{n}_N^I = \{(n^I, n^I)\}$.

- A **parameterised role** is a transitional (functional) role R applied to a name $\underline{n}_N$, i.e. $R \circ \underline{n}_N$.

The name definition $\underline{n}_N$ is derived from the role filler and the identity role definition, i.e. $(\underline{n}_N)^I(n^I) = (id : n)^I$.

With names and parameters our *Grid service composition language* is now complete. We can define *process expressions* consisting of services that achieve some defined goals. We can now express a parameterised role

$$\forall \texttt{create} \circ \underline{\texttt{id}}_N.\texttt{post}$$

for our example document storage and access services, defined by

$$\{x|\forall y.(x,y) \in (\texttt{create} \circ \underline{\texttt{id}}_N)^I \rightarrow y \in \texttt{post}^I\}$$

which is equal to $\{\texttt{id}^I | y \in \texttt{post}^I\}$, where y is a *postState* element that could be further described by roles such as $y = \forall \texttt{postCond.post} \sqcap \forall \texttt{outSign.out}$. With names and role composition *parameterised role chains* can be expressed:

$$\forall\ \texttt{update} \circ (\underline{\texttt{id}}_N, \underline{\texttt{doc}}_N); \texttt{postCond}\ .\ \texttt{equal(retrieve(id),doc)}$$

The expression $\forall$ $\texttt{retrieve} \circ (\underline{\texttt{id}}_N) \circ \texttt{outSign.(Doc)}$ is another example[3].

The *tractability of reasoning* about descriptions is a central issue for description logic. The richness of our description logic has some negative implications for the complexity of reasoning. However, some aspects help to reduce the complexity. We can restrict roles to functional roles. Another beneficial factor is that for composite roles negation is not required. The defined language is therefore *decidable*, i.e. the satisfiability problem is decidable. It is based on the language $\mathcal{ALC}$ introduced in [10]. It introduces additionally name and parameterisation constructs based on functional roles, avoiding negation – which preserves the decidability in our extension.

5 Matching of Semantic Grid Service Processes

Dynamic assembly of services, for instance to higher-level services, is a central feature of Grid service architectures. The virtualisation of services through the Web Services Framework enables composition; specific semantic support for matching is, however, desirable.

The *activities* that we are concerned with are *service description, composition* and *matching*. Central *reasoning constructs* of description logics to support these are equivalence and subsumption. In this section, we look at service matching based on interaction protocols and how it relates to subsumption reasoning.

[3] We often drop the N-annotation if it is clear that a name is under consideration.

5.1 Subsumption

Subsumption is the central inference construct in description logics [10]. Subsumption is the *subclass relationship*. It is often used to describe classification hierarchies. **Axioms** based on subsumption and equivalence are introduced into description logics to reason about concept and role descriptions.

- Concepts: subconcept $C1 \sqsubseteq C2$, concept equality $C1 \equiv C2$,
- Roles: subrole $R1 \sqsubseteq R2$, role equality $R1 \equiv R2$,
- Individuals: individual equality $\{x\} \equiv \{y\}$.

The semantics of these axioms is defined based on set inclusion of interpretations for the **subsumption** $\sqsubseteq$ and equality for **equivalence** for $\equiv$. Therefore, $A \equiv B$ iff $A \sqsubseteq B \sqcap B \sqsubseteq A$ is a consequence of the axiom definitions. Subsumption is not implication. Structural subsumption (subclass) is weaker than logical subsumption (implication). Subsumption is defined by subset inclusions for concepts and roles:

- A **subsumption** $C_1 \sqsubseteq C_2$ between two concepts C_1 and C_2 is defined through set inclusion for the interpretations $C_1^I \subseteq C_2^I$.
- A **subsumption** $R_1 \sqsubseteq R_2$ between two roles R_1 and R_2 holds, if $R_1^I \subseteq R_2^I$.

We can embed these axioms into the reasoning framework. For instance $C_1 \sqcap C_2 \sqsubseteq C_1$ or $C_2 \rightarrow C_1$ implies $C_2 \sqsubseteq C_1$ holds for concepts C_1 and C_2. We can use subsumption to reason about matching of two service process descriptions (defined as transitional roles).

5.2 Matching of Service Process Descriptions

A notion of *consistency of composite roles* that define interaction protocols or higher-level services through process expressions relates to the underlying service properties, which could be based on semantical contract-related properties. Often, states or state transitions are constrained through invariants and pre- and postconditions[4].

A concept description $\forall P(R_1, \ldots, R_n).C$ with composite transitional role P is **reachable** if $\{(a,b) \in P^I | \exists b.b \in C^I\}$ is not empty. A composite role $P(R_1, \ldots, R_n)$ is **consistent**, if the last state is reachable.

For instance, in the presence of pre- and postconditions, a composite transitional role P is **consistent** if the following (sufficient) conditions are satisfied:

- for each sequence $R; S$ in P : $\forall postCond.post_R \sqsubseteq \forall preCond.pre_S$
- for each iteration $!R$ in P : $\forall postCond.post_R \sqsubseteq \forall preCond.pre_R$
- for each choice $R + S$ in P : $\forall preCond.pre_R \sqcap \forall preCond.pre_S$ and $\forall postCond.post_R \sqcap \forall postCond.post_S$

[4] Even though we do not fully formalise a framework for pre- and postconditions, we consider these to be of importance for the Semantic Grid [1, 2]. Consequently, we prepare our ontology for future extensions in this direction; see also Section 6.

We can now define *consistent services processes.* A **service process** is a consistent composite role expression $P(R_1, \ldots, R_n)$ constructed from transitional role names $R_1, \ldots, R_n$ and connectors ; , ! , and + [5]. The specification of service processes describes the ordering of observable activities of the service process that implements the process expression.

A **protocol transition graph** $G = (N, E)$ for composite transitional roles is a graph that represents all possible process executions. A *transition graph* $G = (N, E)$ can be *constructed inductively* over the syntactical structure of a composite role expression. This transition graph can be related to Kripke transition systems in which we interpret expressions: $N \subseteq S$ is a subset of states; $E \subseteq R$ is a subset of relations for a KTS M with states S and roles R.

The next step is to define *matching* of *consistent service processes.* The matching approach here serves two purposes:

- Does an existing process that realises some goal matches some given requirements? Can this process be selected from a repository?
- What is the relation between two given process expressions? Can one be considered as a refinement of an other?

Process calculi suggest *simulations* and *bisimulations* as constructs to address the *subsumption* and *equivalence* of service processes [15]. We will use a notion of simulation between processes to define service process matching.

- A provider service process $P(S_1, \ldots, S_k)$ **simulates** a requested service process $R(T_1, \ldots, T_l)$, if there exists a homomorphism μ from the transition graph of R to the transition graph of P, i.e. if for each $R_g \xrightarrow{T_i} R_h$ there is a $P_k \xrightarrow{S_j} P_l$ such that $R_g = \mu(P_k)$ and $R_h = \mu(P_l)$.
- We say that a provided service process $P(S_1, \ldots, S_k)$ **matches** a requested service process $R(T_1, \ldots, T_l)$, if $P(S_1, \ldots, S_k)$ simulates $R(T_1, \ldots, T_l)$.

The form of this definition originates from the simulation definition of the π-calculus [15]. The provider needs to be able to simulate the request, i.e. needs to meet the expected behaviour of the requested process. The problem with this definition is that it involves a semantical structure. We can, however, construct a transition graph based on the syntactical representation.

In our document service example, the provider might require the *interaction protocol* `crtDoc;!(rtrDoc+updDoc);delDoc` and the requestor might formulate a *higher-level service* `create;!(retrieve+update)`. Assuming that the operation pairs `crtDoc/create`, `rtrDoc/retrieve`, and `updDoc/update` match based on their contract-relevant descriptions, we can see that the provider matches (i.e. simulates) the required server interaction protocols. `delDoc` is not requested.

We can expect service process *matching* not to be the same as *subsumption.* Subsumption on roles is input/output-oriented, whereas the simulation needs to consider internal states of the composite role execution. For each request in a

[5] We often drop service parameters in expressions if only the ordering is relevant.

process expression, there needs to be a corresponding provided service. However, matching is a *sufficient condition* for subsumption.

If service process $P(S_1, \ldots, S_k)$ simulates service process $R(T_1, \ldots, T_l)$, then $R \sqsubseteq P$. If $P(S_1, \ldots, S_k)$ simulates $R(T_1, \ldots, T_l)$, then for each $(a, b) \in R^I$ there is a pair $(a, b) \in P^I$. Therefore, $R^I \subseteq P^I$, and consequently $R \sqsubseteq P$ follow.

6 Semantics – The Wider Picture

Supporting the Semantic Grid [1, 2] is one of your key objectives. In this section, we will briefly address wider implications of semantics in the Grid context. We will also discuss related work in this context.

6.1 The Semantic Web

The Semantic Web initiative [4] bases the formulation of ontologies on two Web technologies for content description: XML and RDF/RDF Schema. RDF Schema is an ontology language providing classes and properties, range and domain notions, and a sub/superclass relationship. Web ontologies can be defined in OWL – an ontology language whose primitives are based on XML and RDF/RDF Schema, which provides a much richer set of description primitives. OWL can be defined in terms of description logics. However, OWL uses a different terminology; corresponding notions are class/concept or property/role.

With the current wide acceptance of the Web and the potential of the Semantic Web as an ontology framework, the combination of Semantic Web and Grids to the Semantic Grid [1] is the obvious choice. We have developed our ontology within this context.

6.2 Semantic Service Contracts

Service level agreements are called contracts. We have already mentioned pre- and postconditions as possible, behaviourally oriented properties that form part of a contract between service provider and service user. For instance, our matching notion depends on a consistency notion capturing these types of descriptions.

We could add pre/postcondition specifications to our basic ontology language – as indicated in Fig. 2, see [16] for details. Then, the formula

$$\forall \texttt{update}\circ\texttt{(id,doc)}.\forall \texttt{postCond.equal(retrieve(id),doc)}$$

in our description logic corresponds to

$$[\texttt{update(id,doc)}][\texttt{postCond}]\ \texttt{retrieve(id)=doc}$$

in a dynamic (modal) logic. Schild [12] points out that some description logics are notational variants of modal logics. This correspondence allows us to integrate modal axioms and inference rules about processes into description logics.

6.3 Semantic Services Ontologies

Some effort has already been made to exploit ontology technology for the software domain [9, 17], mainly for the Web Services Framework [18]. Compositionality has, however, often not been at the centre of these investigations.

OWL-S [9] (aka DAML-S) is an OWL ontology for describing properties and capabilities of Web services. OWL-S represents services as concepts. Knowledge about a service is divided into two parts. A service profile is a class that describes what a service requires and what it provides, i.e. external properties. A service model is a class that describes workflows and possible execution paths of a service, i.e. properties that concern the implementation. OWL-S provides to some extend what we aim at for Semantic Grid services. However, our reasoning and ontology support is not possible in OWL-S, since services are modelled as concepts and not rules in the OWL-S ontology. Only considering services as roles makes modal reasoning about process behaviour possible.

7 Conclusions

Grids are services-based infrastructures. In order to make full use of this infrastructure, services need to be composable. Users of a Grid infrastructure need to be able to compose services, i.e. define processes that specify the execution of a composed higher-level service process based on a number of individual services. These processes implement more comprehensive goals and business processes. We have defined a service composition language for Grid services.

Our aim is to support the Semantic Grid – knowledge and semantics are expected to be of importance in the future. Consequently, we have embedded our service composition language into a process-oriented ontological framework that allows the intrinsic description of and reasoning about Semantic Grid services. This ontological framework enables the integration with other semantical aspects, e.g. property descriptions that are relevant for contract formulations in Grid marketplaces. With Grid service technology moving towards Web services, in particular semantic Web service techniques can provide solutions.

We have focused our investigation on an abstract service composition framework, neglecting detailed explorations of different types of concrete services of the individual Grid architecture layers. Addressing these different service types is an issue that we will look at in the future. Equally important is the further study of a variety of Grid application domains. So far, we have combined a case study with experience in other service-oriented architectures.

References

1. D. De Roure, N. Jennings, and N. Shadbolt. The Semantic Grid: A Future e-Science Infrastructure. *International Journal of Concurrency and Computation: Practice and Experience*, 2003.

2. H. Tangmunarunkit, S. Decker, and C. Kesselman. Ontology-Based Resource Matching in the Grid - The Grid Meets the Semantic Web. In D. Fensel, K.P. Sycara, and J. Mylopoulos, editors, *Proc. International Semantic Web Conference ISWC'2003*, pages 706–737. Springer-Verlag, LNCS 2870, 2003.
3. T. Berners-Lee, J. Hendler, and O. Lassila. The Semantic Web. *Scientific American*, 284(5), May 2001.
4. W3C Semantic Web Activity. Semantic Web Activity Statement, 2002. http://www.w3.org/sw.
5. I. Foster, C. Kesselman, J. Nick, and S. Tuecke. The Physiology of the Grid: Open Grid Services Architecture for Distribution Systems Integration. In *Proceedings GGF4 Conference, February 2002*. http://www.globus.og/research/papers/ogsa.pdf, 2002.
6. F. Bonnassieux, R. Harakaly, and P. Primet. Automatic Services Discovery, Monitoring and Visualisation of Grid Environments: The MapCenter Approach. In *Proc. European Across Grids Conference 2003*, pages 222–229. Springer-Verlag, LNCS 2970, 2004.
7. W. Poompatanapong and B. Piyatamrong. A Web Service Approach to Grid Information Service. In *Proc. Int. Conference in Web Services ICWS'2003*. 2003.
8. N. Jennings. An Agent-based Approach for Building Complex Software Systems. *Communications of the ACM*, 44(4), 2001.
9. DAML-S Coalition. DAML-S: Web Services Description for the Semantic Web. In I. Horrocks and J. Hendler, editors, *Proc. First International Semantic Web Conference ISWC 2002*, LNCS 2342, pages 279–291. Springer-Verlag, 2002.
10. F. Baader, D. McGuiness, D. Nardi, and P.P. Schneider, editors. *The Description Logic Handbook*. Cambridge University Press, 2003.
11. C. Pahl. Components, Contracts and Connectors for the Unified Modelling Language. In *Proc. Symposium Formal Methods Europe 2001, Berlin, Germany*. Springer-Verlag, LNCS-Series, 2001.
12. K. Schild. A Correspondence Theory for Terminological Logics: Preliminary Report. In *Proc. 12th Int. Joint Conference on Artificial Intelligence*. 1991.
13. Dexter Kozen and Jerzy Tiuryn. Logics of programs. In J. van Leeuwen, editor, *Handbook of Theoretical Computer Science, Vol. B*, pages 789–840. Elsevier, 1990.
14. V. Issamy and C. Kloukinas. Automating the Composition of Middleware Configurations. In *15th International Conference on Automated Software Engineering ASE'00*. IEEE, 2000.
15. D. Sangiorgi and D. Walker. *The π-calculus - A Theory of Mobile Processes*. Cambridge University Press, 2001.
16. C. Pahl. An Ontology for Software Component Matching. In *Proc. Fundamental Approaches to Software Engineering FASE'2003*. Springer-Verlag, LNCS Series, 2003.
17. A. Felfernig, G. Friedrich, D. Jannach, and M. Zanker. Semantic Configuration Web Services in the CAWICOMS Project. In I. Horrocks and J. Hendler, editors, *Proc. First International Semantic Web Conference ISWC 2002*, LNCS 2342, pages 279–291. Springer-Verlag, 2002.
18. World Wide Web Consortium. *Web Services Framework*. http://www.w3.org/2002/ws, 2003.

Towards a Metamodeling Based Method for Representing and Selecting Grid Services

Sergio Andreozzi[1,2], Paolo Ciancarini[1], Danilo Montesi[3], and Rocco Moretti[1]

[1] University of Bologna, Department of Computer Science, 40127 Bologna, Italy*
{cianca,moretti}@cs.unibo.it
[2] Istituto Nazionale di Fisica Nucleare-CNAF, 40127 Bologna, Italy**
sergio.andreozzi@cnaf.infn.it
[3] University of Camerino, Department of Mathematics and Informatics
62032 Camerino (MC), Italy***
danilo.montesi@unicam.it

Abstract. The service oriented model is the emerging approach adopted by Web and Grid services where parties act as service requestors and service providers. A meaningful aspect to consider consists in improving machine-to-machine interaction by enabling an automatic evaluation and selection of available services with respect to a set of expectations. In this context, it can be useful to raise the modeling abstraction level by considering the metamodeling theory principles by which to enhance the modeling constructs. The goal of this paper is to present a method for the rigorous representation and selection of service characteristics in the area of Grid computing. Such a method relies on the measurement theory and the Logic Scoring of Preferences (LSP). Moreover, relying on the metamodeling theory provided by the OMG Model Driven Architecture (MDA), a prototype tool for mapping MOF based Grid services metamodels in domain specific textual languages is presented.

1 Introduction

The service oriented model is the emerging approach adopted by Web and Grid services where parties act as service requestors and service providers. A meaningful aspect to consider consists in improving machine-to-machine interaction by enabling an automatic evaluation and selection of available services with respect to a set of expectations. In this context, it can be useful to raise the modeling abstraction level by considering the metamodeling theory principles by which to enhance the modeling constructs. The goal of this paper is to present a method for the rigorous representation and selection of service characteristics in the area of Grid computing. Such a method relies on the measurement theory [1] and

* This research was partially funded by the SAHARA project.
** This research was partially funded by the IST Programme of the European Union under grant IST-2001-32459 (DataTAG project).
*** This research was partially funded by the projects 'GERONACCESS', 'Implementing background for innovation Technology' and 'ISPI'.

M. Jeckle, R. Kowalczyk, and P. Braun (Eds.): GSEM 2004, LNCS 3270, pp. 78–93, 2004.

on the Logic Scoring of Preferences (LSP) [2,3]. We start by considering the systems that are involved in our study.

Web services are software systems having interfaces described in a machine processable format designed to support message based interoperable interactions over a network. The World Wide Web Consortium (W3C) is defining the Web Service Architecture (WSA) [4], consisting of a conceptual stack of interrelated standard protocols where upper layers rely on the capabilities provided by the lower layers. The downmost layer is the 'message' concerning mechanisms for communicating document-centric messages that are based on the Simple Object Access Protocol (SOAP) [5]. The 'description' layer allows to define a set of description documents using the Web Services Description Language (WSDL) [6]. Finally, the 'process' layer concerns process descriptions like, for instance, the discovery of service descriptions satisfying specified criteria.

Grid services consist in coordinating services not subject to centralized control within multi-institutional Virtual Organizations (VO) spanning locations, machine architectures and software boundaries [7]. The current production systems (e.g., LHC Computing Grid [8], INFN-GRID [9]) are based on the de-facto standard Globus Toolkit 2. It relies on a layered architecture where the downmost layer is the 'Fabric' providing shared access mediated by Grid protocols to operations on local resources. The 'Connectivity' layer defines core communication protocols to enable the exchange of data between resources of the Fabric layer. The 'Resource' layer defines protocols for the secure negotiation, initiation, monitoring, control, accounting and payment of sharing operations on individual resources. The 'Collection' layer contains global protocols and services capturing interactions among collections of resources. Finally, the 'Application' layer involves user applications operating within a VO environment [7].

The new emerging Grid infrastructure is the Open Grid Services Architecture (OGSA) [10] where the basic layer is provided by Web services standards. They have been recently extended by a set of specifications globally called Web Services Resource Framework (WSRF) [11] supporting the capability of representing stateful resources and managing resource lifetime. It also provides a common notification model. Preliminary implementations supporting the new standards are already available (e.g., Globus Toolkit 3.9.1 Java WSRF Core [12], WSRF.NET [13]).

In the infrastructures given above, the concept of 'quality' can be considered from different perspectives. The approach presented in this paper considers quality as an aggregation of satisfactions associated to the values returned by measurements of the attributes under investigation. Among the multi-criteria evaluation methods present in the literature [14,15], the Logic Scoring of Preferences (LSP) has been selected. It is a quantitative decision method for evaluation, comparison and selection of hardware and software systems. LSP can be enriched by the measurement theory, meant as the set of concepts and rules by which to define a mapping between empirical and formal systems, thus enabling a machine evaluation of quality. Relying on such an approach, we present the current status of a method for the representation and selection of Grid services considered from a satisfaction perspective. Moreover, we present the architecture of a prototype tool for mapping Grid services metamodels in domain specific textual languages is presented.

In Section 2, a scenario motivating the work presented in this paper is considered. Section 3 introduces a method for satisfaction based quality evaluation. Section 4 explains how metamodeling principles can be considered in the context of our method and present the prototype tool. Finally, in Section 5 conclusions and ongoing activities are summarized.

2 Discovery for Selection of Grid Services

In a Grid environment, resources are dynamically contributed by different owner institutions to VOs, thus forming virtual pools to be assigned to VO users. The key functionality of providing information about the structure and state of available resources is provided by the Grid Information Service (GIS) [16]. Available resources can be dynamically selected and composed on the basis of user requirements to set up and provide complex and on-demand services.

Due to the open nature of the Grid (e.g., resources can dynamically join or leave) and due to the virtual nature of services (e.g., users are not aware of which resources will be assigned to their applications), it is a vital determinant the capability of describing both user requirements and service properties in order to decide if a profitable interaction can take place. Further, the possibility that parties can be unknown to each other implies a more stringent need for representing not only functional, but also non-functional properties.

As an example, we select the simple use case of a user asking to the Grid the execution of a single application by means of a 'Computing Service' (i.e., a uniquely identified Grid service that can provide a user software application for computing power in a certain execution environment). Concerning the execution environment, the user can require a specific operating system type. Moreover, it is desirable that the application is assigned to the less loaded resource among those available.

The operation of selection and brokering is typically provided by a Grid collective service called 'Broker Service'. Using it, a Grid user can submit a document called 'Job Submission Description' (JSD) describing the expected complex Grid service. Based on the available Grid services and on the JSD, the broker service executes a matchmaking phase during which suitable solutions are prepared. Then, it executes a brokering phase where one solution is selected. This decision can take into account not only the user requirements, but also general aspects related to the Grid behavior. The main objective of a broker service is both to fulfill user requests and balance the workload of the system. The service selection requires the ability of aggregating the satisfaction degree concerning a set of attributes of interest. The final decision can take into account a combined satisfaction degree. For instance, if several solutions satisfying the user expectations exist, the broker can use a further satisfaction criterion favoring the less loaded services.

In order to provide a practical example, we refer to a language that has been widely used in the area of Grid computing [17] for describing both services and service agreement proposals: the Classified Advertisement (ClassAd) language [18]. It has been designed in the context of the Condor distributed computing system [19], where it is used for discovery and allocation of resources. Its usage consists of the following phases: (1) providers of computing resources submit advertisements describing their capabilities and declaring constraints and preferences for jobs that they are willing to run; (2) consumers submit advertisements describing their jobs and constraints or preferences regarding execution sites; (3) a matchmaker process matches the resource and consumer request advertisements. Recently, a mechanism called gang-matching has been added to the ClassAd language [20]. It extends the bilateral matchmaking approach to a multilateral model that allows the description of the relations holding between several participants in the match. Both a computing service and a JSD can be represented using the ClassAd language as follows:

```
[
 Type            = "computing service";
 URI             = "serviceURI1";
 OSType          = 0; # RedHat Linux
 ProcessorFamily = 0; # Pentium(R)
 FreeJobSlots    = 56;
 RunningJobs     = 25;
 WaitingJobs     =  0
]
```

(CL.1)

```
[
 Type          = "job submission description";
 Executable    = "/usr/local/myApplication";
 Arguments     = "--config /home/ui/my.cfg";
 FileStageIn   = {"fileURI1"};
 FileStageOut  = {"fileURI2"};
 Constraint    = cs.Type == "computing service"
                 && cs.OSType == 0;
 Rank=cs.FreeJobSlots;
]
```

(CL.2)

As regards the ClassAd `CL.1`, a computing service can be expressed by its category (`Type`), a unique identifier (`URI`), the operating system type of the offered execution environment (`OSType`), the processor family of the underlying system (`ProcessorFamily`), the number of free slots that can accommodate new running jobs (`FreeJobSlots`), the number of jobs that are being executed (`RunningJobs`) and the number of jobs that have been queued and whose execution is not yet started (`WaitingJobs`). As regards the ClassAd `Cl.2`, the JSD is characterized by the full path name of the user job (`Executable`), the set of arguments (`Arguments`) for the user job, the set of input files (`FileStageIn`) for the user job, the set of output files (`FileStageOut`) for the user job. The basic assumption is that the file expressed in `FileStageIn` will be copied in the same execution directory of the job. Moreover, the name of output file generated in the execution directory of the job is expressed by the `FileStageOut`.

Constraints are boolean expressions involving constants and ClassAd attributes of the service of interest. The rank consists in defining an arithmetic expression synthesizing values used for sorting the services satisfying the constraints. In the JSD given above, the `Constraint` expression contains the operating system requirements. Further matching CSs are ranked considering the amount of `FreeJobSlots`. The JSD is written using a set of attributes that are unambiguously shared between the service requestor and the service provider and it represents an agreement proposal. This document is sent to the broker service. The task of the broker is to control whether, among the set of available services, there is a suitable solution that can satisfy the service request.

3 Satisfaction Based Service Evaluation

In this section, we present the model for the representation and evaluation of quality in Web and Grid services. It relies on the measurement theory and the LSP method. The fundamental assumption consists in considering the concept of quality of a service in terms of the 'satisfaction degree' concerning the admissible measurement values of its attributes of interest.

3.1 Measurement Theory Background

We start by introducing the concepts of 'entity' and 'attribute'. The former is an object or event of the real world, whereas the latter is a feature of this object or event. For each attribute, a 'measurement' can be defined as the process by which numbers or symbols are assigned to attributes of entities in the real world in such a way as to describe them according to clearly defined rules [1]. It is important to clearly define the boundaries of the reality under investigation. For this purpose, we introduce the concept of 'empirical relational system'.

Definition 1 (Empirical Relational System). *An empirical relational system is an ordered tuple* $\mathcal{ERS} = (\mathcal{EO}, er_1, \ldots, er_n, \star_1, \ldots, \star_m)$ *where* $\mathcal{EO}$ *is a set of empirical objects,* er_i $(i = 1, \ldots, n)$ *are k-ary empirical relationships* $(k \geq 2)$ *defined in* $\mathcal{EO}$, $\star_j$ $(j = 1, \ldots, m)$ *are binary closed operations between empirical objects in* $\mathcal{EO}$.

An empirical relational system describes the objects of the real world that must be measured ($\mathcal{EO}$) and our empirical knowledge of their attributes (the empirical relationships er_i). For instance, if we are interested in the 'availability' attribute of the 'service' entity, we will use the 'more available than' empirical relationship (i.e., 'the service S_1 is more available than the service S_2'). Binary operations can be considered as particular ternary relationships among objects. For instance, if $\star_1$ is the operation of sequential composition of services, we can consider the following ternary relationship among them: $SeqComp(S_1, S_2, S_3)$, where S_3 is the result of the sequential composition of S_1 and S_2 (i.e., $S_3 = S_1 \star_1 S_2$). In order to carry out meaningful analyses, the empirical relational system given above must be mapped onto a 'formal relational system'.

Definition 2 (Formal Relational System). *A formal relational system is an ordered tuple* $\mathcal{FRS} = (\mathcal{FO}, fr_1, \ldots, fr_n, \diamond_1, \ldots, \diamond_m)$ *where* $\mathcal{FO}$ *is a set of formal objects,* fr_i $(i = 1, \ldots, n)$ *are k-ary formal relationships* $(k \geq 2)$ *defined in* $\mathcal{FO}$, $\diamond_j$ $(j = 1, \ldots, m)$ *are binary closed operations between formal objects in* $\mathcal{FO}$.

In the formal relational system, empirical objects are mapped in the set of formal objects $\mathcal{FO}$; empirical relationships are modeled by the respective formal relationships fr_i and operations between empirical objects are mapped in the formal operations $\diamond_j$. It is important to remark that the same objects can be intended as empirical or formal depending on the entities and attributes they relate to. The link between the empirical relational system and the formal relational system is represented by the concepts of 'measure' and 'measurement scale' that we are going to introduce.

Definition 3 (Measure μ). *Let $\mathcal{EO}$ and $\mathcal{FO}$ be a set of empirical objects and a set of formal objects respectively. A measure $\mu\colon \mathcal{EO} \to \mathcal{FO}$ is a function mapping each empirical object $eo \in \mathcal{EO}$ in a formal object $\mu(eo) \in \mathcal{FO}$ (the measurement value).*

The measure μ enables to define the measurement scale expressing a mapping between the empirical and the formal relational system.

Definition 4 (Measurement Scale). *Let $\mathcal{ERS} = (\mathcal{EO}, er_1, \ldots, er_n, \star_1, \ldots, \star_m)$ and $\mathcal{FRS} = (\mathcal{FO}, fr_1, \ldots, fr_n, \diamond_1, \ldots, \diamond_m)$ be an empirical relational system and a formal relational system respectively. Let $\mu : \mathcal{EO} \to \mathcal{FO}$ be a measure. $\mathcal{S} = (\mathcal{ERS}, \mathcal{FRS}, \mu)$ is a measurement scale if and only if $\forall i \in [1, n], \forall j \in [1, m]$ and $\forall eo_1, \ldots, eo_k, b, c \in \mathcal{EO}$ $(k \geq 2)$:*

1. $er_i(eo_1, \ldots, eo_k) \iff fr_i\big(\mu(eo_1), \ldots, \mu(eo_k)\big)$
2. $\mu(b \star_j c) = \mu(b) \diamond_j \mu(c)$

If $\mathcal{FO} = \mathbf{R}$ the measurement scale $\mathcal{S}$ is a real measurement scale.

Each empirical object $eo \in \mathcal{EO}$ is associated with a formal object $\mu(eo) \in \mathcal{FO}$ and each empirical relationship er_i is associated with a formal relationship fr_i. Five measurement scales are reputed to be particularly meaningful [1]: (1) the 'Nominal Scale' is used when the measured objects need to be partitioned in classes; (2) the 'Ordinal Scale' is a nominal scale with an order relation among the classes; (3) the 'Interval Scale' is an ordinal scale that preserves the difference among the values associated to the measured objects; (4) the 'Ratio Scale' is an interval scale that maintain constant the ratio of the values associated to the measured objects; (5) the Absolute Scale' is a ratio scale representing the only possible scale suitable to measure the attribute under investigation.

3.2 Logic Scoring of Preferences

We present two steps included in the Logic Scoring of Preferences (LSP) method [2, 3]. The first step consists in defining the elementary criteria of satisfaction that are specific functions associated to the values of measurements concerning the attributes of the entities to examine. These functions must map each possible value in a number $e \in [0, 1]$ (i.e., $e = 0$ means 'no satisfaction', whereas $e = 1$ means 'full satisfaction') expressing the satisfaction for each possible value. Therefore, the elementary criteria of satisfaction are defined depending on the set of possible measurement values.

The main problem in the definition of these functions is related to the kind of the measurement under investigation. For instance, let us consider the attribute (a_1) 'supported `OSType`' of a computing service and let us suppose that its possible values are 'RedHat Linux', 'Debian Linux' and 'Microsoft Windows XP'. If the user expectation is to run its job on a RedHat Linux environment, then its elementary criterion of satisfaction can be expressed as follows: $e_1 = 1$ if the supported `OSType`' is 'RedHat Linux', $e_1 = 0$ if the supported `OSType`' is 'Debian Linux' or 'Microsoft Windows XP'. It must be remarked that all possible values returned by a measurement of this attribute can be listed. This is a required feature for using this type of elementary criterion of satisfaction. Examining the attribute (a_2) 'average response time' t of a service, if the average response time is less or equal than the time t_{min}, a full satisfaction ($e_2 = 1$) can be expected; if the average response time is more or equal than the time t_{max}, a satisfaction of no value will be defined ($e_2 = 0$); finally, if the average response time is between t_{min} and t_{max}, a partial satisfaction can be defined by a linear interpolation. In this case, two values have been used in order to evaluate the average response times: t_{min} and t_{max} introducing an absolute classification. The third alterative elementary criterion of satisfaction is exemplified on the attribute (a_3) 'Number of job slots `FreeJobSlots` that can accommodate new running jobs'. In this case, user expectations are fully satisfied (i.e., $e_3 = 1$) when its job is assigned to the computing service with the highest number of free job slots. Let fjs_i be the number of free job slots of the computing service i and let FJS_{MAX} be the maximum fjs_i among the m services ($i = 1, \dots, m$) under examination, if the number of free job slots is 0, then no satisfaction is associated to the value (i.e., $e_3 = 0$). In the other cases, a partial satisfaction is defined by the following function: $e(fjs) = \frac{fjs^2}{FJS_{MAX}^2}$ $(0 < fjs < FJS_{MAX})$. The examples given above represent the three main ways to define an elementary criterion of satisfaction: an enumeration of all possible values returned by a measurement of an attribute, an absolute classification of these values and their relative classification.

The second step of the LSP method consists in synthesizing the satisfaction concerning a feature that can be modelled only by a set of measurements. The method suggested in [2] prescribes the definition of functions returning a global satisfaction $E \in [0, 1]$. They are based on the satisfactions $e_1, \dots, e_n$ defined by n elementary criteria to aggregate and by their respective weights $w_1, \dots, w_n$. These weights can be selected in order to reflect the relevance of the attribute that the satisfaction refers to. Besides, they must be positive (i.e., $w_i > 0 \ \forall i$) and normalized (i.e., $\sum_{i=1}^{n} w_i = 1$). For instance, a possible function to aggregate the satisfactions can be their arithmetic mean ($E = w_1 e_1 + \dots + w_n e_n$). In [2] it is outlined that this function cannot assure that the global satisfaction E will be positive if and only if a certain satisfaction e_i is more than a fixed threshold. Besides, in this function if $e_i = 0$ the global satisfaction E will decrease in value by w_i. This decrease could be inadequate to model the effective relevance of e_i, that is the insufficient presence of a specific attribute can always be compensated by sufficient presence of any other attribute. Therefore, a wider spectrum of nonlinear multi-criteria scoring functions has

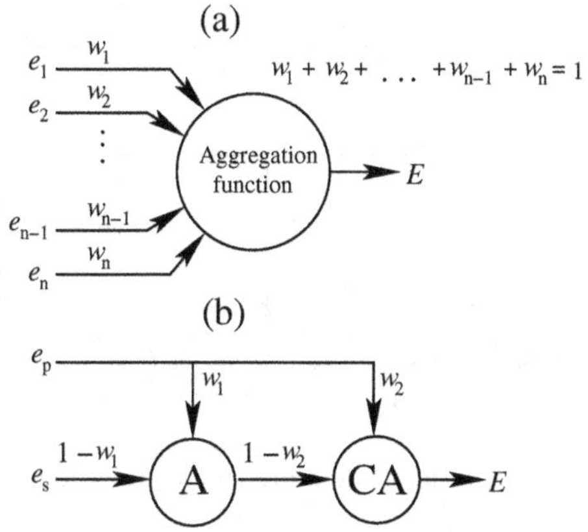

Fig. 1. Aggregation functions (based on [3]): (a) Notation to represent the aggregation functions. (b) The conjunctive partial absorption function.

been defined in order to model 'simultaneity', 'neutrality', 'replaceability' and other input relationships:

$$E = (w_1 e_1{}^r + \ldots + w_n e_n{}^r)^{\frac{1}{r}} \tag{1}$$

where $-\infty \leq r \leq +\infty$. Only certain functions among all possible ones are useful to solve the problems presented above. Therefore, nine basic aggregation functions have been considered [2]: the conjunction (C), the strong quasi-conjunction (C^+), the medium quasi-conjunction (CA), the weak quasi-conjunction (C^-), the arithmetic mean (A), the weak quasi-disjunction (D^-), the medium quasi-disjunction (DA), the strong quasi-disjunction (D^+) and the disjunction (D). The calculation of the r parameter is based on the number n of satisfactions to aggregate and on the expected degree of conjunction [3, 21]. It enables the expression of the desired logical relationship and intensity of polarization of the aggregation function. If $r > 1$, the formula models the disjunction or replaceability of inputs; if $r < 1$, the formula models the conjunction or simultaneity of inputs; if $r = 1$, the formula is neutral in the aggregation. Besides, the aggregation functions can be composed in order to produce other functions enabling to define aggregation criteria based on a particular logic. For instance, if we aggregate a satisfaction e_p that must cross a fixed threshold so that $E > 0$ and a satisfaction e_s for which we admit $E > 0$ even if $e_s = 0$, we will resort to a particular composition: the 'conjunctive partial absorption function' (see Fig. 1).

A useful notation based on [3] is presented in Figure 1a. An aggregation function is represented by a circle; for each satisfaction e_i $(i = 1, \ldots, n)$ a weighted entry arc ($\sum_{i=1}^{n} w_i = 1$) is defined; finally, for each circle we have a single exit arc (the synthesized global satisfaction). We introduce the mentioned conjunctive partial absorption function by this notation (Fig. 1b). The arithmetic mean function (A) is the input of the average quasi-conjunction function (CA) and the weights follow the distribution in figure. We have $E = 0$, apart from the

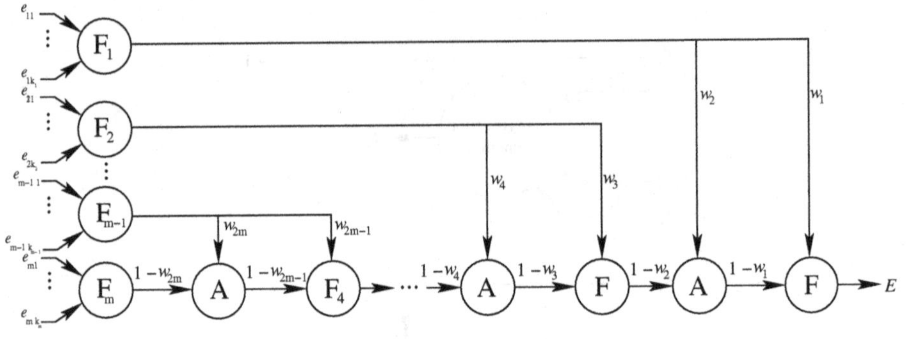

Fig. 2. General pattern for defining the aggregation functions.

value of the secondary satisfaction e_s, if the principal satisfaction e_p is equal to 0. On the contrary, if $e_p > 0$ the global satisfaction E is positive. Finally, we have the largest global satisfaction ($E = 1$) if $e_p = e_s = 1$.

3.3 Service Quality Model

The service quality model is presented in this section. Firstly, we define the set A whose elements are all attributes of entities involved in the quality evaluation. Then, we introduce the set AM of pairs (a, S_a), where $a \in A$ and $S_a = (\mathcal{ERS}_a, \mathcal{FRS}_a, \mu_a)$ is a measurement scale. In the empirical and formal relational systems involved, empirical operations may need to be considered for defining measures and elementary criteria, while their respective formal operations are not defined because they are not used.

By these concepts, we are able to map attributes under evaluation and their values in a formal relational system, that is an important step for the automatic evaluation of services. In this context, the set EC_A of elementary criteria of satisfaction for each $a \in A$ must be considered. It enables the expression of satisfactions for the evaluation. These satisfactions can be categorized by defining an equivalent relevance relation $\sim_{REL}$, that is a collection of pairs (a_i, a_j) $(a_i, a_j \in A)$, where $a_i \sim_{REL} a_j$ means: 'the satisfaction concerning the values of a_i is as relevant as the satisfaction concerning the values of a_j'.

Given these categories of satisfaction, they must be aggregated in an overall score by defining a proper 'Aggregation Functions Set' AF_{EC_A} enabling the expression of a specific aggregation logic. Therefore, the service quality model can be summarized by the following function:

$$SQM : (AM, \sim_{REL}, EC_A, AF_{EC_A}) \rightarrow [0, 1] \tag{2}$$

Considering the following scheme from the left to the right, in the part preceding $\sim_{REL}$, the measurement scales for the attributes under investigation are defined and the satisfaction concerning the value of each attribute is produced by the elementary criteria of satisfaction.

$$\left.\begin{array}{c}
\underbrace{(a_1,\mathcal{ERS}_{a_1})\overset{\mu_{a_1}}{\longrightarrow}(a_1,\mathcal{FRS}_{a_1})}_{(a_1,S_{a_1})}\overset{ec_{a_1}}{\longrightarrow}e_{a_1}\\
\underbrace{(a_2,\mathcal{ERS}_{a_2})\overset{\mu_{a_2}}{\longrightarrow}(a_2,\mathcal{FRS}_{a_2})}_{(a_2,S_{a_2})}\overset{ec_{a_2}}{\longrightarrow}e_{a_2}\\
\vdots\\
\underbrace{(a_n,\mathcal{ERS}_{a_n})\overset{\mu_{a_n}}{\longrightarrow}(a_n,\mathcal{FRS}_{a_n})}_{(a_n,S_{a_n})}\overset{ec_{a_n}}{\longrightarrow}e_{a_n}
\end{array}\right\} \sim_{REL} \begin{array}{c}
\begin{pmatrix} a_2 \rightarrow e_{11}\\ \cdots \\ a_5 \rightarrow e_{1k_1}\end{pmatrix}\\
\begin{pmatrix} a_4 \rightarrow e_{21}\\ \cdots \\ a_9 \rightarrow e_{2k_2}\end{pmatrix}\\
\vdots\\
\begin{pmatrix} a_1 \rightarrow e_{m1}\\ \cdots \\ a_7 \rightarrow e_{mk_m}\end{pmatrix}
\end{array} \tag{3}$$

In the part of the scheme following $\sim_{REL}$, the satisfactions reputed to be of the same relevance are grouped together to start the aggregation for obtaining the global satisfaction. To carry out this phase, the pattern exemplified in Figure 2 is adopted. As discussed in [3], the first step consists in aggregating the satisfactions belonging to the same category. It can be done by defining the equivalence relevance relation $\sim_{REL}$ partitioning the set of satisfactions involved in the evaluation. The number and the type of such categories is not constrained by the model. In order to perform the aggregation of the satisfactions synthesized for each category, intermediate aggregation steps are needed. They must start from the satisfactions concerning the two less relevant categories and arrive to the global satisfaction E.

The proposed model affects the Grid architecture in the following parts: (1) Grid services should be able to measure the attributes meaningful for their evaluation and they should publish their values (for instance, by using the GIS [16]); (2) the user interface should support the selection of the attributes of interest for the user, then it should enable the association of the user satisfaction to the attributes values, after that it should support the creation of the overall aggregation pattern; (3) the broker service should be extended to evaluate the user request translated in a machine-processable language against the service description accessible by the GIS.

As an example, let us consider a user requiring the execution of a job by means of a computing service available in the Grid and selected from a virtual pool on the base of a set of constraints. The aim is to show how the model can be applied to the selection use case and to present the benefits of its usage. The first step is to identify the set of entities and their related attributes that are meaningful for a service requestor in order to evaluate the global satisfaction as regards a service offering. The meaningful attributes of the entities involved in the scenario under investigation are identifiable in the JSD. Considering the computing service entity, the relevant attributes are: (a_1) 'Supported `OSType`' and (a_2) 'Number of job slots that can accommodate new running jobs `FreeJobSlots`'. The second step is the definition of a measurement scale for each attribute. In the empirical and formal relational systems presented below, empirical operations are considered only when they are needed for the definition of measures and elementary criteria, while formal operations are not considered.

a_1 'Supported `OSType`'
- $\mathcal{ERS}_{a_1}$: (1) $\mathcal{EO}_{a_1}$ is {RedHat Linux, Debian Linux, Microsoft Windows XP}; (2) er_{a_1} = 'is equal to'.
- $\mathcal{FRS}_{a_1}$: (1) $\mathcal{FO}_{a_1} = \{0, 1, 2\}$; (2) fr_{a_1} ='='.
- The measure $\mu_{a_1} : \mathcal{EO}_{a_1} \rightarrow \mathcal{FO}_{a_1}$ is:

$$\mu_{a_1}(x) = \begin{cases} 0 & \text{if } x = \text{RedHat Linux} \\ 1 & \text{if } x = \text{Debian Linux} \\ 2 & \text{if } x = \text{MS Windows XP} \end{cases}$$

a_2 'Number of job slots `FreeJobSlots` that can accommodate new running jobs'
- $\mathcal{ERS}_{a_2}$: (1) $\mathcal{EO}_{a_2} = \{x \mid x \in \mathbb{N}\}$; (2) er_{a_2} = 'is greater than'.
- $\mathcal{FRS}_{a_2}$: (1) $\mathcal{FO}_{a_2} = \{x \mid x \in \mathbb{N}\}$; (2) fr_{a_2} ='>'.
- The measure $\mu_{a_5} : \mathcal{EO}_{a_5} \rightarrow \mathcal{FO}_{a_5}$ is $\mu_{a_5}(x) = x$.

The third step is the association of a satisfaction degree to each formal object using the elementary criteria of satisfaction. For the attribute $\mathbf{a_1}$, a meaningful elementary criteria is $f_{a_1} : \mathcal{FO}_{a_1} \rightarrow [0, 1]$ defined as follows:

$$f_{a_1}(y) = \begin{cases} 1 & \text{if } y = 0 \\ 0 & \text{otherwise} \end{cases}$$

while for the attribute $\mathbf{a_2}$, a meaningful elementary criteria of satisfaction is $f_{a_2} : \mathcal{FO}_{a_2} \rightarrow [0, 1]$ defined as follows:

$$f_{a_2}(y) = \begin{cases} \frac{y^2}{FJS_{MAX}^2} & \text{if } 0 \leq y < FJS_{MAX} \\ 1 & \text{if } y \geq FJS_{MAX} \end{cases}$$

where $FJS_{MAX} \in \mathcal{FO}_{a_2}$ is the maximum number of free job slots among the available computing services.

The last step is the aggregation of satisfactions by defining aggregation functions expressing the selected logic of aggregation. For the equivalence relevance relation $\sim_{REL}$, we identify two satisfaction categories: (1) 'essential', that is if a not satisfying value is offered by the service provider, then the global satisfaction will be insufficient and no agreement can be reached and (2) 'desired', that is if a not satisfying value is offered by the service provider, then the global satisfaction can still be sufficient and the agreement can be reached, even if the global satisfaction decreases. In our example, the essential attribute is (a_1) `OSType`, while the desired attribute is (a_2) `FreeJobSlots`. Summarizing the foregoing list, the adopted equivalence relevance relation $\sim_{REL}$ induces the following partition: (1) 'essential' $\{a_1 \rightarrow e_{11}\}$, (2) 'desired' $\{a_2 \rightarrow e_{21}\}$. The adopted aggregation function is the conjunctive partial absorbtion function presented in Figure 1 and instantiated below:

$$E = \left((1 - w_2) \Big((1 - w_1) e_{21} + w_1 e_{11} \Big)^{-0.72} + w_2 e_{11}^{-0.72} \right)^{\frac{1}{-0.72}} \tag{4}$$

The weights are selected as follows: $w_1 = 0.6$; $w_2 = 0.3$; $r = 1$ for A, $r = -0.72$ for CA. In this paper, we do not consider how to determine values for the weights and the r parameter (see [2]). Finally, it must be remarked that the proposed model allows the representation of both constraints and preferences in a single framework. Given the possibility of defining attributes categories and given the aggregation pattern, we are able to express constraints in terms of 'essential' attributes. Moreover, it is possible to compute the minimum value of the overall satisfaction E for which the 'essential' attributes (i.e., the constraints) are satisfied.

4 MOF Based Models of Grid Services

Grid services enhanced by the measurement theory and the LSP method can be defined by means of the OMG Model Driven Architecture (MDA) [22]. The MDA Meta-Object Facility (MOF) [23] is a specification for expressing concepts useful for defining metamodels (e.g., Unified Modeling Language [24]) that can be stored in repositories where they can be created, read, updated and deleted. In this way, a better expression of systems and requirements can be defined, an easier analysis of the properties under investigation is possible, the porting to different platforms is enabled and technological changes are supported by testing techniques. MOF based metamodels can be associated with Grid services features in order to consider mapping techniques for expressing properties and constraints of interest in Grid architectures. It enables to study the enactment of such features in Grid services languages and technologies. This approach can be applied in order to define MOF based metamodels including the measurement theory and the LSP method for representing and selecting Grid services. Such metamodels can then be mapped in target technologies, like, for instance, services and service requests expressed using the ClassAd language.

Tools supporting such an approach must enable the expression in Grid architectures of properties and constraints of interest. In this context, we are developing a prototype that relies on dMOF [25], TokTok [26] and ModFact [27] (see Figure 3). The dMOF tool provides a MOF implementation by which it is possible to create repositories of MOF based metamodels using the Meta-Object Definition Language (MODL) [28] that is defined by the Distributed Systems Technology Centre (DSTC). TokTok is a DSTC implementation of the OMG Human-Usable Textual Notation (HUTN) [29, 30]. It specifies a standard mapping from a MOF based metamodel expressed by MODL to a textual notation for representing models corresponding to that metamodel. Such a mapping is based on a number of usability principles enabling to produce languages that can be customized in order to better represent specific application domains. Finally, ModFact [27] is a software library developed by the 'Laboratoire d'Informatique Paris 6' (LIP6) that provides a rule based model transformation tool.

Our prototype includes several components. The `sourcemetamodel` can be expressed by the MODL model definition language or other proprietary languages like the Rational Rose Model Definition Language (MDL) [31]. The

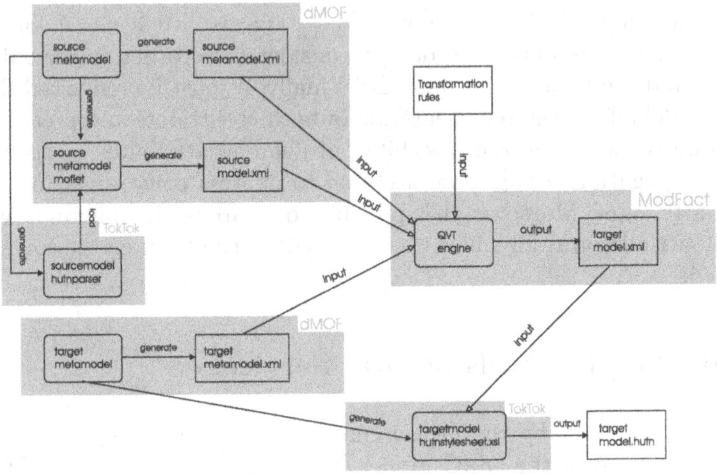

Fig. 3. The metamodeling framework prototype.

`sourcemetamodel.xmi` is the source metamodel in XMI format. Depending on the adopted model definition language (e.g., MODL or MDL), the transformation can be done by different tools like, for instance, dMOF or Rational Rose (in Figure 3 we consider dMOF). The `sourcemetamodelmoflet` is the moflet of the source metamodel (a moflet is the implementation of the repository meta-objects representing a user metamodel). It enables to manage models complying with the source metamodel. The `sourcemodel.xmi` is the model produced by the moflet in XMI format. The `sourcemodelhutnparser` is the parser whose source code is generated by TokTok enabling to load the source models complying with the source metamodel in the moflet. The `targetmetamodel` is the target metamodel expressed by MODL to which models produced by the transformation must comply with. The `targetmetamodel.xmi` is the target metamodel in XMI format produced by the dMOF tool. The `QVTengine` (Query View Transformation engine) is the ModFact transformation tool. It has four inputs: (1) the `sourcemetamodel.xmi`, (2) the `sourcemodel.xmi`, (3) the `targetmetamodel.xmi` and (4) the transformation rules. Such transformation rules are written in the Simple Transformation Rule Language (Simple TRL) that is a contribution of the ModFact project [27]. By this language, it is possible to specify the mappings between concepts of the source metamodel and those of the target metamodel. The output of the transformation is one or more XMI models complying with the target metamodel. The `targetmodel.xmi` is the target model in XMI format complying with the target metamodel produced by the transformation. The `targetmetamodelstylesheet.xsl` is the stylesheet produced by TokTok enabling to transform the target XMI model in textual form. Finally, the `targetmodel.hutn` is the target model in textual form.

The metamodel specification language that we use is MODL with the Object Constraint Language (OCL) [24] for representing constraints that apply to the modeled entities. The direct correspondence of MODL with MOF metamodeling constructs enables to specify metamodels regulating models of the entities involved in the Grid services scenario and models of concepts involved in the LSP method for Grid services ranking. In order to exemplify this approach, we present two fragments that are part of the `sourcemetamodel`:

```
abstract class Resource {
  attribute string URI; };

class GridService: Resource {
  attribute string Type;
};

class ComputingService : GridService {
  enum t_OS {0,1,2};
  enum t_ProcessorFamily {0,1,2,3};

  attribute t_OS OS;
  attribute ProcessorFamily t_ProcessorFamily;
  attribute unsigned short FreeJobSlots;
  attribute unsigned short RunningJobs;
  attribute unsigned short WaitingJobs;
};

        (MODL.1)
```

```
abstract class MeasurementValue { };

class Satisfaction {
    attribute float value;
    constraint between0and1 "OCL" value : "context satisfaction"
      "inv: self.value >= 0 and self.value <= 1";
};

abstract class ElementaryCriterion {
  Satisfaction evaluate(in MeasurementValue MeasurementValueIn);
};

class DiscreteAbsoluteElementaryCriterion: ElementaryCriterion {
  struct ElementType {
    MeasurementValue MeasurementValueItem;
    Satisfaction SatisfactionItem;
  }

  attribute ordered set [1..*] of ElementType Element;
};
        (MODL.2)
```

In `MODL.1`, the class `Resource` defines a conceptual mapping to an entity or set of entities that have an identity [32]. The class `GridService` is a specialization of `Resource` defining the `Type` of Grid services. Finally, the class `ComputingService` specializing `GridService` introduces a set of attributes of interest for a computing service. Such classes and attributes have a direct correspondence with the ClassAd representation presented in Section 2 adding the modeling of attributes types. In the same way, entities involved in the LSP method can be modeled by MODL. According to the principles for expressing elementary criteria of satisfaction (see Section 3.2), the fragment `MODL.2` captures the rules for defining an elementary criterion enabling to express an absolute classification of a finite set of measurement values. `MeasurementValue` is an abstract class presenting the result returned by the application of a measurement process. The class `Satisfaction` expresses the concept of satisfaction as a value $E \in [0,1]$. `ElementaryCriterion` defines the general concept of an elementary criterion that should be specialized in more specific criteria, like the `DiscreteAbsoluteElementaryCriterion` where the possible measurement values are finite and for each of them a certain satisfaction is given.

5 Conclusions

In this paper we have presented a method dealing with the representation and selection of Grid services based on quality aspects. Quality has been defined in terms of the user satisfaction measurement by means of the measurement theory and the LSP method.

Relying on the metamodeling theory provided by the OMG Model Driven Architecture (MDA), a prototype tool for mapping MOF based Grid services metamodels in domain specific textual languages like the ClassAd language has been presented.

Ongoing work aims at fully including the measurement theory and the LSP method in the Grid services metamodel enabling rigorous analyses of Grid services properties. Further work is also targeted at adapting the method to the evaluation of services defined in terms of other services. This process requires the ability of capturing not only component services properties, but also their inter-relationships that affect the global satisfaction.

References

1. Fenton N. E., Pfleeger S. L.: Software Metrics: A Rigorous and Practical Approach. 2nd edn. PWS Publishing Company, Los Alamitos (California) (1997)
2. Dujmovic J. J.: A Method for Evaluation and Selection of Complex Hardware and Software Systems. In: Intenational Conference for the Resource Management and Performance Evaluation of Enterprise Computing Systems. Volume 1. (1996) 368–378
3. Su S. W., Dujmovic J. J., Batory D. S., Navathe S. B., Elnicki R.: A Cost-Benefit Decision Model: Analysis, Comparison, and Selection of Data Management Systems. ACM Transaction on Database Systems **12** (1987) 472–520
4. Booth, D., Champion M., Ferris, C., Haas, H., McCabe, F., Newcomer E., Orchard D.: Web Services Architecture (2004) W3C Working Group Note 11 February 2004.
5. W3C XML Protocol Working Group: SOAP Version 1.2 Part 0: Primer (2003) W3C Recommendation.
6. Chinnici R., Gudgina M., Moreau J. J., Weerawarana S.: Web Services Description Language (WSDL) Version 2.0 Part 1: Core Language (2003) Working Draft.
7. Foster I., Kesselman C., Tuecke S.: The Anatomy of the Grid: Enabling Scalable Virtual Organizations. In: International J. Supercomputer Applications. Volume 15(3). (2001)
8. Large Hadron Collider Computing Grid: (http://www.cern.ch/lcg)
9. Italian National Institute for Nuclear Physics Computing Grid: (http://grid.infn.it/)
10. Foster, I., Kishimoto, H.: The Open Grid Services Architecture - Version 1.0 (2004) GGF Draft.
11. Czajkowski K., Ferguson D., Foster I., Frey J., Graham S., Sedukhin I., Snelling D., Tuecke S., Vambenepe W.: Web Services Resource Framework (2004) White Paper - Version 1.0.
12. The Globus Alliance: (Globus Toolkit Development Homepage) http://www-unix.globus.org/toolkit/downloads/development/.
13. University of Virginia Grid Computing Group: (WSRF.NET Project) http://www.ws-rf.net/.
14. Fagin R.: Combining fuzzy information from multiple systems. Journal of Computer and Systems Sciences (1999)
15. Triantaphyllou, E.: Multi-Criteria Decision Making Methods: A Comparative Study. Kluwer Academic Publishers (2002)
16. Czajkowski K., Fitzgerald S., Foster I., Kesselman C.: Grid Information Services for Distributed Resource Sharing. In: Proceedings of the Tenth IEEE International Symposium on High-Performance Distributed Computing (HPDC-10), IEEE Press (2001)
17. Prelz F. et Al.: The EU DataGrid Workload Management System: towards the second major release. In: Computing in High Energy and Nuclear Physics, 24-28 March 2003, La Jolla, California. (2003)

18. Solomon M.: The ClassAd Language Reference Manual. Computer Sciences Department, University of Wisconsin, Madison. (2003)
19. Litzkow, M., Livny, M., Mutka, M.: Condor - A Hunter of Idle Workstations. In: Proceedings of the 8th International Conference of Distributed Computing Systems. (1988)
20. Litzkow M. J., Livny M., Mutka M. W.: Policy Driven Heterogeneous Resource Co-Allocation with Gangmatching. In: Proceedings of the Twelfth IEEE International Symposium on High-Performance Distributed Computing, Seattle, WA. (2003)
21. Dujmovic J. J., Erdeljan A.: A Comparison of Training Methods for Preferential Neural Networks. In Press, I.A., ed.: IASTED International Conference on Artificial Intelligence, Expert Systems and Neural Networks. Volume 2. (1996) 924–935
22. Object Management Group: Model Driven Architecture (MDA). Technical report (2003) ver. 1.0.
23. Object Management Group: Meta Object Facility (MOF) specification (2002) Rev. 1.4.
24. Object Management Group: Unified Modeling Language (UML) Specification (2003) Version 1.5.
25. Distributed Systems Technology Group (DSTC): DSTC's MOF product suite (dMOF). Technical report, DSTC (2001) ver. 1.1.
26. PEGAMENTO Project: TokTok. (http://www.dstc.edu.au/TokTok)
27. Laboratoire d'Informatique Paris 6 (LIP6): The ModFact project. (http://modfact.lip6.fr/ModFactWeb)
28. Distributed Systems Technology Centre: dMOF User Guide - version 1.1. (2002)
29. Object Management Group: Human Usable Textual Notation (HUTN) (2002) ver. 1.4.
30. Raymond K., Stee J.: Generating Human-Usable Textual Notations for Information Models. In: Fifth IEEE International Enterprise Distributed Object Computing Conference, Seattle, Washington. (2001) 250–261
31. IBM: Rational Software. (http://www.rational.com)
32. Berners-Lee T., Fielding R., Irvine U. C., Masinter L.: Uniform Resource Identifiers (URI): Generic Syntax (1998) Internet RFC 2396.

Towards a Flexible Trust Model for Grid Environments

Elvis Papalilo[1] and Bernd Freisleben[1,2]

[1] SFB/FK 615, University of Siegen, D-57068 Siegen, Germany
[2] Dept. of Mathematics and Computer Science, University of Marburg
Hans-Meerwein-Str., D-35032 Marburg, Germany
{elvis,freisleb}@informatik.uni-marburg.de

Abstract. An important problem in Grid computing is the management of trust among the entities (e.g. users, resources) involved in a collaboration or computation. In this paper, we present a trust model for Grid environments where trust is calculated based on the trust of the entity itself, its trust towards other entities and the trust of others towards the entity. The proposed approach uses the functionalities of Bayesian networks to be able to dynamically calculate and assign trust values to entities and also to evaluate their capabilities in different scenarios. An implementation of our approach using the GridSim toolkit is presented, and experimental results are shown to illustrate how Grid entities build up their trust values in selected interaction scenarios.

Keywords: Grid Computing, Trust, Bayesian Networks.

1 Introduction

According to [1, 2], the *Grid computing* paradigm is aimed at (a) providing flexible, secure, coordinated resource sharing among dynamic collections of individuals, institutions and resources, and (b) enabling communities ("virtual organizations" (VOs)) to share geographically distributed resources as they pursue common goals, assuming the absence of central location, central control, omniscience, and existing trust relationships.

This paper deals with the problem of managing trust relationships in Grid environments. Trust is a complex issue in a Grid, because there are many uncertainties with respect to the level of reliability that the participants should assign to each other. In practice, it is not possible to know in advance whether a certain entity can be trusted or not. To illustrate the issues involved, consider two VOs with a certain number of participants. Some of them offer various services and resources with different quality, processing speeds, cost etc. Some others want to take advantage of these facilities and use services or processing resources offered by the providers. At the base of every decision for an interaction between the two parties, trust considerations should reside. The level of trust represents the level of intention of computational entities or participants to collaborate. These trust values can be accumulated and calculated based on past direct reciprocal interactions or indirect interactions.

In this paper, we present an approach to manage trust in Grid environments that not only is based on the past behavior of entities, but also on the uncertainties of future actions. The basic idea of our proposal is to make use of *Bayesian networks* [3] which offer the possibility to construct and continuously update tables with values that rep-

M. Jeckle, R. Kowalczyk, and P. Braun (Eds.): GSEM 2004, LNCS 3270, pp. 94–106, 2004.

resent the success or non-success of an interaction regarding specific requirements such as service quality, processing speed, processing cost etc. In this way, each of the entities is able to predict the percentage of having a successful collaboration and thus determine the most suitable partner in an interaction through specific scheduling policies. The proposed approach is illustrated by presenting examples of simulated trust management scenarios using the GridSim toolkit [4].

The paper is organized as follows. In section 2, related work is discussed. Section 3 presents the proposed trust model based on functionalities of Bayesian networks. In section 4, several examples are presented to show how an entity can build up its trust values. Section 5 concludes the paper and outlines areas for future research.

2 Related Work

The problems of managing trust in Grid environments are discussed by Azzedin and Maheswaran [5, 6, 7] who define the notion of trust as consisting of *identity trust* and *behavior trust*. They separate the "Grid domain" into a "client domain" and a "resource domain", and the way they calculate trust is limited in terms of computational scalability, because they try to consider all domains in the network; as the number of domains grows, the computational overhead grows as well. Hwang and Tanachaiwiwat [8] and Goel and Sobolewski [9] try to build trust and security models for Grid environments, using trust metrics based on e-business criteria. Alunkal et al. [10] propose to build an infrastructure called "Grid Eigentrust" using a hierarchical model in which entities are connected to institutions which then form a VO. They conclude with the realization of a "Reputation Service", however, without providing mechanisms that automatically can update trust values.

Apart from the Grid domain, there are several proposals for managing trust and reputation in peer-to-peer (P2P) systems which are likely to converge with Grid computing systems. For example, Aberer and Despotovic [11] try to build a trust and reputation system based on complaints or "negative feedbacks" against peers in cases where something went wrong, resulting in the lack of possibilities for a positive peer to improve its social position through propagation of its good name. Kamvar et al. [12] present the "EigenTrust" algorithm which evaluates the trust information provided by the peers according to their trustworthiness, using trust ratings for credibility. Damiani et al. [13] propose the idea of maintaining reputations for resources as well as for peers, but their developed system is vulnerable to active attacks and there is no possibility to authenticate the identity of participants. The work done by Xiong and Liu [14, 15] is concerned with the evaluation of the identity and the reputation of the peer that gives trust information about the other peers. Finally, Wang and Vassileva [16, 17] use "Bayesian Networks" for enabling peers to develop trust and reputation, especially with respect to the competence and capability of peers to offer high-quality files and valuable recommendations in a P2P file sharing application.

3 A Grid Trust Model Based on Bayesian Networks

Trust is a complex subject relating to belief in the honesty, truthfulness, competence, reliability, etc., of the trusted person or service. In the literature there is no consensus on the definition of trust, though its importance is widely recognized. According to [18], in information technology, trust can be defined as *"the firm belief in the competence of an entity to act dependably, securely, and reliably within a specified context"*. Trust is usually specified in terms of a relationship between a "*trustor*", the subject that trusts a target entity, and a "*trustee*" (i.e., the entity that is trusted). Trust forms the basis for allowing a trustee to use or manipulate resources owned by a trustor or may influence a trustor's decision to use a service provided by a trustee.

Socially inspired trust models are useful for Grid environments, especially for the ease of efficiency in supporting the management of trust requirements. An important step to be taken in a Grid environment deals with the "decentralization" and "generalization" of the notion of trust. Each of the entities should be able to decide on its own regarding to its policies. Although in this case more responsibility and expertise is assigned to an entity, at least each of them has a chance to manage their own trust relationships.

In today's Grids, two types of participants can be identified: *clients* and *providers* of services and resources for storage or computational purposes. It is in best interest of all participants that both clients and providers know that they are dealing with single identities in the Grid. Individual actions performed under a particular identity influence the "good name" of the identity itself and as a result the relationships of this identity with others in the community. Each participant can identify itself as a client, as a provider or as both (if services or resources can be offered by clients).

For each of the participants, their identity and their behavior must be considered to establish trust among them. When trusting an entity, it is important to know which aspect we are referring to. There are instances where one entity is trusted more than the others regarding to different levels of trust. There must be the possibility to specify in which aspect of trust entities are interested in and at which level. Trust towards a participant should be handled in different contexts. These contexts should be used to decide whether a participant is eligible for a certain activity and the overall value of trust of a participant should interfere with the decision of improving the social position among the others. Thus, trust is a social value that pushes entities to collaborate with each other, assuming that their identities are already verified and that the kind of offered goods are of sufficient quality. There is the need to separate different activities in which a participant is involved, and the need to consider not only the behavior of the participant in offering and requesting services or resources but the quality of goods as well. Two participants continue to collaborate or set collaboration with each other thanks to direct or indirect good experiences they formerly had. The bigger the level of accumulated trust of a participant, the better will be its social value and position in the system. Thus, for each entity its social position in the community is important and must be determined upon the calculated level of trust that this entity acquired in the community. The importance of a "good" or "bad name" is crucial in further decisions about the interactions with the entities involved. However, apart from giving the possibility to an entity to gain a better social position and the possibility to be decorated according to the level of trust, such a system should also include sanctions to entities or even entire VOs in case of misconduct or a lower level of participation and interest in the community.

It is also important to underline that just like in our society it is good to have a percentage of risk involved which is derived from some useful social aspects such as reciprocity and altruism. In general, Grid systems can be seen as *uncertain environ-*

ments with casual relationships based on the "good name" of entities at the moment of collaboration.

3.1 Bayesian Trust Model

Apart from the past behavior of entities, there are several uncertainties and thus every future action can be subject to probability theory. Values assigned and accumulated can express the ratio of success or failure of the interaction that is going to take place in a certain moment of time.

The idea of using *Bayesian networks* [3] for managing trust in an uncertain Grid environment as explained above is motivated by the fact that Bayesian networks allow decisions to be taken based on the accumulated and processed experience through:

- interpreting situations through observations and continuous gathering of information
- handling future actions through recommendations and interventions
- adaptation to changing environments, and
- possibly learning from past experience.

The main advantage is that Bayesian Networks offer the possibility to construct and continuously update tables with values that represent the success or failure of an interaction regarding specific requests, such as service quality (high, medium or low), processing speed (fast, medium, low), processing cost (high, acceptable, low), etc. according to the needs. In this way, each of the entities is able to predict the percentage of having a successful collaboration and also trying to decide by itself about the most suitable partner in an interaction through specific scheduling policies.

A Bayesian network can be defined as follows:

- Given is a set of variables and a set of directed edges between the variables.
- Each variable has a finite set of mutually exclusive states.
- The variables together with the directed edges form a directed acyclic graph (DAG).
- To each variable A with parents $B_1, \ldots\ldots, B_n$, the potential table $P(A \mid B_1, \ldots., B_n)$ is attached. If A has no parents, then the table reduces to unconditional probabilities $P(A)$.

Our Bayesian network Grid trust model is based on the Bayes rule:

$$P(b \mid a) = \frac{P(a \mid b)P(b)}{P(a)} \tag{1}$$

where P(a) and P(b) are the probabilities of the events (e.g. successful interaction) a and b, P(a | b) is the probability of event a given event b and P(b | a) is the probability of event b given event a.

As mentioned above, trust is a property that consists of *identity* and *behavior* trust. Using a Bayesian network, the trust value of an entity can thus be modeled as shown in Fig. 1, where the node "Trust" represents the general trust of an entity, the node "Identity Trust" represents the trust on the identity of a certain entity (user or processing entity) and node "Behavior Trust" represents the overall trust value of the compound behavior trust. The arrows indicate that the trust values e.g. of "Behavior Trust" are influenced by the trust values of "Identity Trust".

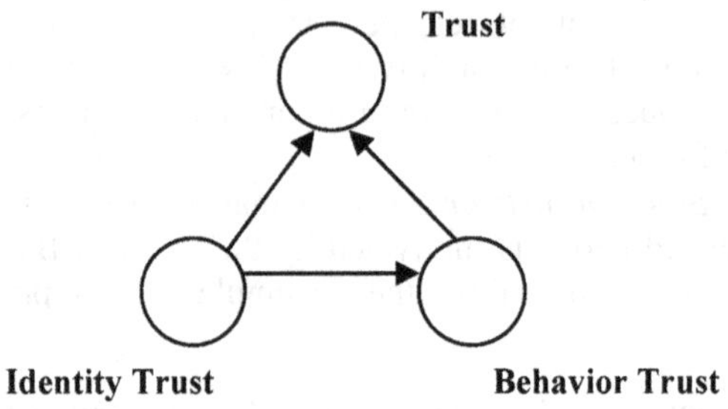

Fig. 1. Bayesian network model for the overall trust value of an entity

Although identity trust is part of the Grid authentication and authorization process, its value is nevertheless related to the overall trust value. Behavior trust depends on different aspects, such as type of connection, type and quality of services offered, computing power, quality of resources etc. In different situations, users can have different needs with respect to the overall capabilities of an entity, e.g.:

- the user may want to use some computing power in the shortest time possibly at the lowest cost,
- the user may want to take advantage of any special service with a certain quality of service offered by one or more entities,
- the user may want to save critical data at some entity and in this case is more interested in the overall trust value of the entity regarding identity and behavior trust.

In Fig. 2, a simplified model of behavior trust using selected aspects and constraints is presented:

In Fig. 2, nodes with the names "Processing Speed", "Processing Cost", "Service *i*", "Service Quality", "…." represent some of the "constraints" or "contexts". Node "Service *i*" represents a normal service, e.g. math service, or a system properties ser-

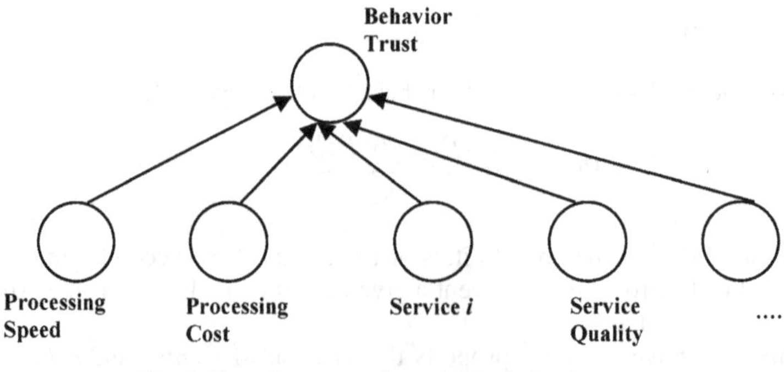

Fig. 2. Bayesian network model for behavior trust

vice in a service-oriented grid environment, where *i* serves as an identifier for that particular service. The last node "….." shows that other elements can be added to the network.

Apart from identity and behavior trust, we consider two additional types of trust. The first one is the *direct trust* that each entity has built up for other entities it has collaborated with in different contexts. The second one is the *indirect trust* that other entities have built up for some specific entities the entity in question wants to collaborate with at a certain moment of time in a particular context.

In our approach, each of the entities builds up a Bayesian network for every other entity it has previously collaborated with in a certain scenario. Each of the Bayesian networks has a root node with two values 0 and 1 which represent the success (S = 1) or not (S = 0) of the specific collaboration with the other entity. Clearly,

$$p(S=1)+p(S=0)=1 \tag{2}$$

If an entity needs to be used in a certain context (Cx) within some constraints (Cn), such as e.g. using a "Math service" offered by an entity within the "smallest amount of time", the trust that the chosen entity can complete this task successfully (S = 1) can be calculated as:

$$p(S=1 \mid Cx_i, Cn_i) \tag{3}$$

Every time an entity wants to set up a direct collaboration with another entity, the contexts and constraints can be set to the specific need using formula (3).

Additionally, an entity can ask other entities about their level of trust related to the entity it wants to collaborate with. Each of the entities then offers its Bayesian network values about the "target" entity regarding the context and constraints required.

The level of trust of a successful collaboration with an entity can be calculated as the product of the probabilities of the direct trust between two entities and indirect trust values offered by the other entities which have previously had a similar collaboration with the "target" entity, as expressed with (3).

After each collaboration, the entities update their corresponding Bayesian networks. These values can be used in case of further direct collaborations or can be offered to the other entities that search for previous similar collaborations between entities.

Fig. 2 shows that the "Behavior Trust" (BT) is the result of the trust value of its components. According to the chain rule for Bayesian networks if $U=\{A_1,......,A_n\}$ where U is a universe of variables A_i then

$$P(U)=\prod_i P(A_i \mid pa(A_i)) \tag{4}$$

where $pa(A_i)$ is the parent set of A_i, in our case "Behavior Trust" and its components, whose values affect the "Behavior Trust".

According to (4), the joint probability distribution of BT of an entity is the product of all conditional probabilities specified in its Bayesian network.

Fig. 1 shows that the general "Trust" (T) value of an entity consists of "Identity Trust" (IT) and "Behavior Trust" (BT). According to the Bayes rule (1):

$$P_{BN} = P(T)P(IT \mid T)P(BT, IT) \tag{5}$$

By specifying prior probabilities and conditional probabilities of the Bayesian network, we can model every joint probability distribution of the three variables. For each of the entities, according to specific capabilities, a Bayesian network can be built and will be updated after a collaboration has taken place.

3.2 Discussion

Compared to other proposals [5, 6, 7, 10], our model is more fine-grained, because we consider different aspects of trust, especially the elements that constitute behavior trust. In this way, we offer a flexible way to rate the entities according to their specific capabilities. Our model is easily extensible if further aspects of behavior trust need to be considered.

The work done in the P2P domain [16, 17] is also based on using Bayesian networks for enabling peers to develop trust and reputation among them. Apart from considering Grid environments, the difference to our work is that we calculate the entity trust as the joint probability of the identity and behavior trust, where behavior trust of the entities includes more aspects in Grid environments than in P2P networks.

In Grid environments with continuous interaction among participants, as well as continuous requests for services, computational power and storage, there is the possibility for each of the entities to build up a personal trust value according to its capabilities. The overall trust value of the entity and the values of its elements are easy identifiable. After each interaction, there is also the possibility to update the trust values for the entities involved in an interaction. Thus, we consider the proposed model as very suitable for a Grid environment regarding its flexibility.

4 Implementation

An initial implementation of the proposed approach has been performed using the GridSim toolkit [4]. GridSim simulates real heterogeneous resources and as a result can be used for modeling and simulation of application scheduling on various classes of parallel and distributed computing systems like a Grid. GridSim already offers the possibility to create "processing" entities with different processing speed and cost and also "user" entities with a certain number of jobs and certain constraints regarding the desired deadline and amount of budget that the user assigns for his or her jobs to be completed. The GridSim toolkit provides facilities for modeling and simulating resources and network connectivity with different capabilities, configurations and domains. It supports primitives for application composition, information services for resource discovery and interfaces for assigning application tasks to resources and managing their execution. These features can be used to simulate parallel and distributed scheduling systems such as resource brokers or Grid schedulers for evaluating the performance of scheduling algorithms or heuristics. The GridSim toolkit is part of the Gridbus Project [19], engaged in the design and development of service-oriented cluster and grid middleware technologies to support eScience and eBusiness applications.

All users need to submit their jobs to a central scheduler, which can be targeted to perform global optimization such as higher system utilization and overall user satisfaction. For each of the entities ("user" entity and "resource" entity) hash tables are built for storing the trust values of the entities. Trust values assigned to the entities reflect their level of trust in others. Jobs are assigned to the "processing" entities primarily after sorting them according to the trust values that this entity was able to build on the others. The ratio of the successfully completed jobs and the total number of jobs assigned to that resource is the new trust value that is going to update the old trust value in the "user" entity trust table. This is considered as direct trust among the "user" entity and the specified "processing" entity.

The initial trust values of the entity "user *i*" and the entity "resource *i*" towards other entities in the system is assigned as 0.33 in order to treat all participants as equal. This value is used because it results from the probability table built for a certain trust component that we have chosen, such as processing speed or processing cost. Although they quite often change from one interaction to another, the values for these elements can be categorized as follows:

- Processing Speed (PS*i*): with values "Fast", "Medium" and "Low".
- Processing Cost (PC*i*): with values "High", "Acceptable" and "Low".

where the *i*-factor represents the entity we are dealing with.

For ease of use, this initial value and its later updates are seen as the probability ratio that collaboration among parties was successful (Tab. 1).

Table 1. Representation of a hash table with keys (entity_i) and values P(collaboration | succes1s)

	P(success)
Entity *i*	P(collaboration | success)

In this way, none of the participants is underestimated compared to the others. The "user" entity is the one that requests a collaboration with "processing" entities. Each of the users creates a list of jobs that are distributed to the "processing" entities according to the selected scheduling policy. For each of the users, a hash table named "usertrust_*i*", where *i* represents the user identity, is created. All the "processing" entities are organized under another hash table named "resourcetrust" where as values serve the probability tables (hashtables) that each "processing" entity has build toward other "processing" entities. As constraints for an entity, we currently use *processing cost* and *processing speed,* since GridSim is primarily selects entities based on their processing power (Million Instructions Per Second) and their cost (Grid$ per Million Instructions). Once the tables with trust values for "user" entities and "resource" entities are defined, we implemented a *comparator* which sorts the entities that a user is going to assign jobs to according to the trust values in the hash tables. This comparator serves as the basic object of the scheduling policies offered by the simulator:

- Cost optimization - the cheapest entity is seen as the most suitable one for finishing a job within a certain budget offered
- Deadline optimization - the most powerful entity is seen as the most suitable one for finishing a job within a certain interval of time

In our implementation, we assume that all the participants know their identities among each other. After ordering the trust values of the entities with which the user is going to collaborate, cost and time factors are considered. If the trust values calculated for two entities are the same, then the entities are going to be sorted according to their speed and/or processing cost. After the entities for collaboration are chosen in this way and the simulator has distributed the jobs to them, for each of the entities involved we count the number of jobs assigned and control their status. The ratio of successful jobs executed by an entity and the total number of jobs assigned to that entity is considered as the trust value that the user puts on that entity. If all the jobs are successfully completed, then the trust value of that entity is 1, otherwise if none of the jobs assigned is successfully completed, then the direct trust that a user puts on this entity is 0. The trust value calculated in this way replaces the old trust value that the "user" entity has previously placed for that particular entity. In this phase of our implementation, we have not dealt with the update of the trust values that the entity itself puts on the "user" entity that collaborated with it. In this way, we can always have an updated trust values table for the "user" entity. Similarly, we plan to also update the trust values that the entities place on the user they have collaborated with.

Table 2. Modeled simulation "resource" entities

Resource Name	**Resource Characteristics**	**MIPS rating**	**Resource Manager Type**	**Price (G$ / PE)**	**MIPS/G$**
Resource1	Sun Ultra, OS-Solaris	198	Time-shared	3	66.0
Resource2	Compaq Alpha Server, OS-OSF1	284	Time-shared	5	56.8
Resource3	Compaq Alpha Server, OS-OSF1	362	Time-shared	4	90.5
Resource4	SGI Origin, OS-Irix	460	Time-shared	5	92.0
Resource5	Intel Pentium, OS-Linux	386	Time-shared	2	193.0
Resource6	Sun Ultra, OS-Solaris	335	Time-shared	6	55.33
Resource7	Sun Ultra, OS-Solaris	277	Time-shared	3	92.33
Resource8	SGI Origin, OS-Irix	418	Time-shared	6	69.66

5 Experimental Results

To test our approach, we have modeled a set of resources using GridSim with different characteristics of resources and the respective costs per time unit G$ (Grid Dollar; the chosen currency) of their processing elements created for simulation purposes. These simulated resources with their names and characteristics are shown in Table 2. All values are generated by the Visual Modeler [20]. The brokers translate the cost into Grid currency (G$) per million instructions (MI) for each resource. Such a translation helps in identifying the relative cost of resources for processing the jobs assigned to them.

In the experiments, the GridSim scheduling strategy applied for a single modeled user is "scheduleWithDBC_CostOptimization()". The idea behind this scheduling strategy is that the "processing" entities are sorted according to the price they charge for their service.

For the user, a different number of jobs varying from 3 to 100 are created and. deadline and budget values are assigned. The starting values for the deadline is 674.0 (in terms of simulation time) and for the budget 6552.0 (in terms of G$). These values are modified in steps of 500 and 1000 for the time and budget factors, respectively. We are not trying to show what the impact of budget and time constraints on the selection of the entities is, but rather to show how each entity, in our case "processing" entities, according to their capabilities (processing power and cost), can build their trust values on the trust values of their collaborators (in our case the "user" entity as a requestor for a collaboration).

Inside this scheduling strategy, we have applied our "comparator". This means that at the moment when "processing" entities are created, the trust tables for the "user" entity and for each of the "processing" entities are created (Fig. 3).

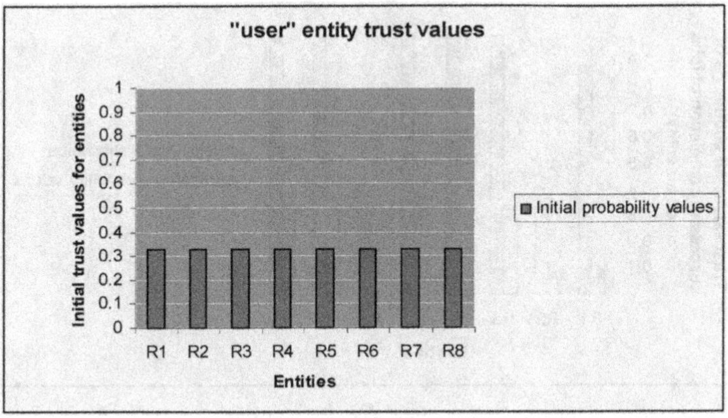

Fig. 3. Initial trust values for the "user" entity; each "processing" entity builds similar tables

The simulation shows that for a small number of assigned jobs (e.g. 3 jobs) the jobs are processed only in a particular entity, the one that offers the best price according to the "cost-optimization" strategy, since the trust values in the tables of the entities "user" and "resource" are the same (the initially assigned value of 0.33). In our case, the "processing" entity "Resource5" offers the best price. After a successful interaction, the trust values for this entity are going to be updated in the "usertrust" table and the other values remain unchanged since there was no interaction between them and the user (see Fig. 4).

Increasing the number of jobs that the "user" entity creates and needs to process, there is also the need to increase the budget and/or deadline values that the "user" entity places for the completion of the jobs. In this moment, according to the output file generated by GridSim, a lot of collaboration takes place. In order to finish the task

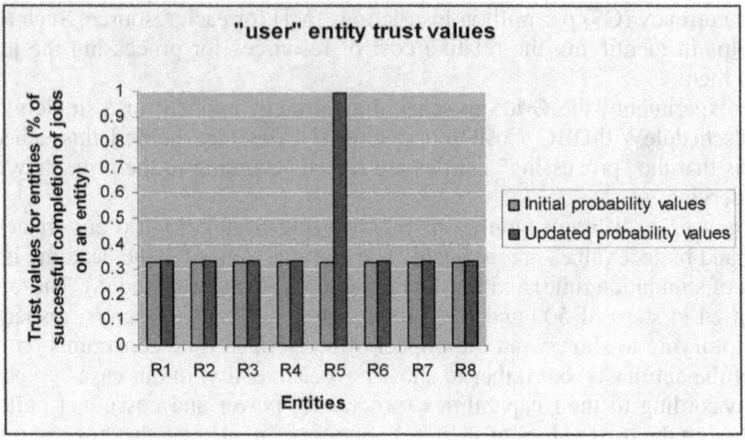

Fig. 4. Updated trust values for the "user" entity; "R5" has a greater probability value than the others, thanks to a successful interaction

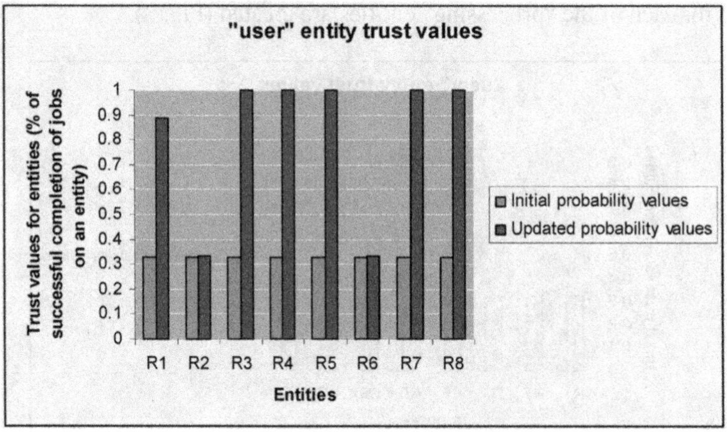

Fig. 5. Accumulated trust values for the "processing" entities in the "user" entity trust table

within the assigned budget and deadline, the scheduler invokes more "processing" entities. Initially, since the trust values in the corresponding tables are the same (assigned by us), the jobs are assigned to cheaper "processing" entities. In order to meet the deadline constraint, the scheduler also invokes more expensive "processing" entities. Once a certain job is completed by an entity, we check its status, and if it is successful, the ratio of the successful jobs executed on that resource grows. We use this value as the trust value that the "user" entity places for that entity in his or her table of direct trusts. After executing all the jobs, in our experiment with 100 jobs and an assigned deadline value of 1800 and a budget value of 18000, the updated "user" entity trust table ("usertrust" hash table) is as shown in Fig. 5.

From Fig. 5 we can see that the "user" entity has not placed a collaboration with the "processing" entities R2 and R6, it has successfully collaborated with R3, R4, R5, R7, R8 and for some reasons the collaboration with R1 was not completely successful, but this result has influenced the trust value that the "user" entity places on the entity.

The results have shown that the so called "direct" trust values that the "user" entity places on the entities it has previously collaborated with changes conform the success ratio of the collaboration. In this way, we have presented an initial implementation of how the entity, in our case a "processing" entity, can build its trust value to another entity that had previously interacted or needs at a certain moment to interact with it.

6 Conclusions

In this paper, we have presented a Bayesian network approach to manage trust in Grid environments. The proposed trust model separates each of the participants based on the role they are playing at a certain moment of time. The functionalities offered by Bayesian networks were used to calculate trust of the entities in different scenarios in a fine-grained way, according to the collaboration between the entities. Using the GridSim toolkit, we have demonstrated how the trust of the elements that constitute the overall trust of the entities and the trust of the entities itself changes according to simulated "past interactions", offering possibilities for the entities to choose the most suitable ones according to specific needs.

There are several areas for future work. For example, we plan to conduct further experiments using more complex test cases, involving multiple users and a greater number of "processing" entities. Furthermore, an implementation of the proposed model in real scenarios other than in a simulated Grid environment is an interesting issue. This could be also used as the basis for building a "recommender system" based on the calculated trust values of the entities. By comparing the values of their Bayesian networks, each of the entities, except of contributing to the calculation of the trust that a certain task is going to be successfully completed, can contribute also to choose or recommend the most suitable of the entities for a certain action as well. Finally, another issue is to investigate whether our Bayesian network approach can contribute to identifying possible malicious behavior of the entities.

Acknowledgements

This work is financially supported by the Deutsche Forschungsgemeinschaft (SFB/FK 615, Teilprojekt MT) and by Deutscher Akademischer Austauschdienst (DAAD, Stability Pact South-Eastern Europe). The authors would like to thank M. Gollnick, M. Grauer, F. Mansouri, E. Papalilo, R. Sennert and J. Wagner for their valuable support.

References

1. Foster, I., Kesselman, C., Tuecke, S.: The Anatomy of the Grid: Enabling Scalable Virtual Organizations. In: International J. Supercomputer Applications (2001)
2. Foster, I., Kesselman, C., Nick, J.M., Tuecke, S.: The Physiology of the Grid: An Open Grid Services Architecture for Distributed Systems Integration. In: Open Grid Service Infrastructure WG, Global Grid Forum (2002)

3. Jensen, F.V.: Bayesian Networks and Decision Graphs. Springer-Verlag (2001)
4. http://www.gridbus.org/gridsim
5. Azzedin, F., Maheswaran, M.: Evolving and Managing Trust in Grid Computing Systems. In: Conference on Electrical and Computer Engineering, Canada. IEEE Computer Society Press (2002) 1424–1429
6. Azzedin, F., Maheswaran, M.: Towards Trust-Aware Resource Management in Grid Computing Systems. In: Second IEEE/ACM International Symposium on Cluster Computing and the Grid (CCGRID), Berlin, Germany. IEEE Computer Society (2002) 452–457
7. Azzedin, F., Maheswaran, M.: Integrating Trust into Grid Resource Management Systems. In: International Conference on Parallel Processing, Vancouver, B.C., Canada. The International Association for Computers and Communications. IEEE Computer Society Press (2002) 47–54
8. Hwang, K., Tanachaiwiwat, S.: Trust Models and NetShield Architecture for Securing Grid Computing. In: Journal of Grid Computing (2003)
9. Goel, S., Sobolewski, M.: Trust and Security in Enterprise Grid Computing Environment. In: Proceedings of the IASTED International Conference on Communication, Network and Information Security, New York, USA (2003)
10. Alunkal, B., Veljkovic, I., von Laszewski, G.: Reputation-Based Grid Resource Selection. In: Workshop on Adaptive Grid Middleware (AgridM), New Orleans, Louisiana, USA (2003)
11. Aberer, K., Despotovic, Z.: Managing Trust in a Peer-2-Peer Information System. In: Ninth International Conference on Information and Knowledge Management (CIKM), Atlanta, Georgia, USA (2001) 310-317
12. Kamvar, S.D., Schlosser M.T., Garcia-Molina, H.: The Eigentrust Algorithm for Reputation Management in P2P Networks. In: Proceedings of the Twelfth International World Wide Web Conference (WWW), Budapest, Hungary (2003) 640-651
13. Damiani, E., di Vimercati, S.D.C., Paraboschi, S., Samarati, P., Violante, F.: Reputation-Based Approach for Choosing Reliable Resources in Peer-to-Peer Networks. In: Proceedings of the Ninth ACM Conference on Computer and Communications Security, Washington, DC, USA (2002) 207-216
14. Xiong, L., Liu, L.: A Reputation-Based Trust Model for Peer-to-Peer eCommerce Communities. In: IEEE Conference on E-Commerce (CEC), Newport Beach, California, USA. IEEE Press (2003) 275-284
15. Xiong, L., Liu, L.: Building Trust in Decentralized Peer-to-Peer Electronic Communities. In: Fifth International Conference on Electronic Commerce Research (ICECR-5), Montreal, Canada. ACM Press (2002)
16. Wang, Y., Vassileva, J.: Trust and Reputation Model in Peer-to-Peer Networks. In: Peer-to-Peer Computing, Linköping, Sweden (2003) 150-
17. Wang, Y., Vassileva, J.: Bayesian Network-Based Trust Model. In: Web Intelligence, Halifax, Canada (2003) 372-378
18. Grandison, T., Sloman, M.: A Survey of Trust in Internet Applications. In: Vol. 3, Number 4 of IEEE Communications Surveys & Tutorials (2000)
19. Buyya, R., Venugopal, S.: The Gridbus Toolkit for Service-Oriented Grid and Utility Computing: An Overview and Status Report. In: Proceedings of the First IEEE International Workshop on Grid Economics and Business Models (GECON), Seoul, Korea. IEEE Press (2004) 19-36
20. Sulistio, A., Yeo, C.S., Buyya, R.: Visual Modeler for Grid Modeling and Simulation (GridSim) Toolkit. In: Proceedings of Third International Conference on Computational Science (ICCS), Saint Petersburg, Russia / Melbourne, Australia. Springer-Verlag (2003) 1123-1132

Decentralized, Adaptive Services: The AspectIX Approach for a Flexible and Secure Grid Environment

Rüdiger Kapitza[1], Franz J. Hauck[2], and Hans Reiser[1]

[1] Dept. of Comp. Sciences 4, University of Erlangen-Nürnberg, Germany
{rrkapitz,reiser}@cs.fau.de
[2] Distributed Systems Lab, University of Ulm, Germany
hauck@informatik.uni-ulm.de

Abstract. In this paper we present EDAS, an environment for decentralized, adaptive services. This environment offers flexible service models based on distributed mobile objects ranging from a traditional client-server scenario to a fully peer-to-peer based approach. Automatic, dynamic resource management allows optimized use of available resources while minimizing the administrative complexity. Furthermore the environment supports a trust-based distinction of peers and enables a trust-based usage of resources.

1 Introduction

In the past few years, many research activities have been initiated to create new infrastructures for distributed applications. The primary goals are to overcome limitations of traditional client/server-structured systems, to increase flexibility, to reduce administrative cost, and to enable a better utilization of all available resources, possibly distributed world-wide.

The utilization of client-side resources is specifically addressed by the increasingly popular peer-to-peer systems. In such systems every peer has similar responsibilities and provides resources for the whole system. Frequent changes of participating nodes are supported by the protocols. However, severe degradation of the overall system performance or even a collapse of the system may happen if too many nodes participate only for very short periods of time. More severely, using all available peer resources means that all peers have the potential of attacking the system. In many systems, a single attacker may even counterfeit multiple identities in the system and thus control a significant part of the whole system. As a result, the advantage of using peer resources easily is being paid for with severe difficulties in controlling security and privacy concerns.

Infrastructures for grid computing aim at virtualizing a group of computers, servers, and storage as one large computing system. Resource management is a key issue in such systems, needed for an efficient and automated distribution of tasks on the grid. Such grid infrastructures are often deployed at enterprise level, but projects like SETI@home [1] have demonstrated the feasibility of more decentralized grids as well. Research on ubiquitous computing, autonomous computing, or spontaneous networks concentrates more on problems caused by the dynamicity in a network with a large number of devices, many of them mobile, and with huge differences in networking facilities, architecture and computational resources.

M. Jeckle, R. Kowalczyk, and P. Braun (Eds.): GSEM 2004, LNCS 3270, pp. 107–118, 2004.

There is a tendency towards growing overlaps between all these different areas. Consequently future systems will demand a generic infrastructure that is able to fulfill the requirements of all such application types. Such next generation infrastructure will be confronted with the following challenges:

- First of all, faced with large systems with constantly growing complexity, it must keep the administrative complexity at an easily manageable level. A high degree of automation of management tasks is necessary, without loosing controllability of the system.
- Second, it has to provide mechanisms for a controlled usage of resources. On the one hand, it should be possible to make use of all peer resources available anywhere the distributed system. On the other hand, security and confidentiality concerns must be respected.
- Furthermore, it should allow easy and flexible adaptation to changing circumstances. One example of such dynamic reconfigurations is migration of service provision between rapidly changing participants (e.g., mobile devices). Similarly one can consider compensating reactions to failures, changes in available resources, or varying utilization of a service. The aspects of adaptation and resource control cannot be solved each on its own, but influence each other mutually.

In this paper, we present our *Environment for Distributed, Adaptive Services (EDAS)*. This environment allows the usage of client-side resources in a controlled, secure fashion. It supports dynamic adaptation at run-time, provides a management infrastructure, and offers system-level support for scalability and fault tolerance. The environment is built upon our AspectIX middleware infrastructure, which directly supports QoS-based, dynamic reconfiguration of services. It supports flexible service models, including a fully centralized client/server structure, completely peer-to-peer based systems, and various configurations "in between" that allow a controlled use of peer resources. The overall goal is do provide a generic service architecture that allows to implement the service functionality once, and then, ideally, run this service with different service models and adapt it at run-time.

We support explicit management of available resources via a *home service*. Using this home service, domain administrators can provide resources for application services or service classes. For simplicity of administration, a set of nodes within one administrative domain is managed jointly. Furthermore, the home service is responsible for local resource monitoring (e.g., currently available memory, CPU resources, and network bandwidth) and notification about resource-specific events (e.g., addition or removal of resources, node shutdown).

The second key component is the *service environment*. Its task is to provide the environment in which services can be hosted. It manages the available execution locations, depending on resource offers by home services and trust specifications of the administrator of the service environment. It also reacts to notification from the home services, and suggests, for instance, that a service should be migrated to another available node as a reaction to a shutdown notification. The service environment is also able to consider different trust levels for the service. For example, the core of a service (e.g., all of its primary data replicas) might be located at highly trusted nodes only, whereas some caching or secondary read-only replicas might be placed on other available nodes as well.

This paper is structured as follows: The next section gives a short overview over the AspectIX middleware infrastructure. Section 3 presents the core architecture of EDAS. Section 4 illustrates the structure and properties of the environment with a sample service. Section 5 surveys related work. Section 6 summarizes our contribution and gives some concluding remarks on the status of our prototype implementation.

2 Basics Middleware Infrastructure

The EDAS environment is based on our AspectIX middleware [2]. At its core, it provides a CORBA-compliant ORB and, as such, supports heterogeneous distributed systems. There are extensions which allow direct interoperation with Java RMI or .NET applications. These extensions may be encapsulated in a transparent way for any client or service implementation. Our fragmented object model, which we will explain in the next subsection, provides a generic abstraction for services with arbitrary internal structure. Furthermore, AspectIX provides useful basic mechanisms for distributed adaptive services. A dynamic loading service (DLS) allows loading of service-specific code at the client side respecting local platform dependencies [3]. A generic architecture with state transfer mechanisms supports migration and replication of service fragments. These will be explained afterwards.

2.1 The Fragmented Object Model

In a traditional, RPC-based client-server structure, the complete functionality of an object resides on a single node. For transparent access to an object, a client instantiates a stub that handles remote invocations (Fig. 2.1 A). The stub code is usually generated automatically from an interface specification.

In the fragmented object model, the distinction between client stubs and the server object is no longer present. From an abstract point of view, a fragmented object is a unit with unique identity, interface, behavior, and state, like in classic object-oriented design. The implementation of these properties however is not bound to a specific location, but may be distributed arbitrarily on various *fragments* (Fig. 2.1 B). Any client that wants to access the fragmented object needs a local fragment, which provides an interface identical to that of a traditional stub. However the local fragment may be specific for exactly that object. Two objects with the same interface may lead to completely different local fragments. This internal structure allows a high degree of freedom on where the state and functionality is provided, and how the interaction between fragments is done. The internal distribution and interaction is not only transparent on the outer interface of the distributed object, but may even change dynamically at runtime. This allows the fragmented object model to adapt to changing environment conditions or quality of service requirements.

In the context of EDAS a decentralized, adaptive service is modeled as fragmented object. This offers the possibility to change the service model on demand from traditional client-server to a peer-to-peer based approach and all kind of intermediate stages by migrating and exchanging fragments.

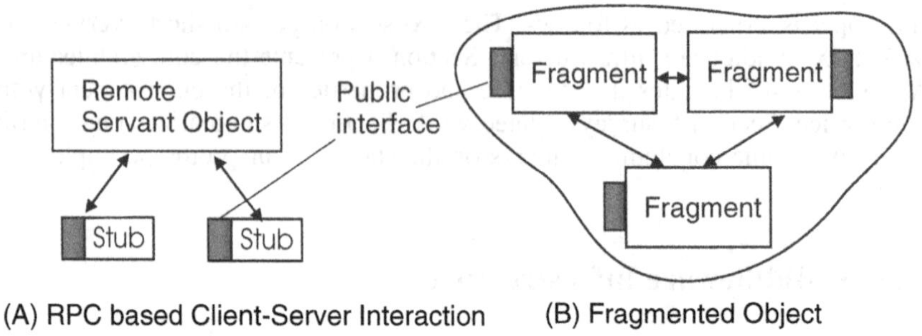

Fig. 2.1. RPC-based Client-Server Interaction vs. Fragmented Object

```
interface Checkpointable {
     void setState(in byte[] state);
     byte[] getState();
};
```

Fig. 2.2. `Checkpointable` Interface

2.2 AspectIX Services for Migration and Replication

The migration and replication of fragments or fragment implementations can be divided into three steps: First of all, an appropriate target system has to be found. After that, unless the necessary code is already available at the target system, it has to be loaded on demand. Finally, the corresponding fragment has to be instantiated and the state has to be transferred to the new location.

To solve these tasks the AspectIX middleware provides an extended version of the CORBA lifecycle service [4]. If a fragment has to be replicated or migrated a factory finder is consulted. Such a factory finder is responsible for locating factories within a defined scope. In the context of the AspectIX middleware, this factory finder consults special factory finder objects that reside on each node of the scope. These factory finders cooperate with the Dynamic Loading Service (DLS) to instantiate a factory for the needed fragment on demand, provided that the requirements of the fragment are met and the fragment code could be loaded and executed in the context of the target system. To achieve this, the DLS queries an implementation repository for all available implementations of the needed fragment. Then, the DLS checks the requirements of each implementation and selects the implementation that fits best to the local node. With the help of the factory a new fragment is instantiated.

After creation, the new fragment needs to be informed about its state. Our state transfer mechanism adheres to the according elements in the FT-CORBA standard [5]. That is, any service object that can be relocated or replicated has to implement a `Checkpointable` interface (see Fig. 2.2).

This interface is used for all kinds of state transfer, both for exchanging the local fragment implementation with a different one, and for remote state transfer for migration or replication. Special care has to be taken about concurrency between method invocations at the service and state transfer actions. Appropriate synchronization mechanisms are provided at the middleware level.

In the simplest case, the state is completely encoded into an octet sequence with `get_state` and decoded with `set_state`. Please note, however, that more sophisticated models are possible. `get_state` might, e.g., simply return a FTP address where to get the state, and `set_state` could use this address for the actual state transfer. For an exchange of the local implementation, `get_state` might simply encode the location on the local disk where the state resides, and `set_state` just feeds this information to the new local implementation.

3 Architecture of EDAS

Our environment for decentralized, adaptive services (EDAS) aims at providing a generic platform for services in a distributed system. Any EDAS-based services may be spread over a set of peers and combines available resources for service provision. Administrative complexity is minimized by automation of management tasks, like reconfiguration in reaction to failures, high load, or system policy modifications. Mechanisms for migration and replication of service components are available. The process of selecting execution locations considers trust metrics of peers that offer resources, to fulfill reliability requirements of a service.

The EDAS platform has three major components (Fig. 3.1): The *home service* is provided by every peer that actively supports decentralized, adaptive services. It basically manages resources of one or more peers belonging to the same administrative domain. The *service environment* is spread over a set of domains that support a group of decentralized, adaptive services run by one organization or community. Finally, the *decentralized, adaptive service* is dynamically distributed within the scope of an associated service environment.

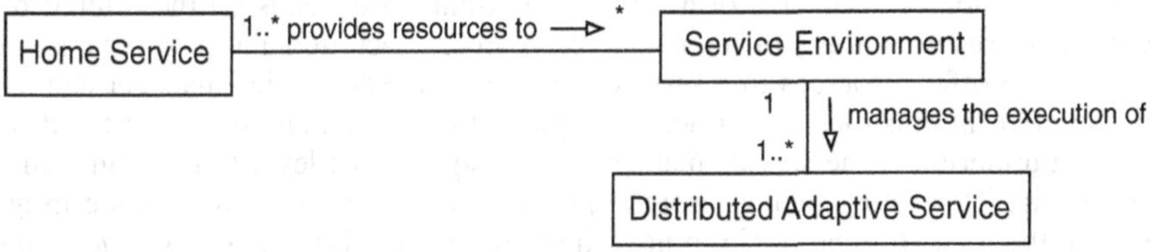

Fig. 3.1. Core Components

3.1 Home Service

The home service represents a mediator between the peers of an administrative domain and one or more service environments, each running a set of decentralized, adaptive services (Fig. 3.1). Fig. 3.2 shows three domains each running a home service which spans all peers of the respective domains. Every peer provides a set of resources. These resources are combined and monitored by the associated home service. Each domain has a manager who can use that home service to assign resources to service environments and to revoke them. Furthermore, the home service provides system information about each peer to the involved service environments and to the domain manager. This includes system load and all kinds of resource usage information but also the notification about important system events. For example, if a peer is shut down all affected service environments are notified and can migrate affected service components as needed.

3.2 Service Environment

A service environment represents a scope of distribution for one or more decentralized, adaptive services. Usually, a service environment is owned by one organization or community and managed by an individual called service manager. Such a manager can start, stop, and configure services through the interface of the service environment and decides which resources provided by home services are accepted (Fig 3.3). The main goal of the service environment is to support the seamless and easy distribution and management of distributed, adaptive services.

In most cases a service environment is spread over more than one administrative domain as shown in Fig. 3.2. One task of the service environment is to collect the system and resource information of the supporting home services. Another task is to manage the migration of services or service components, based on available resources, the needs of the services, and the policies provided by the service manager. The migration of service components can be necessary for various reasons, like peer shutdown, load balancing, or the growth or shrinkage of a service environment. For this purpose the service environment implements a generic factory for service components. If a new replica has to be created or a service component needs to be migrated, the service asks the service environment for a new service component instance. The service environment now has to determine which node provides sufficient resources and fulfills the system requirements of the service component. Further basic requirements have to be taken into account, like not to place replicas of the same component on the same node. To achieve this, a component specific factory has to be instantiated on all suitable hosts. The factory provides information about the resource requirements of the service component and checks in co-operation with the service environment if additional runtime requirements are fulfilled.

The expansion or shrinkage of a service environment depends on the offered resources and trustworthiness of the resource provider. Each domain manager has the possibility to offer resources to a service environment. The service manager can accept the offer and instruct the service environment to expand and use the offered resources. Furthermore, the service manager can assign a trust level to the administrative domain. This rating of the resource provider allows an explicit resource usage based on the trustworthiness. Up to now the rating is based on the knowledge of the service provider but we currently evaluate how and based on what information this could be done automatically. The shrinkage of a domain can be caused by an administrative domain revoking the usage permission or simply by decision of the service administrator. If a service component is migrated or a new replicate is instantiated, this is done in a trust-level conform way. A new component will always be placed on nodes with the same or higher trust level.

It is obvious that there could be situations where the available resources are not sufficient or severe problems occur like a network partition. In these cases, where the service environment cannot autonomously solve the problem, the service environment notifies the service administrator. The service administrator can now fix the problem manually (e.g., accept resource offers by other domains). The service environment also detects failures like a crashed node. In such a case the affected services are notified. Then it is up to the service to cope with the situation; for example, a service could request a new replicate.

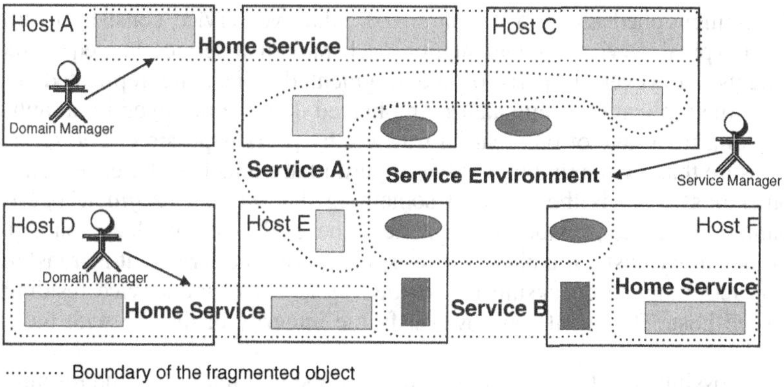

Fig. 3.2. EDAS Scenario

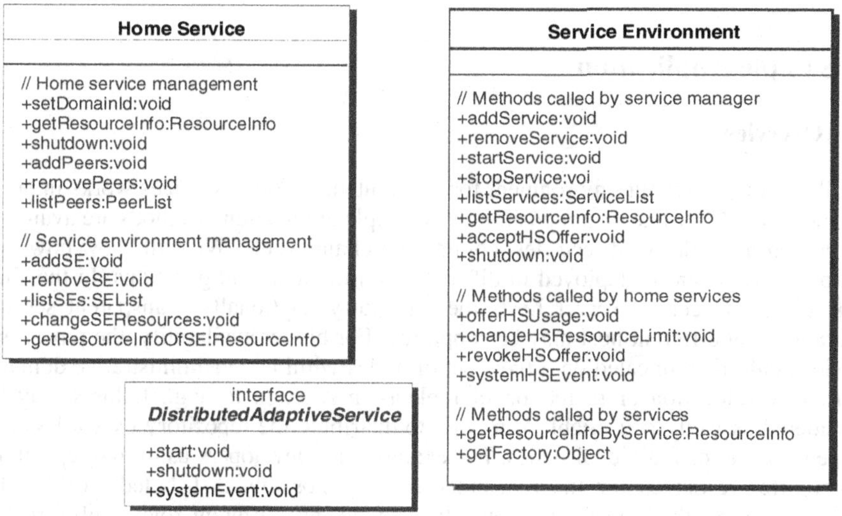

Fig. 3.3. Interfaces

3.3 Decentralized, Adaptive Services

In EDAS a decentralized, adaptive service normally matches a traditional service accessed by users like a web server, an instant messaging server or a source code repository. Such a service is represented by a fragmented object. This object expands or shrinks in the scope spanned by the associated service environment depending on the service demands and for fault-tolerance reasons. Usually every part of the object is mobile and is migrated if necessary. Each service has at least two interfaces: one for management tasks and another service specific for the end user. The management interface offers methods to start, stop, and configure service instances.

In the preceding section we already mentioned that each supporting domain has an assigned trust level. This level is used for a secure and fault tolerant distribution of a service. As mentioned above a decentralized, adaptive service consists of different parts. In a typical service implementation each part of a service has equal security requirements. However, if parts of the fragmented object are replicated and the changes to the replication group and the replicated data are managed by a fault tolerant algorithm, the usage of only partial trustworthy peers is possible. The service has only to ensure that the maximum number of permitted faults is never exceeded.

Another possibility is the usage of something that we call *verifiable operations*. For example, a service provides a set of files. These files can be placed on a number of less trustworthy hosts. If a client requests a file from the service, it is transferred to the client and a signed checksum is provided by a part of the service residing on a fully trusted host. The client can now verify the integrity of the file with the checksum.

A third possibility is the distribution based on the self-interest of the resource provider. If the service can be structured in a way that parts of the service are only responsible for request issued by clients within a domain, then these parts should be hosted by peers of the associated domain whether they are trustworthy or not.

4 Sample Application

4.1 Overview

For illustrating how our environment for distributed, adaptive services works in practice, we use a CVS-like data repository as a sample application. Methods are available for adding new files or directories, committing changes, etc. We will show how this sample service can be deployed in different environment configurations. In the simplest case, one central server hosts the repository. Optionally, transparent service migration to a different host may be supported. For higher availability, the repository service could be replicated on a fixed set of nodes within one administrative domain. Automatic relocation or recreation of replicas in reaction to, e.g., failures may be considered as well. You might even want to distribute the repository over a less homogeneous set of individual nodes. For example, all developers using the repository might offer resources for the repository service, possibly distributed world-wide. Furthermore, available resources could be divided into different roles: Fully trusted nodes are allowed to host primary replicas, and other nodes are available for "mirrors", i.e., secondary read-only replicas which simply copy the state of the primary ones. In the ultimate case, you might want to use the data storage of a peer-to-peer network for hosting the repository.

4.2 Central Repository Implementation

For a central client-server implementation, only a very simple variant of the home service and service environment are needed: The home service is a simple, local fragment that allows the use of the local resources (disk, network) to a local service environment, which in turn hosts the repository service locally. No interaction with other nodes is necessary. The repository service itself is implemented in exactly the same way as one would do with traditional client/server middleware infrastructures.

If such basic service implementation additionally implements our standard interface for state transfer (see Section 2.2), migration is automatically supported in EDAS, without any modifications to the service implementation. Figure 4.2 illustrates the steps necessary for a service migration.

First of all (step 1), a second node has to offer resources for the service. This might be the case automatically, if Node 2 is managed via the same home service. Otherwise, the administrator of the home service of the second node has to offer its resources explicitly.

As a second step, the service environment needs to be expanded to the second node. This may happen automatically as soon as the service environment is notified of the resource offer, provided that the home service is sufficiently trusted. Otherwise, an explicit administrator action of the service environment can accept the new home service as a potential execution location for its services.

In a third step, the migration itself has to be triggered. This is either done explicitly by an administrator, or it is initiated automatically based on notifications ("*Node 1 will be shut down for maintenance*") or policies ("*Trigger migration if load on Node 1 exceed limits and another Node with significantly less load is available*"). The migration itself is done by accessing a factory on Node 2, which will use the DLS to load the repository service implementation on that node. After that, the service environment controls the state transfer using the mechanisms described in Section 2.2.

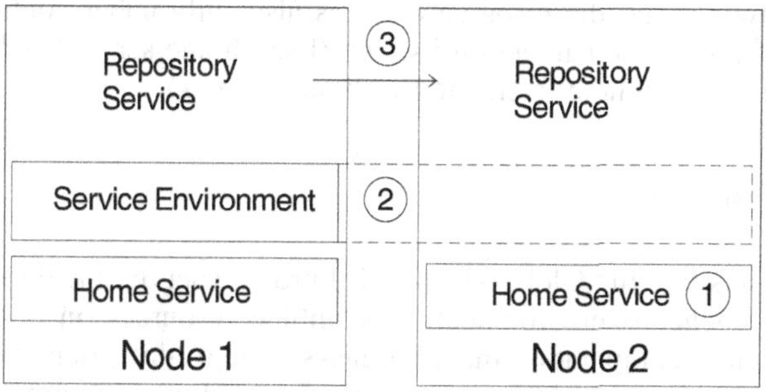

Fig. 4.1. Migration of a Central Repository Service

4.3 Replicated Service

It might be desirable to replicate the repository service for fault-tolerance or performance reasons. The AspectIX middleware provides basic services for passive or active replication strategies. These again relay on the `Checkpointable` interface described above. The EDAS environment is responsible for the management of the replication.

A sufficient number of nodes have to offer resources to the service environment of the repository service. The administrator of a service environment has to decide, which home services are to be considered when locating resources for service fragments. Furthermore, he may express policies for preferred locations and can define a desired degree of replication for a specific service.

Based in this information, the service environment is able to select execution locations for the service automatically. Using the factory and state transfer mechanisms already described before, the necessary number of replicas will be created. In contrast to the migration example in 4.2, the DLS needs to load enhanced fragment code that uses some consistency protocol to ensure replica consistency. Such protocols are provided in the fault tolerance framework of the AspectIX middleware.

The service environment may perform dynamic reconfigurations – like migration or creation of replica – automatically. Such actions are initiated by notifications about shutdown or crash of a node, by overload of nodes, or when the service administrator adjusts the desired number of replicas.

An extension to such basic replication infrastructure is the introduction of a second trust level. In such a scenario, the service environment will always place the core parts of the repository service at fully trusted nodes. In addition, secondary replicas or caches might be created automatically in the system for load balancing reasons.

4.4 Peer-to-Peer-Based Repository

A general peer-to-peer based data store might be used for storing the repository. This implies all the security and confidentiality problems outlined in the introduction. To some extent, these may be overcome with adequate cryptographic mechanisms and massive replication. We are working on a Byzantine fault tolerant replication service that might be used in such situations. From an EDAS point of view, this is a rather simple variant: No state transfer is required as all data is available anywhere in the peer-to-peer network, and the resource usage is also fully under control of the P2P network, so that each node can act on its own (local home service and service environment on each node without interaction with other nodes).

5 Related Work

Grid infrastructures like the Globus-Toolkit [6] provide services and mechanisms for distributed heterogeneous environments to combine resources on demand to solve resource consuming, computation intensive tasks. Due to this orientation, grid infrastructures lack techniques for using resources of partially trustworthy peers and the usage of client-side resources in general. These systems also do not provide support for mobile objects or mobile agents. JavaSymphony [7] and Ibis [8] provide object mobility but are limited to the Java programming language and provide no distributed object model.

The CORBA middleware offers the interaction of objects across heterogeneous environments via generated stubs. The CORBA Life-Cycle Service [4] and the Fault Tolerant CORBA [5] extension provide a basic support for decentralized, adaptive services, but CORBA also lacks a distributed object model which enables the usage of client-side resources.

Previous mobile agent systems like Aglets [9] , Moa [10] or Mole [11] offer state and code migration of objects and special communication mechanisms for agent interaction. To support the implementation of distributed adaptive services, these systems lack a distributed object model and also flexible mechanisms for the utilization of client-side resources provided by partially trusted peers.

Peer-to-peer systems like CAN [12], Chord [13], or Pastry [14] construct an overlay topology and force each peer to collaborate if using the system. This has certain drawbacks if many peers participate only a short period of time or don't behave well.

The proposed concept of distributed, adaptive services offers each peer the possibility to provide resources or not. Moreover the participation of peers is controlled by a service manager. The peer-to-peer infrastructure JXTA [15] partly addresses this necessity through membership protected peer-groups. This offers the possibility to control participation, but also strongly limits the usage because only group members can use the services of a peer-group. Furthermore JXTA lacks any mechanisms for mobile objects.

6 Conclusions

We presented the architecture of EDAS, an environment for decentralized, adaptive services. This environment makes the following contributions. It provides a generic platform that allows using flexible service models ranging from a traditional client-server scenario to a fully peer-to-peer based approach. Based on the fragmented object model, it supports scalable services and mobility of service fragments. The administrative complexity of EDAS-based applications is minimized by its management infrastructure. It allows domain-based joint management of resource offers, supports an inter-domain resource selection taking into account assigned trust levels, and automates reconfigurations in reaction to events like failures, resource shortages, or explicit policy changes.

The EDAS prototype is based on our AspectIX middleware, which has been published under the LGPL licenses. It is available for download, together with further information, at `http://www.aspectix.org`. We plan to make the EDAS system software available as well. A first public release is scheduled for the end of 2004 after internal verification. Further steps will a better notion of trust and to provide mechanisms for trust aware distribution at the middleware level.

References

1. W. T. Sullivan, III, D. Werthimer, S. Bowyer, J. Cobb, D. Gedye, D. Anderson: "A new major SETI project based on Project Serendip data and 100,000 personal computers." In *Proc. of the Fifth Intl. Conf. on Bioastronomy*,1997.
2. H. Reiser, F. J. Hauck, R. Kapitza, A. I. Schmied: "Integrating Fragmented Objects into a CORBA Environment." In *Proceedings of the Net.Object Days*, Erfurt, 2003
3. R. Kapitza, F. J. Hauck: "DLS: a CORBA service for dynamic loading of code." In *Proc. of the OTM Confederated International Conferences*, Sicily, Italy,2003
4. Object Management Group: *Life Cycle Service Specification.* Ver. 1.1, OMG Doc, formal/00-06-18, Framingham, MA, April 2002.
5. Object Management Group: *The Common Object Request Broker Architectur and Specification.* Ver. 2.6, OMG Doc. formal/01-12-35, Framingham, MA, Dec. 2001.
6. I. Foster, C. Kesselman, S. Tuecke: "The Anatomy of the Grid: Enabling Scalable Virtual Organizations." In *International J. Supercomputer Applications*, 15(3), 2001
7. T. Fahringer: "JavaSymphony: A System for Development of Locality-Oriented Distributed and Parallel Java Applications." In *Proceedings of the IEEE International Conference on Cluster Computing CLUSTER 2000*, Chemnitz, Germany, Dec. 2000.
8. R. V. van Nieuwpoort, J. Maassen, R. Hofman, T. Kielmann, H. E. Bal: "Ibis: an efficient Java-based grid programming environment." In *Proceedings of the 2002 joint ACM-ISCOPE conference on Java Grand*, Washington, USA, 2002.

9. D. Lange, M. Oshima: "Programming and Deploying Java? Mobile Agents with Aglets." Addison Wesley, 1999
10. D. Milojicic, W. LaForge, D. Chauhan: "Mobile Objects and Agents (MOA)." In *Proc. of USENIX COOTS '98*, Santa Fe, 1998
11. M. Strasser, J. Baumann, F. Hohl: "Mole - A Java based Mobile Agent System." In: *M. Mühlhäuser: (ed.), Special Issues in Object Oriented Programming*, dpunkt-Verlag 1997
12. S. Ratnasamy, P. Francis, M. Handley, R. Karp, S. Shenker: "A Scalable Content-Addressable Network." In *Proceedings of the ACM SIGCOMM '01 Conference*, San Diego, August 2001
13. I. Stoica, R. Morris, D. Karger, M. F. Kaashoek, H. Balakrishnan: "Chord: A Scalable Peer-to-peer Lookup Service for Internet Applications." In *Proceedings of the ACM SIGCOMM '01 Conference*, San Diego, August 2001
14. A. Rowstron, P. Druschel, "Pastry: Scalable, distributed object location and routing for large-scale peer-to-peer systems." In *IFIP/ACM International Conference on Distributed Systems Platforms (Middleware)*, Heidelberg, Germany, November, 2001.
15. L. Gong. "JXTA: A network programming environment." In *IEEE Internet Computing*, v. 5, 2001

A Specification for Security Services on Computational Grids

Franco Arcieri[1], Fabio Fioravanti[2], Enrico Nardelli[1], and Maurizio Talamo[1]

[1] NESTOR - Laboratorio Sperimentale per la Sicurezza e la Certificazione di Servizi Telematici Multimediali - Univ. of Roma "Tor Vergata", Roma, Italia
[2] Dipartimento di Informatica, Univ. of L'Aquila, L'Aquila, Italia

Abstract. In this paper we present a computational infrastructure, the Security Backbone, which is able to satisfy security requirements arising from resource sharing and services interoperability in Grid-like environments, without having to rely on a Public-Key Infrastructure (PKI). Motivation of our approach is rooted in the well-known difficulties encountered to show that interoperability of PKIs is effective or efficient in real-world environments.
The proposed solution uses a security layer, lying between the communication and the application level, which provides confidentiality, integrity and authentication services in a fully transparent way from the application point of view, thus enabling the deployment of distributed network applications satisfying the highest security constraints, at a very low organizational and financial cost.
Moreover, we have designed a service for scalable and flexible management of authorization policies governing access to resources shared by members of a Virtual Organization, by improving on the Community Authorization Service distributed with the Globus Toolkit[1].

Computational resources sharing between different organizations in an untrusted environment arises several issues related to information security. This is especially true on *computational grids* [26] where members of different organizations join a *Virtual Organization* (VO) for performing collaborative tasks, and users and resources can be dynamically added to or removed from a VO.

In this paper we address the problem of managing certification and security-related operations on grid infrastructures, with a particular focus on specific needs arising from inter-organizational cooperation.

We have studied how to protect interactions between computational entities belonging to different organizations when such interactions take place over unsecure public networks. Typical examples of critical interaction where security is a primary concern are: (i) transactions involving transfer of funds, (ii) transactions where parties commit to action or contracts that may give rise to financial or legal liability, and (iii) transactions involving information protected under privacy regulations, or information with national security sensitivity.

[1] This work has been partially supported by the Grant MIUR L.449/97, CNR Project "P1 - INTERNET networks: efficiency, integration and security", Research Action "Security Services" and by the Grant MIUR PNR 2001-2003, FIRB Project RBNE01KNFP "GRID.IT: Enabling Platforms for High-Performance Computational Grids Oriented to Scalable Virtual Organizations".

M. Jeckle, R. Kowalczyk, and P. Braun (Eds.): GSEM 2004, LNCS 3270, pp. 119–135, 2004.

In order to enable secure interactions between network applications in multi-organizational environments with large and rapidly evolving communities, the following standard requirements have to be met:

Confidentiality: nobody but the intended recipient can read the content of a message travelling over an insecure communication network. **Integrity:** unauthorized alteration of messages must be detected and traced. **Authentication:** subjects (i.e. persons or processes) participating in a communication must be sure about the identity of all involved parties. **Authorization:** resources and services can only be accessed by authorized subjects. **Auditing:** the information flow associated with an interaction must be audited either for certifying correct service provision or for identifying who is responsible for failure. Timestamped audits can also be used for a-posteriori monitoring the performance of service provision. **Single sign-on:** users should be able to authenticate themselves only once, at the beginning of the work session. Notice that this behavior may require a mechanism for delegating credentials to remote processes running on behalf of the user.

In this paper we present an architecture which is able to satisfy security requirements arising from resource sharing and service interoperability in inter-organizational cooperation, without having to rely on the existence of a Public Key Infrastructure (PKI) shared by all involved organizations. Indeed, the adoption of a single PKI by different and autonomous organizations would be the source for many technical and organizational difficulties, like certificate usage and management of certificate validity (see Section 1 for details).

The proposed solution uses an infrastructural layer (called *Security Backbone*) for managing security-related functions. The Security Backbone provides services which are needed for secure service interoperability in a completely transparent way from the application point of view, thus allowing for deployment of network applications which satisfy strict security requirements with very low financial and organizational costs.

Moreover, we propose a scalable and flexible system for the management of authorization policies governing coordinated resource sharing in Virtual Organizations, which allows one to specify authorization rights granted by Virtual Organizations to their members, as well as authorization rights granted by resource owners to Virtual Organizations. The proposed solution does not depend on the existence of a PKI shared by all "real world" organizations for performing the signing of authorization credentials or for verifying the identity of a subject. Instead, the system for authorization management we have devised leverages the security services provided by the Security Backbone, thereby avoiding the PKI-specific problems which are present in the Globus Toolkit [25] version of the Community Authorization Service [36].

The Globus Toolkit (GT), by relying on a general-purpose security API (GSS-API) [29], allows security services to be implemented by using different security protocols (like Kerberos, for example). However, in its current implementation, GT's security services heavily rely on the availability of PKIs and using different security mechanisms still requires huge implementation efforts [30,3]. Moreover, GSSAPI does not remove the need for credential translation when enabling interoperability between subjects using different security technologies.

In Section 1 we survey on PKI features and shortcomings. In Section 2 we present our solution for infrastructural security services provision. In Section 3 we describe the authorization model used by the Security Backbone and we present some example scenarios. Moreover, we give a description of the authorization service as a Web Service by using WSDL [18]. We designed our solution dealing with security issues in grids within a very large (8.1 milion Euro) Italian national research project on High-Performance Computational Grids [1] involving the Italian National Research Council (CNR), the Italian Institute for Nuclear Physics (INFN), the Italian Space Agency (ASI), the Photonic Networks Laboratory (CNIT) and many Italian universities. Our group is responsible for research related to grid security issues.

1 Problems with Current PKI Technology

The PKI-based approach is suitable for use in well-structured and trusted environments like scientific communities, but it has demonstrated to be unable to effectively or efficiently support secure interactions when deployed in an open and dynamic environment like the Internet, both for technical and organizational reasons. For a detailed survey on the shortcomings of current PKI technology we refer the interested reader to [28].

1.1 PKI Technical Problems

The most important technical obstacles to the success of the PKI approach in real-world inter-organizational environments are the following:

(i) there are still several open issues about interoperability between PKIs operated by different organizations, and
(ii) the predominant use of Certificate Revocation Lists (CRLs) for handling the (in)validity of certificates makes the PKI not scalable,
(iii) PKI technology is too hard for end-users [27].

In the real world, when members of different organizations join to form a Virtual Organization, they establish a network of relations enjoying a structure which is much richer than the tree-like schema of *hierarchical* PKI. In this scenario *mesh* PKIs seem to be more appropriate, but their adoption dramatically increases the complexity of certificate *path discovery* (the process of constructing the chain of certificates leading to a subject) and *path validation* (the process of checking the validity of each certificate in the path). It is also natural to assume that if a PKI-based grid is to be deployed in a large, world-wide scale, there can be no single top-level CA. Instead several independently managed PKIs will be created, just like it has happened on the Internet for many other services.

In this more general and realistic setting, interoperability can only be enabled by using cross-certification techniques between independent PKIs. However, achieving cross-certification is very hard because of (i) the organizational obstacles deriving from the fact that two or more organizations are forced to trust each other, (ii) the increased computational effort needed for verifying longer chains of certificates, and (iii) the lack of scalability of this approach which requires each CA to recognize each CA it wants to interoperate with.

We want to remark the problems and the risks associated with the existence of a single PKI by quoting P. Alterman, member of the U.S. Federal PKI Steering Committee and Federal Bridge Certification Authority: "There are strong arguments against fielding a U.S. Federal PKI, especially under a single root".

The most relevant of these problems is that a single nation-wide Certification Authority represents an actual threat to individual privacy, as it will enable the government and security agencies to collect personal information of any kind.

Such a single CA would also violate organizational autonomy, as most organizations are reluctant to participate in a single PKI run by an entity other than themselves.

Moreover, the existence of a single supplier of PKI services would generate disastrous consequences to other suppliers: it is easy to imagine the lobbying activity which will be performed by suppliers for winning such a competition.

Also, the overall deployment and operational cost of this approach would be an obstacle to the wide adoption of security services in inter-organizational cooperation. The cheapest solution will be the most popular, and PKI is not by any means the cheapest solution.

We should not forget that "The purpose of deploying a PKI is to provide a secure electronic government utilizing Internet technology, not only to satisfy the little hearts of a dedicated cadre of techno-nerds and paranoiac security gurus but to serve the citizenry", as Alterman states.

Recently proposed solutions try to mitigate scalability and interoperability issues of PKIs by using *bridge certification authorities* [16,37] and *validation authorities* [38]. Bridge CAs do not issue certificates to users, but they are used for creating *bridges of trust* between PKIs operated by different organizations and for translating between different security policies. Validation authorities are entities which are responsible for performing resource consuming tasks like path construction and path validation on behalf of users, possibly by interacting with PKIs using different technologies. Although use of the above solutions can enable better interoperability of PKIs on a large scale, they are currently supported only by very few applications, thus the benefits which can be obtained in the short term by following this approach are minimal. Moreover, the feasability of the approach based on Bridge CAs is currently being tested by the U.S. Federal Bridge Certification Authority [11], but it is still not clear which would be its performance when deployed to support applications' needs on a large scale.

In a PKI each Certification Authority (CA) manages the validity of certificates it releases by making Certificate Revocation Lists (CRLs) available for download on the network. CRLs are large documents signed by the issuing CA containing a list of certificates released by the CA itself which are not to be considered valid anymore. Unfortunately, CRLs suffer from the following serious problems: (i) they do not provide real-time information about the validity of certificates, (ii) their distribution and checking is expensive, and (iii) they are extremely vulnerable to denial-of-service attacks.

The intrinsic problem with the CRL-based approach is that only negative information is provided: if a certificate is in the CRL then it must not be considered valid, but if it is not listed therein then no warranty is given about its validity as, for example, the list may simply be not recent enough. However maintaining CRLs fresh generates very high loads for servers distributing them, due to the simultaneous requests for CRL update by PKI-enabled clients.

Since there is no real economic advantage for CAs which update their CRLs most frequently (except for having a good reputation, of course), currently deployed attempts to solve this problem try to reduce the size of CRLs by grouping certificates in classes or by publishing only changes with respect to previously issued CRLs. However, in the real-world scenario many high-value transactions rely on the validity of certificates and the need for real-time validity assertions is ever increasing.

The CRL-based approach is also exposed to paradoxical situations like the existence of a CRL containing the certificate which was used to sign the CRL itself. Moreover, non-standard situations like this are not handled uniformly by applications.

A more radical solution to manage certificate validity would be not to use CRLs at all, and adopt a protocol which can provide real-time information about the validity of a certificate, like the Online Certificate Status Protocol (OCSP) [23]. This approach, which is encountering an increasing support by vendors, is anyhow not yet a standard component of certificate validation client software installed in the more common applications. Also, OCSP server may be subject to "denial of service" attacks and must satisfy the same strict security requirements of a Certification Authority.

Another obstacle to the adoption of PKI technology is that it is too complex for use by average end-users [27]. Indeed, for example, there is no procedure which allows the end-user to obtain a PKI certificate in an automated, transparent way, like DHCP does for configuration of networking parameters on workstations.

1.2 PKI Organizational Problems

A pure PKI-based approach also suffers from an important organizational problem which is rarely addressed in the literature but is often the culprit of unsuccessful secure service interoperability: Trust in a CA can be established unilaterally.

Any entity in an organization can indeed decide to trust any CA, independently of the organization security policies and without necessarily asking for authorization (see Figure 1).

This behavior is clearly only acceptable in no-profit scientific communities where reliance on security service is non-critical. Indeed, when we focus on the reality of business cooperation it becomes evident that security services can be established only after some kind of agreement among involved organizations is formally in place, that is, *trust between members of different institutions always requires a bilateral agreement at the organizational level.*

This aspect was a further motivation for our choice of putting security services in a layer fully independent from the application one.

A notable exemplification of this organizational requirement is mobile phone roaming in a foreign country, where access to local resources is granted only if an agreement exists between the local company and the home-base one, and it becomes impossible for the user to by-pass the local infrastructure.

In conclusion, PKI technology, despite of considerable recent developments, is not yet to be considered mature for deployment in large and dynamic environments like the grids. An alternative solution to PKI infrastructures for providing security services on a grid is presented in Section 2.

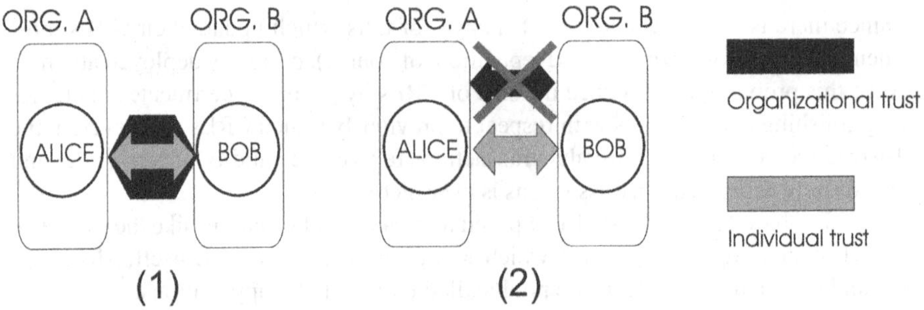

Fig. 1. Organizational and individual trust: (1) the reality of business cooperation, and (2) the approach allowed by PKIs.

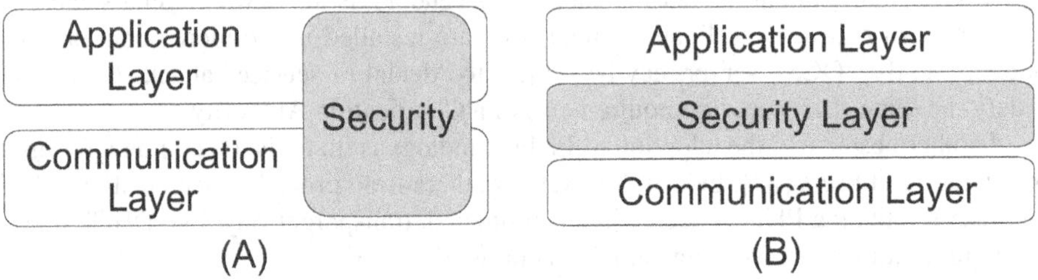

Fig. 2. Provision of security services: the standard approach (A) and the Security Backbone approach (B).

2 The Security Backbone

In this section we present the Security Backbone, an alternative approach for easy and transparent provision of security services at the infrastructure level, independently from locally deployed network technology and topology. In the proposed architecture security services are provided by a layer lying between the application and the communication layers (see Figure 2.B), which is in charge of monitoring network connections directed to or originating from the application level and securing them according to the policies of the Security Backbone.

In our view *security is an infrastructural service of inter-organizational communication, not an add-on service*. Notice how our position is similar to the requirement expressed in the WS-Security roadmap document [19]: "What is needed in a comprehensive Web service security architecture is a mechanism that provides end-to-end security".

Our approach, by making security services readily available to applications in a completely transparent, infrastructural way, allows for separation of issues related to security services and business logic, relieving developers of the burden of managing security-related mechanisms and thereby reducing the risks of introducing security flaws. This is in contrast with the standard approach, where security services are usually provided at different levels in the protocol stack (see Figure 2.A).

Moreover, our approach also solves the organizational problems of PKIs by allowing cooperation between members of different organizations only on top of the Security Backbone layer, which is set up only after a bilateral agreement is formally in place between their organizations. This represents a reasonable trade-off between freedom granted to users by PKI technology and the functionalities needed by business-to-business cooperation.

The Security Backbone also provides auditing services, thus making it possible to certify successful e-services interaction and composition, to identify culprits of bad service provision, as well as monitoring the actual performance of the service as perceived by end-users. There is an increasing interest in techniques which are able to certify correct service execution [31] and this is especially important for composite services, which result from the composition of simpler subservices provided by different organizations [17].

We also want to point out that our solution for security services provision is currently in use within large Italian e-government projects [6,4].

2.1 The Security Backbone Technical Details

The Security Backbone contains the following functional subsystems: (i) confidentiality and integrity services, (ii) authorization service, (iii) authentication service, (iv) documentation subsystem, (v) access policy management, (vi) quality of service monitoring.

We now give some detail on the functions executed by the subsystems and how they have been realized.

Confidentiality and Integrity Services. A mechanism similar to SSL/TLS is used for guaranteeing integrity and confidentiality of exchanged messages: before being transmitted over an insecure communication channel, TCP packets are encrypted by using symmetric cryptography based on session keys which are generated anew for each session and exchanged between communicating parties using asymmetric cryptography.

A part of each subject's private key is distributed by out-of-band methods. Once this part of a subject's private key is arrived at the destination site, the confidentiality and integrity subsystem at the site has to be activated, as described in the paragraph below on the authorization subsystem. After activation, local and remote modules of the confidentiality and integrity subsystem are fully operational.

Authorization Service. This subsystem takes care of the initial set-up of functions in the security layer. On the basis of the part of the private key obtained by out-of-band methods, an exchange of encrypted messages between the local subsystem and a central control server happens, aiming at registering the local subsystem at the central control server. Hardware identifiers of the communicating machines are exchanged during this phase, so that it is possible to uniquely identify physical sites having the right to access the communication network. After successful completion of this registration procedure the site is activated, its private key is complete and bound both to registered end-user(s) and registered machine(s), and the client is authorized to securely exchange messages.

Authentication Service. Guarantee of the identification of message source and destination is implemented by having local and remote modules of the authentication subsystem exchange messages over an encrypted tunnel: TCP packets are encrypted and transmitted as payload of IP packets addressed to the other endpoint of the tunnel. Again, encryption uses symmetric cryptography based on session keys, securely exchanged using private keys. In this way, whenever IP packets arrive at the destination endpoint, only those originating from authenticated sources are accepted, while the other ones get discarded.

Documentation Subsystem. A dedicated subsystem of the Security Backbone records application-level messages exchanged between authorized access points of the communication network, so that documentation can be produced on actually exchanged data. In fact, since service provision is often bound to contractual or legal obligations, it becomes extremely important to certify, when a problem is later found, if and when data were sent and received.

The documentation subsystem is based on an architecture using network probes at network access points for recording exchanged application-level messages. This solution has been extensively described elsewhere [8,9,10]. Here we just want to recall that it works without any change to existing applications, it performs filtering of selected IP packets and reconstructs messages exchanged at the application-level, using highly efficient algorithmic solutions [32], which make the solution scalable and with a very low overhead.

Access Policy Management. It is also possible to define and enforce the desired policy for access management at a central control point. In fact, both authorization and documentation services are fully parameterized, making it possible to implement various access control policies.

For example, users or groups of users can be given different rights (e.g. read-only, write, publish, query) to different resources in a dynamic and flexible way, without requiring any modifications at the application level. After the initial set-up and registration phase of the access point, end-users' access rights can be dynamically established by means of a communication between the local and the central modules of the access policy management subsystem.

Quality of Service Monitoring. Quality of service measuring and monitoring in a business cooperation scenario needs techniques which measure and certify *actual* application level performance of service flows spreading on a network in consequence of a service request. To obtain precise measurements, it is then needed to record the actual behaviour in the network of IP packets corresponding to service flows, while it is not possible to use estimation based approaches, where sophisticate techniques have been proposed for accounting and billing [21,22]. The same reasons prevent the use of flow statistics like those being provided by Cisco NetFlow [40].

To the best of our knowledge no solution for the problem of actual performance measurement of distributed e-services is known in the literature beyond ours: our solution is based on the same technique used to provide documentation services (see paragraph above) and is described in more detail in [7,5].

3 Authorization Management on a Computational Grid with the Security Backbone

The Security Backbone can be easily deployed for creating a computational grid which allows secure utilization of resources shared by members of a Virtual Organization. In this scenario, the configuration of the Security Bacbone is managed by the VO administrator and each non-virtual organization which wants to allow access to the grid to some of its members, or make some of its resources available, will have to join the Security Backbone infrastructure which transparently provides, among other services, mutual authentication, integrity and confidentiality for network communication.

In this section we present a model for authorization management and we show it in action in two different usage scenarios: in the first scenario, the set of authorization rights granted to VO users does not change over time, while in the second authorization rights can be dynamically managed.

3.1 An Authorization Model

In the following we use a simple yet flexible authorization model, inspired by the requirements which led to the development of languages [34,33,24] and models [39,2] for management of authorization rights in distributed network environments.

In the considered authorization model we can identify three main entities: *subjects*, *resources* and *actions*. Entities are specified by a set of *attributes* of the form $\langle n, v \rangle$, where n is the attribute name and v is the attribute value.

A *subject* is an entity which wants to perform an action on a resource. It can be specified by using a name and, optionally, a host or a role. For example, a valid subject may be the attribute $\langle$*"name"*, *"John Smith"*$\rangle$, and $\langle$*"host"*, *"jsmith.employees.mycompany .com"*$\rangle$.

A *resource* is a computational entity which is available for use to members of a VO. A resource is typically specified by using the following information: the name of the resource, the host where it is located, and the application protocol and the network port which must be used for performing actions on the resource. Example of resources are FTP directories, filesystems and web applications.

An *action* is an operation which a subject wants to perform on a resource. Actions can be specific to a particular application protocol and thus, not all actions can be performed on a given resource. The complete set of actions which can potentially be performed on a resource must be explicitly agreed upon by the organizations involved and stated in formal agreement documents. Example of actions are the following: read, write, execute, HTTP GET, HTTP POST.

Authorization *policies* are sets of authorization *rules* which specify if and how subjects can perform actions on resources by using constraints on resource and action attributes (f.e. "read-write access is granted to FTP directories below /pub/incoming on host A"), or time related constraints (f.e. "access is only granted between 9 AM and 7 PM", or "access is granted for a maximum time period of two hours").

In order to ease the definition of authorization policies, authorization rules need not refer to every particular instance of subjects, resources or actions but can refer to classes of subjects. When evaluating an authorization policy, rules can be combined in different ways. We assume that the authorization rights granted by an authorization policy consists of the union of the authorization rights granted by each applicable authorization rule herein contained.

We now illustrate two different usage scenarios: a scenario where authorization rights are statically defined and cannot be changed, and a scenario where authorization rights can be dynamically modified. In both cases, users are authenticated by the Security Backbone at the beginning of the session, by performing the single sign-on procedure described above. Notice that, by following this approach, each organization still retains full control of the hosts operating on the grid, and, as already mentioned, no changes to applications or to intra-organizational architectures are required.

3.2 A Static Authorization Scenario

In a simple scenario, the set of authorization rights owned by users of a VO is statically determined by the configuration of the Security Backbone, and does not change during the lifecycle of a VO unless the Backbone is externally reconfigured by manual intervention.

The authorization rights owned by the user are not limited to those which are explicitly created according to the Backbone configuration. Indeed, a user process running at a remote site can access resources located at other sites if the configuration of the Security Backbone which controls communication between the host where the process is running and the host where the resource is located permits so. The newly requested resource can be a process itself which may require access to further resources, and so on (see Figure 3).

From a mathematical model point of view we can represent this authorization relation as a labeled directed graph where nodes can be labeled by subjects and resources and edeges are labeled by actions. Then, the set of authorization rights owned by each

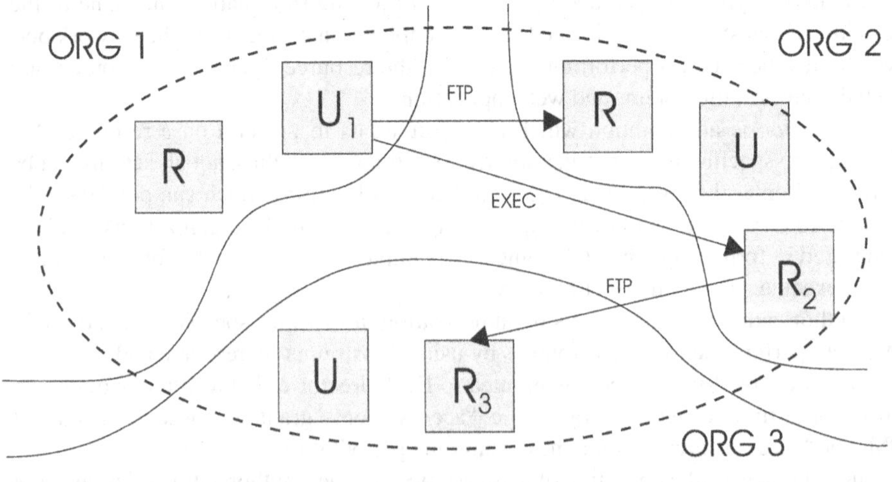

Fig. 3. A Static Authorization Scenario: although there is no direct agreement between Org1 and Org3, U_1 can leverage authorization rights owned by R_2 for accessing R_3.

subject can be thought of as the transitive closure of the peer-to-peer authorization relation constructed by starting with the authorizations for the resources which can be directly accessed by the subject: a subject s can perform an action a on a resource r iff there exists a path from s to r labeled $a_0, \ldots, a_n, a$ where, for all $i = 1, \ldots, n$, if action a_i is performed then action a_{i+1} can also be performed.

In this scenario, differently from what happens on Globus grids, requests for access to resources are not mediated by a user-proxy. This enables enhanced scalability, as there is no single point of failure, while retaining control of authorization policies. Moreover, interactions between hosts can be audited and documented by the Security Backbone in real-time, thus providing a useful tool for detecting possible anomalies and for providing legal evidence in case of judicial dispute.

3.3 A Dynamic Authorization Scenario

In this section we illustrate a scenario where authorization rights can be dynamically managed by interacting with the Security Backbone.

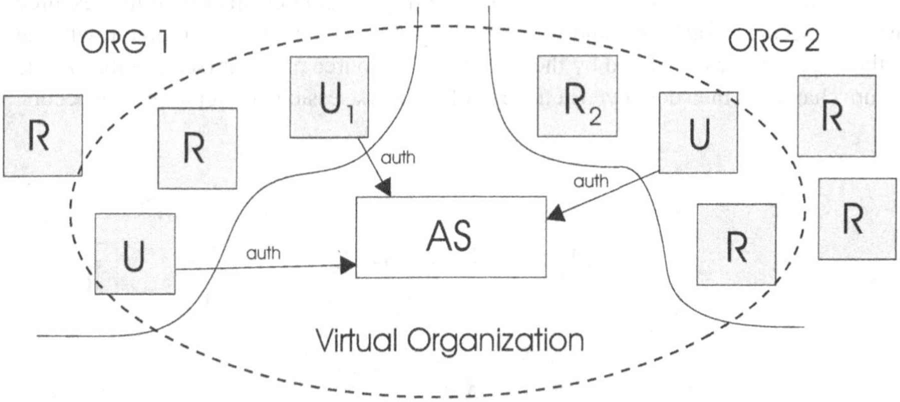

Fig. 4. The configuration of the Security Backbone in the initial state of the Virtual Organization.

In the initial state of the considered scenario, i.e. when a Virtual Organization is created, the only interactions allowed by the Security Backbone are authorization requests from members of the VO to the VO's authorization server, also referred to as the Policy Decision Point (PDP), that is the machine which accepts authorization requests, evaluates authorization policies and replies with authorization decisions (see Figure 4). The VO's administrator is the unique responsible for management of the VO's authorization server.

For issues of reliability, the VO authorization server may be replicated on different machines. In this case, members should be allowed to send authorization requests to all authorization servers used by the VO and standard replication techniques should be used for ensuring overall consistency of the authorization servers.

Notice that the set-up phase of a Virtual Organization, which involves configuring the PDP as well as user and resource sites, cannot be completely automated as it relies on the existence of credentials which must be obtained by out-of-band methods (see Section 2.1). Offline procedures must also be performed when users or resources belonging to new organizations want to join an existing VO. However, apart from the cases mentioned above, by following our approach one can dynamically modify the set of authorization rights granted to users of a VO, as described below.

When a subject (a member, or a process running on a member's behalf) wants to perform an action on a resource, it sends an authorization request containing attributes of the resource, action, and other relevant information to the authorization server. The authorization server, upon receiving the request for authorization, examines it and retrieves policies which are relevant for determining whether and how to satisfy the request.

As a result of the decision process, the authorization server sends back to the requesting subject a response containing the authorization decision (which f.e. can be one of *Permit, Deny, Don't Know, Error*). If the authorization request is accepted the authorization server proceeds in activating a procedure which reconfigures some software components affecting the behavior of the Security Backbone. Only after this reconfiguration process, the subject is allowed to establish a secure channel with the resource over the Security Backbone and to perform operations which are compliant with the authorization policies defined by the VO and the resource provider (see Figure 5). The secure channel is then destroyed at the end of the work session or after a timeout occurs.

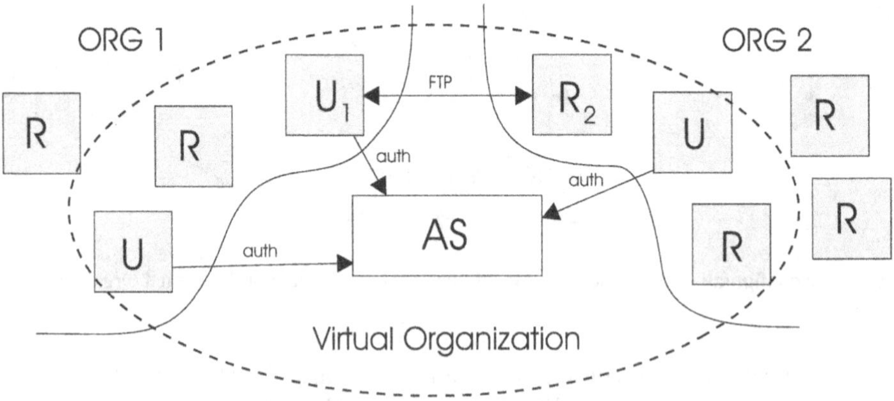

Fig. 5. The configuration of the Security Backbone after creation of a secure FTP channel between member U_1 and resource R_2.

Notice that in our framework it is not needed to include information about the requester's identity as this can be obtained by the Security Backbone itself when the request is evaluated (recall that authorization requests are performed over secure channels). In some cases however, in order to manage requests performed by processes with delegated rights, it might also be useful to specify the identity of the requesting subject.

Our authorization model enjoys the same flexibility of the CAS system [35,36], while allowing non grid-aware applications to securely access and share resources on the grid.

Indeed, management of a VO authorization policies can be performed at the authorization server by extending the model described above to consider management services as resources. Thus, in the initial state of the VO, the VO administrator is granted access to the services for managing the VO itself (adding, removing users and groups) and its authorization policies. On the other hand, each resource owner must only recognize those VO's which will be using its resources and need not be concerned about their dynamics.

Moreover, by following our approach, security services can be provided both to applications which are able to interact with the Security Backbone, as well as to applications which were not developed to manage security related issues. In the former case, for example, applications can perform authorization requests by interacting with the authorization server as a Web Service (see Section 4 for details), while in the latter case authorization requests can be performed by using special purpose client application similar in concept to those distributed with the CAS system.

The architectural solution we propose uses techniques and technologies which are well-known in network security, but is novel as it makes security services available at the infrastructure level, thus enabling secure interoperability between legacy network applications in a non-intrusive and cost-effective manner.

Other systems provide security services at the network level (like IPSec or IPv6) or at the transport level (like TLS [20]) but they require changes at the application level. Thus, they do not represent an effective solution for providing security to existing applications which are expensive, and often impossible, to modify. On the contrary, the Security Backbone, does not require any change to existing applications and can coexist with locally deployed security solutions.

4 Specification of the Authorization Service as a Web Service

In this Section we introduce some basic concepts about web services and we present a simple WSDL document describing the authorization service used for creating a secure channel for accessing a resource by using the FTP protocol.

The problem of enabling interoperability between e-business applications on the World Wide Web is currently being addressed by using XML-based [15] standards like the Web Service Definition Language (WSDL) [18] and the Simple Object Access Protocol (SOAP) [14]. These technologies provide a framework within which it is possible to expose existing network applications in a uniform and abstract manner.

A WSDL document contains the definition of the message exchange pattern between a service requester and a service provider (one-way, request/response, or publish/subscribe), together with the definition of the structure of the messages, the message data types and the bindings to concrete network protocols (HTTP GET/POST, SOAP, MIME) to be used for communication of messages. Messages exchanged by the service requester and provider are typically formatted according to the SOAP protocol. SOAP messages are XML documents consisting of three parts: (*i*) an envelope describing the message content and the rules for processing it, (*ii*) an optional header for extending a message with new features like authentication and transaction management, and (*iii*) a body containing data related to service requests or responses. Although HTTP is used as the main network protocol, SOAP can potentially be used in combination with a variety of other protocols, like FTP, SMTP or RPC.

In a Web Service architecture [13], if a service requester wants to use a web service, it must first obtain the WSDL document containing the service description, either from the service provider itself or from a network-accessible catalog where service providers publish their service descriptions, like UDDI [12]. In order to successfully complete the service invocation, interaction between requester and provider must adhere to the service specifications contained in the WSDL document. As long as the parties involved in service provision adhere to the same service description, the software systems actually providing the Web services can be implemented by using any technical solution, ranging from Java Servlets to legacy applications.

In the case of the FTP protocol, resources can be described by using the name or the address of a host and the path of a file or directory on the host filesystem, while actions are described by a single attribute which can take one of the following values: READ, STOR, WRITE, MKD, DELE.

Below, we present a simple WSDL document describing how interaction takes place between a subject requesting access to a FTP resource and the FTP authorization service.

```
<?xml version="1.0" encoding="UTF-8"?> <wsdl:definitions
targetNamespace="http://DefaultNamespace"
xmlns="http://schemas.xmlsoap.org/wsdl/"
xmlns:apachesoap="http://xml.apache.org/xml-soap"
xmlns:impl="http://DefaultNamespace"
xmlns:intf="http://DefaultNamespace"
xmlns:wsdl="http://schemas.xmlsoap.org/wsdl/"
xmlns:wsdlsoap="http://schemas.xmlsoap.org/wsdl/soap/"
xmlns:xsd="http://www.w3.org/2001/XMLSchema">
 <wsdl:types>
  <schema elementFormDefault="qualified"
  targetNamespace="http://DefaultNamespace"
  xmlns="http://www.w3.org/2001/XMLSchema">
   <element name="createSecureChannel">
    <complexType>
     <sequence>
      <element name="host" nillable="true" type="xsd:string"/>
      <element name="resource" nillable="true"
      type="xsd:string"/>
      <element name="action" nillable="true" type="xsd:string"/>
     </sequence>
    </complexType>
   </element>
   <element name="createSecureChannelResponse">
    <complexType>
     <sequence>
```

```
      <element name="createSecureChannelReturn" nillable="true"
      type="xsd:string"/>
      </sequence>
     </complexType>
    </element>
   </schema>
  </wsdl:types>


   <wsdl:message name="createSecureChannelResponse">
      <wsdl:part element="intf:createSecureChannelResponse"
      name="parameters"/>
   </wsdl:message>
   <wsdl:message name="createSecureChannelRequest">
      <wsdl:part element="intf:createSecureChannel"
      name="parameters"/>
   </wsdl:message>
   <wsdl:portType name="gridBackbone">
      <wsdl:operation name="createSecureChannel">
         <wsdl:input message="intf:createSecureChannelRequest"
         name="createSecureChannelRequest"/>
         <wsdl:output message="intf:createSecureChannelResponse"
         name="createSecureChannelResponse"/>
      </wsdl:operation>
   </wsdl:portType>
   <wsdl:binding name="gridBackboneSoapBinding"
   type="intf:gridBackbone">
      <wsdlsoap:binding style="document"
      transport="http://schemas.xmlsoap.org/soap/http"/>
      <wsdl:operation name="createSecureChannel">
         <wsdlsoap:operation soapAction=""/>
         <wsdl:input name="createSecureChannelRequest">
            <wsdlsoap:body use="literal"/>
         </wsdl:input>
         <wsdl:output name="createSecureChannelResponse">
            <wsdlsoap:body use="literal"/>
         </wsdl:output>
      </wsdl:operation>
   </wsdl:binding>
   <wsdl:service name="gridBackboneService">
     <wsdl:port binding="intf:gridBackboneSoapBinding"
     name="gridBackbone">
     <wsdlsoap:address
     location="http://backbone-auth-server:6080/gridBackbone/
     services/gridBackbone"/>
     </wsdl:port>
   </wsdl:service>
</wsdl:definitions>
```

References

1. Grid.it: Enabling platforms for high-performance computational grids oriented to scalable virtual organizations. http://grid.it:8080/InFlow.
2. Gail-Joon Ahn. Specification and Classification of Role-based Authorization Policies. In *Twelfth International Workshop on Enabling Technologies: Infrastructure for Collaborative Enterprises* June 09 - 11, 2003 Linz, Austria, 2003.
3. Edgardo Ambrosi. Creazione di un sistema plug-in di AA in Globus ed aggregazione dinamica di porzioni di griglie computazionali attraverso CAS: Analisi di fattibilita'. Master's thesis, Advanced Master Thesis in Network Security, Univ. Roma "Tor Vergata" and INFN - Frascati, 2004. submitted for partial fullfilment of the Master Degree.
4. F. Arcieri, F. Fioravanti, E. Nardelli, and M. Talamo. The italian electronic identity card: a short introduction. In *The National Conference on Digital Government Research (dg.o2004), May 24-26, 2004, Seattle, Washington, USA*.
5. F. Arcieri, F. Fioravanti, E. Nardelli, and M. Talamo. Inter-organizational e-services accounting management. In *3rd IFIP conference on e-Commerce, e-Business, and e-Government (I3E-03)* Sao Paolo, Brasil. Kluwer Academic Publishers, September 2003.
6. F. Arcieri, F. Fioravanti, E. Nardelli, and M. Talamo. A layered it infrastructure for secure interoperability in personal data registry digital government services. In *14th Int. Workshop on Research Issues on Data Engineering: Web Services for E-Commerce and E-Government Applications (RIDE'04), March 28-29, 2004, Boston, USA*. IEEE Computer Society, 2004.
7. Fabio Arcieri, Fabio Fioravanti, Enrico Nardelli, and Maurizio Talamo. Certifying performance of cooperative services in a digital government framework. In *3rd International Symposium on Applications and the Internet (SAINT'03)*, pages 249–256, Orlando, Florida, USA, January 2003. IEEE Computer Society Press.
8. Franco Arcieri, Elettra Cappadozzi, Enrico Nardelli, and Maurizio Talamo. SIM: a working example of an e-government service infrastructure for mountain communities. In *Workshop Electronic Government (DEXA-eGov'01), associated to the 2001 Conference on Databases and Expert System Applications (DEXA'01)*, pages 407–411, Munich, Germany, September 2001. IEEE Computer Society Press.
9. Franco Arcieri, Giovanna Melideo, Enrico Nardelli, and Maurizio Talamo. Experiences and issues in the realization of e-government services. In *12th Int. Workshop on Research Issues on Data Engineering: Engineering E-Commerce/E-Business Systems (RIDE'02)*, pages 143–150, San Jose, California, USA, February 2002. IEEE Computer Society Press. An extended version is published in the journal "Distributed and Parallel Databases".
10. Franco Arcieri, Giovanna Melideo, Enrico Nardelli, and Maurizio Talamo. A reference architecture for the certification of e-services in a digital government infrastructure. *Distributed and Parallel Databases*, 12:217–234, 2002. A preliminary version was published in the proceedings of the 12th Int. Workshop on Research Issues on Data Engineering (RIDE'02).
11. U.S. Federal Bridge Certification Authority. http://csrc.nist.gov/pki/fbca/welcome.html.
12. T. Bellwood, L. Clement, D. Ehnebuske, A. Hately, M. Hondo, Y. Husband, K. Januszewski, S. Lee, B. McKee, J. Munter, and C. von Riegen. Universal description, discovery and integration of web services (UDDI) version 3. http://uddi.org/pubs/uddi_v3.htm, 2002.
13. D. Boot, M. Champion, C. Ferris, F. McCabe, E. Newcomer, and D. Orchard. Web services architecture. http://www.w3.org/TR/ws-arch, 2002.
14. D. Box, D. Ehnebuske, G. Kakivaya, A. Layman, N. Mendelsohn, H. Frystyk Nielsen, S. Thatte, and D. Winer. Simple object access protocol (soap) 1.1. http://www.w3.org/TR/SOAP, 2000.
15. T. Bray, J. Paoli, C. M. Sperberg-McQueen, and E. Maler. eXtensible Markup Language (XML) 1.0 (Second Edition). http://www.w3.org/TR/REC-xml, 2000.

16. W. E. Burr. Public key infrastructure (PKI) technical specifications: Part a - technical concepts of operations. US Federal Public Key Infrastructure Tech. working group, September 1998.
17. Fabio Casati, Mehmet Sayal, and Ming-Chien Shan. Developing e-services for composing e-services. In *Proceedings of CAISE 2001, Interlaken, Switzerland, June 2001*, 2001.
18. E. Christensen, F. Curbera, G. Meredith, and S. Weerawarana. Web Services Description Language (WSDL) 1.1. http://www.w3.org/TR/wsdl, 2001.
19. IBM Corporation and Microsoft Corporation. Security in a web services world: A proposed architecture and roadmap. ftp://www6.software.ibm.com/software/developer/library/ws-secmap.pdf, 2002.
20. T. Dierks and C. Allen. The TLS Protocol Version 1.0. RFC 2246, January 1999.
21. N. Duffield, C. Lund, and M. Thorup. Charging from sampled network usage. In *ACM-SIGCOMM Internet Measurement Workshop (IMW'01),* San Francisco, Ca., USA, Nov.01.
22. C. Estan and G. Varghese. New directions in traffic measurement and accounting. In *ACM-SIGCOMM Internet Measurement Workshop (IMW'01),* San Francisco, Ca., USA, Nov.01.
23. M. Myers et al. Online Certificate Status Protocol (OCSP). RFC 2560, June 1999.
24. P. Ashley et al. Enterprise Privacy Authorization Language (EPAL). http://www.zurich.ibm.com/security/enterprise-privacy/epal/.
25. Ian Foster and Carl Kesselman. Globus: A metacomputing infrastructure toolkit. *International Journal of Supercomputer Applications*, 2(11):115–129, 1998.
26. Ian Foster, Carl Kesselman, and Steven Tuecke. The anatomy of the grid: Enabling scalable virtual organization. *International Journal of Supercomputer Applications*, 15(3):200–222, 2001.
27. Peter Gutmann. Plug-and-Play PKI: A PKI your Mother can Use. In *Proceedings of the 12th USENIX Security Symposium*, pages 45–58, 2003.
28. Peter Guttman. PKI: It's Not Dead, Just Resting. *IEEE Computer*, pages 41–49, August 2002.
29. J. Linn. Generic Security Service Application Programming Interface (GSSAPI). RFC 2743, January 2000.
30. Patrick Moore, wilbur Johnson, and Richard Detry. Adapting Globus and Kerberos for a Secure ASCI Grid. In *Proceedings of the 2001 ACM/IEEE conference on Supercomputing* Denver, Colorado, 2001.
31. E. Nardelli and M. Talamo editors. *Proceedings of the First International Workshop on Certification and Security in E-Services (CSES 2002), August 28-29, 2002, Montreal, Canada.* Kluwer Academic.
32. Enrico Nardelli, Maurizio Talamo, and Paola Vocca. Efficient searching for multidimensional data made simple. In Jaroslav Nešetřil, editor, *7th Annual European Symposium on Algorithms (ESA'99)*, pages 339–353, Prague, Czech Republic, July 1999. Lecture Notes in Computer Science vol.1643, Springer-Verlag.
33. OASIS. eXtensible Access Control Markup Language (XACML). http://www.oasis-open.org/committees/xacml/.
34. OASIS. Security Assertion Markup Language (SAML). http://www.oasis-open.org/.
35. L. Pearlman, V. Welch, I. Foster, C. Kesselman, and S. Tuecke. A community authorization service for group collaboration. 2002.
36. L. Pearlman, V. Welch, I. Foster, C. Kesselman, and S. Tuecke. The community authorization service: Status and future. In *CHEP03*, La Jolla, California, March 24-28 2003.
37. William Polk and Nelson Hastings. Bridge certification authorities: Connecting b2b public key infrastructures. US National Institute of Standards and Technology, 2001.
38. William Polk, Nelson Hastings, and Ambarish Malpani. Public key infrastructures that satisfy security goals. *IEEE Internet Computing*, pages 60–67, August 2003.
39. Ravi S. Sandhu, Edward J. Coyne, Hal L. Feinstein, and Charles E. Youman. Role-Based Access Control Models. *IEEE Computer*, 29(2):38–47, 1996.
40. Cisco Systems. Netflow. http://www.cisco.com/warp/public/732/Tech/nmp/netflow/.

Grid Service Management by Using Remote Maintenance Shell

Gordan Jezic[1], Mario Kusek[1], Tomislav Marenic[1], Ignac Lovrek[1],
Sasa Desic[2], Krunoslav Trzec[2], and Bjorn Dellas[2]

[1] University of Zagreb, Faculty of Electrical Engineering and Computing
Department of Telecommunications
Unska 3, HR-10000 Zagreb, Croatia
{gordan.jezic,mario.kusek,tomislav.marenic,ignac.lovrek}@fer.hr
[2] Ericsson Nikola Tesla d.d.
Krapinska 45, Zagreb, Croatia
{sasa.desic,krunoslav.trzec}@ericsson.com

Abstract. This paper presents a method called Remote Maintenance Shell (RMS) developed for Grid service management. It allows service management and maintenance of several versions without suspending its regular operation. The method is based on the remote operations performed by mobile agents. The RMS prototype implemented as a multi-agent system with stationary and mobile multi-operation agents is elaborated. A case study of monitoring service managing in the Grid system is included.

Keywords: mobile agents, service management, Grid, multi-agent systems, monitoring service.

1 Introduction

The problem of service management is complex in the Grid environment where service is shared and distributed across the dynamic, heterogeneous and geographically dispersed networks. Therefore, service installation, starting and testing on a large-scale system with many nodes has become the serious problem. The situation is worsened if the shared service malfunctions. Then, more complex operations, e.g. remote service testing or tracing, possibly on every system, are required.

We propose the approach that uses mobile agents for performance of service management in the Grid system. Mobile agent is a program that can autonomously migrate from node to node during execution. Mobile agents are incorporated in a framework we have developed, called Remote Maintenance Shell (RMS). RMS represents a protected environment and supports service migration, remote installation, starting, stopping, tracing, maintenance of several versions of service, selective or parallel execution of two versions and version replacement [1-3].

This paper describes a RMS prototype organized as a team-oriented multi-agent system (MA-RMS), comprising a master agent and a team of cooperative agents. The team agents are implemented as multi-operation agents that mutually communicate using the standardized FIPA ACL language. Our proposal has been verified in a case study for managing of monitoring service in the Grid. RMS is used to manage Mon-

M. Jeckle, R. Kowalczyk, and P. Braun (Eds.): GSEM 2004, LNCS 3270, pp. 136–150, 2004.

ALISA service [4] for monitoring large distributed systems employed in the test Grid environments in CERN.

The paper is organized as follows. Section 2 deals with the agent-based service management; it identifies general requirements for service management in the Grid and describes the related work in the area. Also, it shows the central idea behind RMS and describes the RMS architecture. The RMS prototype, its basic and advanced features, agent coordination and distribution in the Grid environment are elaborated in Section 3. Case study, in Grid monitoring service is installed, started and replaced by a more recent version, is given in Section 4. The achieved results are summarized and plans for future work are given in Section 5.

2 Agent-Based Grid Service Management

Grid infrastructure is a large-scale distributed system that provides high-end computational and storage capabilities to differentiated users [5]. Open Grid Service Architecture (OGSA) [6] defines a Grid service [7] that comprises a set of interfaces and conventions. The interfaces address service discovery, dynamic creation and manageability. The conventions address service naming and upgradeability. Instead of a static set of persistent services we have to handle the complex activity requests from the clients and dynamic creation of new services.

Grid service integrates distributed resources that include hardware and software components. From software viewpoint, service creation includes the actions for software installation and starting. Service manageability and upgradeability support the actions for service tracing, maintenance of several service versions, selective or parallel execution of two versions and version replacement. One and the same service can be installed in several hosting environments where it will be running. Therefore, different users can use the same service.

We have identified several requirements for service management in Grid:

- a complex Grid service must be upgraded independently,
- Grid service must be managed without disrupting regular operation of the hosting environment and other clients,
- an administrator should not be physically present at the location of the managed hosting environment,
- simultaneous management of multiple hosting environments without handling each individually (easy configuration copying) should be enabled,
- Grid service execution should be controlled (service starting and stopping at will),
- Grid service tracing and testing should be performed in the given hosting environment.

2.1 Remote Maintenance Shell Architecture

Basic RMS concept is shown in Figure 1. RMS comprises a management station and remote systems distributed over a network. The management station is responsible for service delivery to remote systems and for remote operations on them. The service under maintenance must be adapted for RMS. Service Testbed, a service-dependent part that has to be created along with service, provides the design for remote maintenance. When service is ready for delivery, it migrates together with Service Testbed to the remote system [1-3].

The Maintenance Environment is a common RMS part, pre-installed on the target remote system(s) in order to enable management actions. It is service independent. The Maintenance Environment is responsible for communication with the management station. Its main tasks are enabling remote operations and storing data about the installed service.

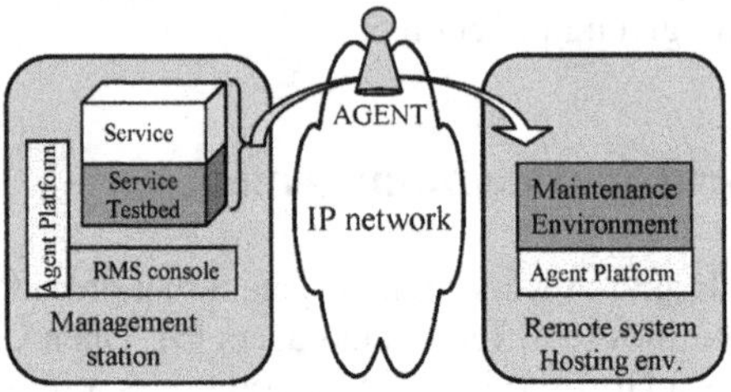

Fig. 1. RMS concept

All of the operations in RMS are executed by mobile agents. The most important characteristic of mobile agents is that they have the ability to autonomously migrate between Grid nodes during execution [8]. Once the Grid administrator defines the operations to be performed on the Grid node(s) they are given to one or several mobile agent, which then migrate to the Grid node(s), cooperate with each other, and perform the operations at the actual target system.

Mobile agents are used because they have some important advantages that make them especially suitable for implementation in the distributed systems. Actually, the use of mobile agents brings the following benefits: completely decentralized operation execution, increased asynchrony, reduced sensibility to the network latency and flexible configuration of the remote testing procedures.

RMS Console is installed on the management station, which serves as a centralized management location. It contains one stationary agent, Management Console agent. RMS Maintenance Environment is the part that must be preinstalled on the remote systems in order for them to be managed by RMS. All service management operations are performed by mobile agents, called multi-operation agents, which migrate from console to the remote system.

Multi-operation Agents. Multi-operation agents are capable of executing multiple operations. Grid administrator inputs the desired end state through the GUI. This end state is passed over to the Management Console agent, which generates necessary operations and assigns them to the cooperative multi-operation agent(s). Each multi-operation agent is assigned one or several operations.

Grid administrator only gives a desired end state of service, without specifying particular operations to be performed. The RMS system automatically determines the operations needed for such transition in service state, as well as the order in which the operations will be executed by the agents performing these operations. Each operation contains the input and output variables. The input variables specify necessary preconditions for the operation execution to begin. The output variables specify the operations that depend on this one, i.e. the operations that have to be notified when this one completes its execution. In this way a net of interdependencies is created between the operations. The operations do not communicate directly, but through their enclosing agents [9].

Besides the input and output variables each operation has a variable defining the Grid node on which it has to be executed. When the input data for that operation are available (i.e. when all preconditions are satisfied), the agent migrates to the node where it must execute the operation and initiates its execution there. When the operation is completed, the system notifies of all the operations defined by the output variables and announces to the agent that the execution is completed. Then the agent checks if there is any other operation ready for execution. If affirmative, the whole process is repeated. If some operation is next in line for execution but its preconditions are not satisfied yet, the agent simply waits for any incoming messages (there is no timeout mechanisms implemented jet). When a message arrives, the agent dispatches it to the appropriate operation and tries to execute it again. In case of multiple unsatisfied preconditions this process may have to be repeated. When all operations are completed, the agent destroys itself.

Maintenance Environment Agents. Maintenance Environment is implemented as an RMS server located on the Grid node (hosting environment, HE). Its main task is to enable service operations on the node. It also handles local database that stores data about the installed service and its status. Remote operations in the Maintenance Environment are provided by stationary agents and two non-agent parts [2,3].

Management Console Agent. RMS Console contains one stationary agent – the Management Console agent. Its responsibility is to act as an intermediary between the GUI (i.e. the user using that GUI) and multi-operation agents that manage the HE.

The RMS user uses RMS GUI to define desired end state of service, without specifying particular operations to be performed, or the sequence of their occurrence. Based on the differences between current and desired service state, Management Console agent generates a set of operations to be executed in order to bring the system to a desired end state. After generating the operations, it distributes them to a set of multi-operation agents, according to the predefined algorithm.

The choice of the algorithm used depends on the number of HEs and the type of operations to be performed. Different distribution strategies can result in significant performance gains. The used algorithm in our prototype assigns all migrate operations to a single agent, while the other operations are assigned according to the HE they relate to – one agent for each HE. The reason for treating migrate operations differently from all the others is the fact that they can cause heavy memory load on the console when transferring large data.

2.2 Related Work

There are several projects and systems that use mobile agents in the Grid environment. *Echelon* is an agent-based Grid infrastructure where a user can state complex problems and computations, allocate all resources needed to solve them and analyze the results [10]. Echelon project defines the agent-based Grid computing architecture in which the agents are used for remote file transfer, superscheduling, distributed visualizations and composition of resources in Grid. *A4* (Agile Architectures for Autonomous Agents) system is a distributed software system based on the idea of federating agents, which can provide services to a large-scale, dynamic multi-agent system [11]. The A4 model comprises a hierarchical model, a discovery model and a coordination model. *ARMS* is an agent-based resource management system for grid computing. Each agent is able to cooperate with others in the provision of service advertisement and discovery for scheduling of applications requiring grid resources [12]. *Agentscape* project provides a multi-agent infrastructure that can be employed to integrate and coordinate distributed resources in a computational Grid environment [13]. None of them uses mobile agents for management in the Grid environment.

Several commercial products for software management in the large distributed environments are available as well. The examples of such products are IBM Tivoli Configuration Manager (part of a larger IBM Tivoli framework) [14], Novadigm Radia [15] and Marimba [16]. None of them uses mobile agents, nor are we aware of any such commercial product that does it. For that reason, we have undertaken a research project to investigate how some generic advantages offered by the mobile agent paradigm can be applied in software management in the large distributed systems. RMS is a prototype implementation developed to validate project results in the real world.

3 Remote Maintenance Shell Prototype

3.1 RMS Features

Basic features of the RMS are service migration, installation, starting, stopping and basic version handling. They include the mechanisms required to bring service to all targeted HEs, configure it properly on each of them, start and stop it. When a new service version is released, it can be installed on the HEs without removal of the old ones. Thus, it is possible to maintain several versions of the same service on each of the HEs, and control which one of them is currently active, i.e. which one gets started. Service must be correctly adapted to allow concomitant existence of multiple versions.

Advanced features of the RMS are tracing, testing and advanced version handling. The important thing about tracing and testing is that they are done on the actual target system. It is of great importance to verify that some service product will function correctly on the target system before it is actually put to work. An appropriate verification environment is often a serious problem, because it is expensive to maintain the test systems capable of defining the required operating environment for all possible target systems.

Experience is a motivation for introduction of these features; it is possible that the same service run on a target node gives the results different from those obtained on the test system. The reasons are mostly in the structural and/or functional differences between both systems. Therefore, actual hosting environment should be verified when new service is being introduced, as well as when introducing new versions of the existing service [17].

The advanced version handling mechanisms aim to provide the support in gradual introduction of new versions, so that the HE can remain operational during testing phase. Besides normal execution mode, where only one version is active, RMS also provides parallel and selective execution modes. In a parallel mode, both versions are executed with the same inputs. The old version is designated as the main version. The output messages from it are sent to the environment, but the outputs from both versions are collected and compared. This enables verification of the correct functioning of the new version. Figure 2 demonstrates service execution in a parallel mode.

The selective mode allows simultaneous execution of two versions with predefined distribution of the incoming requests, as shown in Figure 2. Each input request is sent to only one version that sends the resulting output message back to the environment.

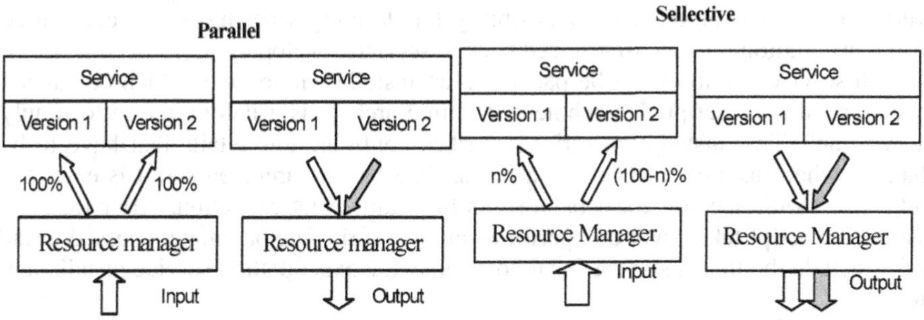

Fig. 2. Parallel and selective execution

These two modes combined allow gradual introduction of new service versions without stronger influence on regular operations. In a typical version replacement scenario [3], a new version is run in the parallel mode with the old one first, so as to verify its correct functioning. Then the versions are switched to the selective mode, in which the execution probability for the new service must be kept low in order to monitor its behavior in real environment. Once the expected results are obtained, the execution probability can be gradually increased, until the complete load is finally turned to the new service.

To use it with the RMS basic features, service itself does not require modifications. Instead, the service developers have to create service testbed, an adaptation layer between RMS and service. The advanced features, however, require service modifications along with writing of the testbed. It should be pointed out that we have developed several demo applications that use the advanced features. One of them is described in [18].

3.2 Prototype Description

Registration of Multiple HEs. RMS Console has to register at the HEs before managing service in it. In order to register, an RMS user has to enter the exact address of the HE. This is time-consuming when a large number of systems have to be contacted, especially if this has to be done each time the console is turned on. Therefore, RMS Console GUI offers the possibility of saving the list of all HEs at which it is currently registered to a configuration file. This file can later be easily loaded, which causes automatic registration in all HEs specified in it. Since this file contains only a plain text, it is possible to manually (or by some other program) edit the list of HEs to be managed.

Configuration Copying. RMS Console GUI offers a dialog in which an RMS user can define a desired end-state (e.g. running or stopped) of the service at the specified location. Bringing service to a desired state does not require specifying the exact list of necessary operations.

Flexible Installation Procedures. One of the main problems that had to be solved in the RMS is providing flexible support to installations. Every service has different configuration requirements, i.e. every service has to be configured differently during installation. It is unfeasible to design a system that knows how to configure literally every service. Therefore, the responsibility for defining what has to be configured during installation must be transferred back to service developers.

Each service version must be packed in an installation archive, which contains a special installation script. The whole installation archive is usually referred to simply as "version". This installation script describes configuration details that have to be changed when installing service. During installation, the archived script is extracted and loaded with specific local parameters that initiate its execution. After that, the installation script takes over and performs all the work. The parameters passed to the script include the things such as local host name, the exact path of service installation, etc.

Writing the installation script is a typical responsibility of those who write service testbed. It is envisaged, as well as with the testbed, that the installation script is written by the service developers, although it is not a firm requirement. Since the installation script describes the parameters to be configured during service installation, its content can be easily extracted from the service documentation, which must specify these details for human users. The format chosen for installation scripts is Ant. Apache Ant [20] is a Java-based build tool, designed for the needs of cross-platform application development.

Both parts of RMS are developed in the Java programming language and use Grasshopper as the underlying agent platform with integrated internal and external security mechanisms [19]. The format chosen for installation scripts is Ant. Apache Ant [20] is a Java-based build tool, designed for the needs of cross-platform application development.

3.3 Agent Organization

There are several basic organizational models used in the multi-agent systems. RMS uses a combination of two basic models. A hybrid between the master/slave and agent team models is used in RMS [9]. A Management Console agent can be viewed as the master agent, because it intelligently decomposes a complex problem into a set of elementary tasks and distributes them to multi-operation agents. However, from that point on a Management Console agent does neither have the control over multi-operation agents, nor is an intermediary for the communication between them. When sent into the network, the multi-operation agents behave as a team with a shared plan. They are aware of interdependencies between them, and directly communicate and coordinate on the achievement of a common goal.

In the RMS the agents communicate in order to execute all operations requested from them. FIPA [21] is the main standardization body which defines standards of inter-agent communication. In the FIPA-compliant agent systems the agents communicate by sending messages. Three fundamental aspects of message communication between the agents are message structure, message representation and message transport.

Message structure is written using the Agent Communication Language (ACL). Message content is expressed in the content language, such as KIF or SL. Content expressions can be grounded on an ontology that defines meaning of each message. To send an ACL message it has to be encoded using the message representation appropriate for the transport e.g. XML, string or bit efficient representation. Transport message consists of the encoded ACL message plus envelope. The envelope includes a sender's and a receiver's transport description with the information about how to send the message. The envelope can also contain additional information, such as the encoding representation, data related security and other realization-specific data that must be visible for transport or recipient(s). A transport message can be sent over the network by different protocols, such as CORBA IIOP or HTTP.

Agent communication in RMS is designed according to the FIPA standards. The agents communicate by exchanging the ACL messages. Message content is expressed in the SL content language, backed up by the RMS ontology. ACL message is represented in XML and transported via IIOP protocol. More information on ACL messages and agent communication can be found in [21]. With the use of Protégé [22] and beangenerator the RMS ontology is defined. The created object of the RMS ontologies is coded by JADE's codec [23] into String object, suitable for transmission through ACL message. The reverse process happens on the other side.

3.4 RMS GUI

RMS GUI is logically separated into two windows, *Remote Locations Status* and *Changes Status List* (Figure 3).

Remote Locations Status window lists the HEs available for management and service currently available at these locations. This information is maintained automatically with the use of *UpdateAgent* that delivers new information to all registered nodes whenever service status changes. An Grid administrator gets a detailed information about current service state, a tracing information and a set execution mode. The user can at any time add a new HE or remove all nodes that are monitored. New locations are entered into a separate dialog window and are kept in *protocol://server:port/agencyName* format.

HEs can be saved in a file with the list of the registered remote locations, for later faster connection to these systems. When a user loads the file that contains only location addresses, the HEs send their current service status to *UpdateAgent*'s and current service status of the remote locations are displayed in the *Remote Locations Status* window.

Changes Status List window displays newly assigned tasks that change service status on the remote nodes. An RMS user adds these tasks through *Add/Edit Remote Location Tasks* button and specifies a desired service status. When all desired final service statuses at all HEs are chosen, the RMS user can execute them. The Grid administrator can also interactively track changes at remote locations, since *Changes Status List* window is refreshed with green checkmarks whenever a service parameter reaches the RMS user's defined final status. When all tasks are completed, the Grid administrator gets a confirmation message.

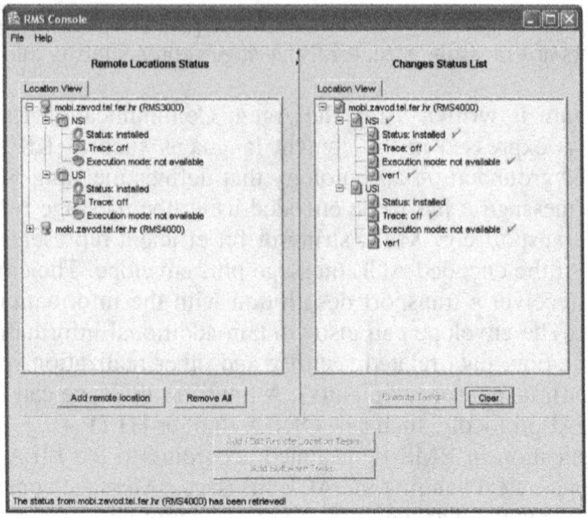

Fig. 3. Graphical User Interface

The Remote Location Tasks dialog enables an Grid administrator to add the ser-voice chosen for installation at a remote location, set its final status (e.g. running), set the execution parameters for each service managed on the HE, and copy service current configuration on any HEs. This feature enables fast and efficient maintenance of all services at all HEs. A user can also get an overview of the selected service's status, including the information as to whether it is traced or not, and the execution mode. Through the *Add Version* button, in the above described way, the user can add a new service version and manageable parameters.

Configuration Copy dialog appears if the Grid administrator wants to copy service configuration at multiple Hes. It enables copying of the selected service configuration on all HEs managed, or copying on some locations by simply choosing the listed ones.

4 Case Study: Monitoring Service Managing

4.1 MonALISA Framework

The MonALISA framework [4] provides a distributed monitoring service system. Each MonALISA server acts as a dynamic service system and provides the functionality to be discovered and used by any other services or clients requiring such information. The goal is to provide the monitoring information from large and distributed systems to a set of loosely coupled "higher level services" in a flexible, self describing way. This is a part of a loosely coupled service architectural model, designed to enable perform effective resource utilization in large, heterogeneous distributed centers. The framework can integrate existing monitoring tools and procedures to collect parameters describing computational nodes, applications and network performance.

MonALISA is currently deployed at many nodes and maintaining and updating such an application at all of them may require a significant effort. For that reason,

MonALISA already contains a mechanism that allows automatic update of the monitoring service. It uses a dedicated thread that periodically checks for the updates on a predefined server. Alternatively, a remote event notification can be used to notify only the selected services to perform an update. When such an event is detected, the running service triggers a restart operation, during which an automatic update is performed.

The provided solution solves the basic problem of service update. However, RMS provides some additional functionality, which allows improvements with more advanced management features:

- Service update is initiated by the Grid administrator, instead of waiting for all installations to check for the updates.
- It is possible to maintain several versions of the same service, instead of overrunning the old version with the new one. This can be especially beneficial if the new version does not function correctly, in which case the old one has to be restored.
- RMS advanced features can help to solve the problem of service malfunction by providing service testing and tracing on the actual target system. It is also possible to gradually replace the old version with the new one, which allows thorough tests in a real environment before the new version is put online.
- Besides solving the installation problem, RMS can also control starting or stopping the service on HEs.

RMS can be used as a unified solution for managing all other service installed on that HE, not just MonALISA.

4.2 Scenario Description

In order to install MonALISA monitoring service at some HE, it is necessary to download the current release from the web, unpack the archive file and configure certain parameters at the target system. Configuration details are specified in the MonALISA installation instructions. When this is done, MonALISA can be started by running a provided script. Even though the described installation routine is not complex, it can be time consuming, especially if it has to be done on a large number of nodes.

A case study presented here attempts to show how RMS can be used to perform Grid service management operations in multiple hosting environments. Even though in most cases the installation of service is simple, it can be time-consuming, especially if it has to be done on a large number of systems. The goal is to install and run MonALISA monitoring service on three HEs, and later replace it with a newer version.

In order to use MonALISA in our case study, a testbed had to be made. Even though we did not participate in developing MonALISA, we were able to make the testbed for MonALISA simply by following the instructions that describe the installation and starting procedures.

The MonALISA testbed employed in this case study supports only basic RMS features, but it can be enhanced to support the advanced features as well. Only one testbed needs to be made for particular service, irrespective of how many versions of that service will be used.

In addition to the testbed, installation archives for both versions had to be created too. The basic idea is the following one: each service version must be packaged in an installation archive, which contains a special installation script. The whole installation archive will usually be referred to simply as "version". That installation script describes the configuration details that have to be changed when installing the service. When an agent executes the installation it extracts the script from the archive, loads it with local specific parameters and initiates its execution. After that the installation script takes over and does all the work. The parameters passed to the script include the things such as local host name, the exact path that service will be installed to etc. The format chosen for installation scripts is Apache Ant [20].

Writing the installation script is typically the responsibility of the same people who write the service testbed. As with the testbed, it is envisaged to be done by the service developers, but it is not necessary. Since the installation script describes the parameters to be configured when installing the service, its content can be easily extracted from the service documentation, which obviously must specify these details for human users.

It should be noted that the installation scripts for the two versions used in this case study are somewhat different. This is so because the configuration requirements have changed between the versions. All the knowledge required to write these scripts comes from the MonALISA documentation describing the "manual" installation procedure.

In addition to specifying configuration details, Ant scripts can be used for other purposes as well. In the case study, we tested a solution that enables migration of large service. Commonly, the agent loads the whole installation archive into the memory and takes it to the HE. However, in case of a really large service, this can cause heavy memory load and lead to the system instability. That is why an alternative approach has been developed, in which the agents transfer only the Ant script. During installation, the script downloads the actual service from a HTTP server to the HE. Both of these approaches are depicted on Figure 4.

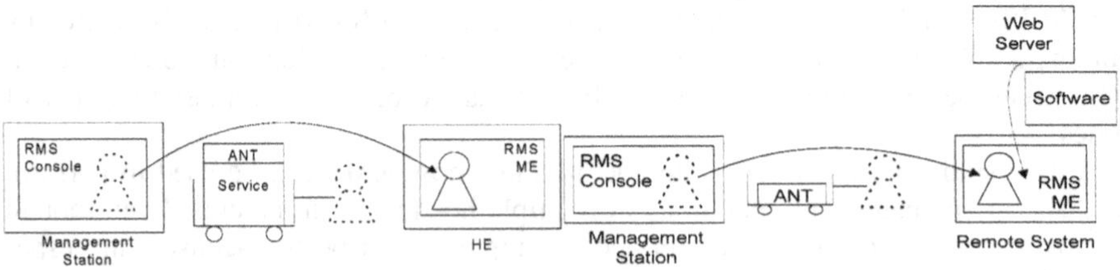

Fig. 4. Alternative service migration scenarios

Imagine a Grid environment with three simple hosting environments, referred to as HE1, HE2 and HE3. All of them should contain the same user application. In the first part of the scenario, Grid administrator wants to run service in the HEs still lacking service. It is supposed that RMS Maintenance Environment is started on all three HEs. At the beginning of the scenario, the RMS user starts the console and registers at all three HEs.

At the beginning of the scenario, RMS Maintenance Environment was started on all three HEs, none containing MonALISA. Grid administrator started the RMS console and registered at all three HEs. To achieve a desired end state, a Management

Console agent generates necessary operations and establishes interdependencies between them. The operations are the following ones: service and testbed migration, installation, setting of the execution parameters and starting.

The service containing testbed has to be picked up and set for start on one of the HEs. After that, the configuration can be easily copied on all other systems. Each operation has two variables, one for the input conditions and other for the output notification. Input variables define the conditions to be fulfilled so that the operation begins execution. After completion, the operation has to notify operations that await it to finish whether they were successful or not. The variables have two values: report for successful completion of the operation, and abort for unsuccessful operation. Once the operation sends the abort variable as its output, that variable propagates through the entire operations communication tree. Thus, all remaining operations fail and the users must be notifieded accordingly.

Figure 5 shows a dependency graph for one HE. The first operation is testbed migration (migrate TB). It is followed by testbed installation (install TB) and version (service) migration (migrate version), which depends on testbed migration. Version installation (install version) depends on version migration, while the operation for setting execution parameters depends on both installation of testbed and installation of version. The last operation is running service (run service) which is executed after setting the execution parameters.

When the RMS user initiates task execution, four cooperative agents are created as a team: Agent1, Agent2, Agent3 and Agent4. The operations are distributed in the following way: a separate agent (Agent1) migrates service to all three hosting environments (HE1, HE2, and HE3), i.e. does the following operations on each of them: testbed migration and version migration. Agent2 migrates to HE1 and when service has migrated to this location (Agent1 notifies it) it performs the following operations: testbed installation, version installation, setting of the execution parameters and starting of service. Similarly, Agent3 migrates to HE2 and performs the same tasks there, while Agent4 migrates to HE3 and performs the equivalent tasks there. Version installation included unpacking of the installation archive and execution of the provided Ant script.

In this part of the scenario, the service was transferred over the network in the usual way – the agent loaded the whole installation archive into the memory. Since MonALISA version 0.9 is about 5 MB in size, there were no significant problems during service migration.

Second part of the scenario deals with service upgrading with a newer version. A Grid administrator wants to terminate the existing user application and to install and run a new version of service in this hosting environment. The following operations must be executed: migrate and install the new version, stop the old one, set the new version to be the active one and start the new version (Figure 5). Initiation of task execution creates four agents. Agent1 carries the installation archive to HE1, HE2 and HE3 (testbed is already migrated). After migration Agent2 performs the following tasks at HE1: new version installation, stopping of service, setting of the execution parameters i.e. setting of the new version to become the active one, and starting of service (now the new version is active). Agent3 and Agent4 carry out the same tasks at HE2 and HE3 respectively.

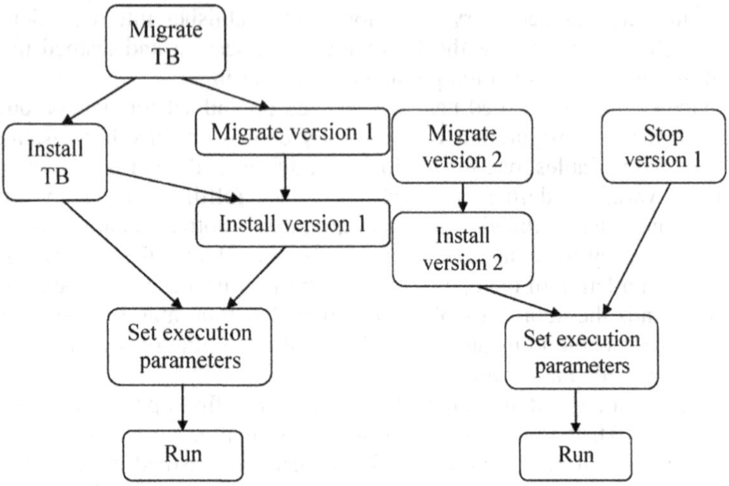

Fig. 5. Scenario graph for service starting and upgrading

This concept, in which the service is downloaded directly from the web, is particularly powerful when it comes to updating multiple HEs running MonALISA as soon as the new version gets released. The important fact to notice is that the service gets downloaded directly from the actual MonALISA home page. That implies that the downloaded archive file is in no way modified for RMS. It is the same publicly available archive file that can be downloaded and manually installed; only RMS does it automatically. So when a new version of some service gets published on the web, the only thing that has to be done is to write a relatively simple Ant script and pack it into an RMS installation archive. Service can then be transferred to the HEs in the same way it would have been done manually, without providing any special distribution channels.

This case study has been implemented in managing MonALISA [4] service from CERN, a distributed monitoring service system used in the real Grid environment.

5 Conclusion

RMS is a framework based on mobile agents, designed to support service management in the large distributed environments. The basics of RMS architecture are presented and the prototype is elaborated. The emphasis is on the prototype that is implemented in the Grid environment and in a case study that describes usage of RMS for service upgrading in several hosting environments. In the given example, RMS has been verified to manage real service for monitoring in Grid.

The case study clearly shows that RMS and mobile agent-based systems can be successfully used in large-scale systems, and that RMS aids significantly in managing service on multiple HEs in Grid. The case study employed basic RMS features, sufficient to solve the commonest real-life problems.

Further research will include a case study in which real world application is adapted to use the advanced RMS features (remote testing and tracing). Future work on RMS will include introduction of the additional management features, such as centralized trace collection from the multiple systems, security mechanisms and system robustness. We are also planning to enable dynamic configuration of the algorithm used for operation distribution on the management station, which would allow testing of different distribution strategies, depending on the environmental specificities.

Acknowledgments

RMS is a result of the joint efforts of the people from Department of Telecommunications and Ericsson Nikola Tesla R&D Center [24]. Special thanks go to Iosif Legrand, Federico Carminati and Predrag Buncic from CERN, for their suggestions about incorporation of RMS into Grid.

References

1. Lovrek, I., A. Carić, D. Huljenic, Remote Maintenance Shell: Software Operations Using Mobile Agents, Proc. of the International Conference on Telecommunications 2002, Yuan'an L.; Yunde, S. (ed.). Peking, China: Publishing House of Electronic Industry, 175-179, 2002.
2. Kusek, M., G. Jezic, I. Ljubi, K. Mlinaric, I. Lovrek, S. Desic, O. Labor, A. Caric, D. Huljenic, "Mobile Agent Based Software Operation and Maintenance", Proceedings of the 7th International Conference on Telecommunications ConTEL 2003, pp. 601-608, Zagreb, 2003.
3. Lovrek, I., G. Jezic, M. Kusek, I. Ljubi, A. Caric, D. Huljenic, S. Desic, O. Labor, "Improving Software Maintenance by Using Agent-based Remote Maintenance Shell", IEEE International Conference on Software Maintenance, ICSM03, IEEE Computer Society Press, Amsterdam, The Netherlands, 2003, pp.440-449.
4. http://monalisa.cacr.caltech.edu/
5. Cao, J., Kerbyson, D.J., Nudd, G.R. Performance evaluation of an agent-based resource management infrastructure for grid computing, Proc. of the First IEEE/ACM International Symposium on Cluster Computing and the Grid, Australia, 2001, pp. 311-318.
6. Foster, I, Keselman, C., Nick, J., Tuecke, S., Grid Services for Distributed System Integration. Computer, 35(6), 2002.
7. Foster, I, Keselman, C., Nick, J., Tuecke, S., The physiology of the grid: An open grid services architecture for distributed systems integration, Technical report, Open Grid Service Infrastructure WG, Global Grid Forum, 2002, http://www. globus.org.
8. Cockayne, W. R., Zyda, M., Mobile Agents, Prentice Hall, 1997.
9. Jezic, G., Kusek, M., Desic, S., Caric, A., Huljenic, D., Multi-Agent System for Remote Software Operation, Lecture Notes in Computer Science, Lecture Notes in Artificial Intelligence, LNAI 2774, Springer-Verlag, 2003, 675-682.
10. http://www.geocities.com/echelongrid/
11. http://www.dcs.warwick.ac.uk/research/hpsg/html/htdocs/public/a4.html
12. Cao, J., Jarvis, S.A, Saini, S., Kerbyson, D.J, ARMS: An agent-based resource management infrastructure for grid computing, 2002. http://www.dcs.warwick.ac.uk/~saj/papers/arms.pdf.
13. Wijngaards, N.J.E., Overeinder, B.J., van Steen, M., Brazier, F.M.T., Supporting Internet-Scale Multi-agent Systems, Data Knowledge Engineering, 41 (2-3), 2002, pp. 229 – 245.
14. http://www.ibm.com/software/tivoli/products/config-mgr/
15. http://www.novadigm.com
16. http://www.marimba.com

17. Mikac, B., I. Lovrek, V. Sinković, Ž. Car, I. Podnar, H. Pehar, A. Carić, A. Burilović, H. Naglić, I. Sinovčić, T. Visković-Huljenić, "Assessing the Process of Telecommunications Software Maintenance", Proceedings of the combined 10th European Software Control and Metrics conference and 2nd SCOPE conference on Software Product Evaluation, pp. 267-275, Herstmonceux, 1999.
18. M. Zivic, L. Rac, A. Medar, M. Kusek, and G. Jezic, Designing of a Distributed Web Application in the Remote Maintenance Shell Environment, accepted for publication at MELECON 2004 (http://www.melecon2004.org/)
19. http://www.grasshopper.de
20. http://ant.apache.org
21. http://www.fipa.org
22. http://protege.stanford.edu/
23. http://sharon.cselt.it/projects/jade/
24. http://agents.tel.fer.hr/rope/index.en.shtml

The Grid-Occam Project

Peter Tröger, Martin von Löwis, and Andreas Polze

Hasso-Plattner-Institute at University of Potsdam
Prof.-Dr.-Helmert-Str. 2-3
14482 Potsdam, Germany
{peter.troeger,martin.vonloewis,andreas.polze}@hpi.uni-potsdam.de

Abstract. We present a new implementation of the old Occam language, using Microsoft .NET as the target platform. We show how Occam can be used to develop cluster and grid applications, and how such applications can be deployed. In particular, we discuss automatic placement of Occam processes onto processing nodes.

1 Introduction

The Occam programming language [17] was developed by INMOS, based on Hoare's idea of CSP [18]. Occam was originally designed for use on transputer systems [14], and the only Occam compiler that was in wide use would generate code only for the INMOS transputers (T222, T414, T800 etc.). Transputers are high-performance microprocessors that support parallel processing through on-chip hardware [28]. According to Michel J. Flynn's taxonomy [6] a transputer system can be declared as a multiple instruction multiple data stream (MIMD) system, more precisely as distributed memory system. Each transputer has four high-speed hardware links, allowing the creation of transputer networks. Communication between unconnected transputers would require routing of messages through intermediate transputers.

While Occam was primarily used on the transputers, its principles extend beyond special-purpose hardware, and Occam programs can be written without a specific interconnection network in mind. In principle, it is possible to execute Occam programs on a single processor, on a multiple-processor system using shared memory, or on a cluster of processor connected through some special-purpose or off-the-shelf interconnection network.

One of our primary aims in the project is the introduction of Occam to current distributed computing environments. We see Occam as a language to describe parallel and distributed algorithms, and we like to support execution of such algorithms in computing clusters and grids. In this context parallel algorithms can either directly be expressed in Occam or consist of a mix of Occam and a traditional sequential language. In that sense, Occam becomes a coordination language for distributed parallel algorithms.

The paper is structured the following way: Section 2 gives an overview of the Occam language in general, while section 3 explains details of the historical INMOS Occam compiler. Section 4 introduces our Grid-Occam concept in detail.

M. Jeckle, R. Kowalczyk, and P. Braun (Eds.): GSEM 2004, LNCS 3270, pp. 151–164, 2004.

After that section 5 discusses concrete implementation details, and section 6 concludes the paper.

2 Occam Overview

The Occam language is based on the idea of communicating sequential processes. Each process has access to a set of (private) variables, and is defined as a sequence of primitive actions, namely

- assignment to variables (variable := value),
- output of a value through a channel (channel ! value),
- input from a channel (channel ? variable),
- SKIP, which does nothing, and
- STOP, which never terminates[1].

The communication through a channel uses the rendezvous style: an output operation will block until an input operation becomes available, and an input operation will block until the corresponding output becomes available. Then, the data is exchanged (i.e. the value of one process is stored into the variable of the other process), and communication succeeds. These primitive actions can be combined through complex processes using three combinators. This is an inductive definition of processes, where complex process can again be combined.

2.1 Sequential Combination of Processes

The keyword *SEQ* identifies a sequential process. The result of the entire process is obtained by executing one of the component processes after another; the entire sequential process terminates when the last subordinate process terminates. The sequence of component processes is indicated with an indentation of two spaces. As a very simple example, the following example shows a process that receives a value from one channel, performs a computation, and outputs a new value to another channel.

```
SEQ
  input ? variable
  variable := variable + 1
  output ! variable
```

2.2 Parallel Combination of Processes

The keyword *PAR* indicates parallel combination of processes. Like *SEQ*, the component processes are denoted by two spaces of indentation. The parallel

[1] This is the formal definition of STOP. STOP indicates that a process is in error, and the typical implementation is that the process stops working, i.e. it ceases to act. Formally, this is the same thing as continuing to do nothing eternally.

statements simultaneously starts execution of all component processes. The entire statement is complete when the last component completes. A very simple example shows the interaction of the sequential process from the previous example in parallel with a process that interacts with the user:

```
PAR
  SEQ
    keyboard ? var1
    to.computer ! var1
    from.computer ? var1
    display ! var1
  SEQ
     to.computer ? var2
     var2 := var2 + 1
     from.computer ! var2
```

The first of the two parallel processes is a sequential one. It interacts with the user, through which it is connected with the channels keyboard and display. This process reads some input from the user, and sends it to the other process. That process performs the computation, and sends the result back to the first process, which then forwards the result to the display.

2.3 Alternative Combination of Processes

If a process has communication channels to many other processes, it needs to select which channel to receive data from. This is done with the *ALT* combinator, which consists of a set of guard inputs and associated processes. The channels are all watched simultaneously. Once a channel is ready, the input is performed, and the associated process is executed. The following process simultaneously guards a channel from the user and from another process, executing, forwarding the data to the other communication partner:

```
ALT
  keyboard ? var1
    to.computer ! var1
  from.computer ? var1
    display ! var1
```

Since the *ALT* statement eventually executes only a single process, it is typically nested within a loop which repeatedly executes the *ALT* statement.

2.4 Repeated Combinators

Each combinator can be defined in a repetitive way. This is often combined with arrays, so that multiple processes operate on array data in parallel. In addition, the parallel processes have their individual channels, which is possible through the notion of channel arrays. The declarations

```
VALUE num.of.fields IS 1024:
[num.of.fields]REAL64 a,b:
[num.of.fields]CHAN OF REAL64 channel:
```

introduce arrays a and b of *REAL64* values, and a single array of channels communicating *REAL64* values. These structures can be used in the following way:

```
INT todo:
REAL64 total, value:
PAR
  SEQ
    todo := num.of.fields
    total  := 0.0
    WHILE todo > 0
      ALT I := 1 FOR num.of.fields
        channel[I] ? value
        total := total + value
        todo := todo - 1
    display ! total
  PAR k := 1 FOR num.of.fields
     channel[k] ! a[k] + b[k]
```

In this process, 1025 parallel processes are created. 1024 of them add two numbers and send the result to a channel. The remaining process receives one result after another and sums them up, eventually sending the total to the display.

2.5 Further Concepts

Occam provides a lot of concepts not presented in this language overview. There are conditional and case statements, loops (used in the previous example), constructed data types, protocols, timers, and many more concepts.

3 INMOS Occam

In the last section we showed that the Occam programming model includes a concept of parallel processes that communicate through unidirectional channels. One of Occam's major advantages with this concept is the abstraction of the parallel execution from the underlying hardware and software environment.

The original INMOS compiler supports the code generation for networks of heterogeneous transputer processors. Therefore the Occam process must be specifically placed on the correct hardware processor. Another problem is the interconnection of processors. A transputer processor can, but need not be connected to its 4 neighbors by the hardware links, which themselves can carry multiple Occam channels. Beside the 4-link star layout, it is possible to have other interconnection schemes for hardware channels, for example a tree or a pipeline scheme. In such cases, the compiler must be able to map the given set of named Occam processes on the right processors for a successful execution of the program. This leads to the need for custom message forwarding, performed by special *routing kernel* code.

The classical Occam solved the problem of process placement by special configuration statements *PLACED PAR* and *PROCESSOR*. Later on, INMOS specified a separate *configuration language*. It supports the design of portable, hardware-independent parallel Occam code. The first part of the configuration (*NETWORK*) describes the interconnection of all available transputer processors. This includes also the specific type of hardware in terms of processor type and memory size. Each defined processor is labeled with a custom name. The second configuration part (*CONFIG*) describes the placement of named Occam processes on virtual processors, identified by the name given in the first part. The usage of a configuration language puts the developer in charge of the process placement. This is uncritical in the context of transputer systems, since the hardware architecture is static and well-known. The execution of such Occam code on another transputer system requires an adaption of the network configuration and a recompilation.

An example for the provisioning of infrastructure-independent Occam environments originates from the Esprit P2701 PUMA project at University of Southampton. They developed a virtual channel router (VCR) software for unrestricted channel communication across a network of transputers [4]. The software is able to map static virtual channels at runtime on communication resources, using a custom kernel on the particular transputer node. The topology of the network is described by an automatically generated network configuration file, after that the VCR generates a set of deadlock-free routes for messages in the system. The resulting message routing is realized during runtime, based on the precomputed informations.

The following section shows that we extend VCR idea of infrastructure-independent Occam execution to cluster and grid environments.

4 The Grid-Occam Approach

The last section showed that the original Occam compiler supports heterogeneity aspects through usage of a static configuration description. It is easy to see that such an approach is not appropriate in heterogeneous cluster or grid environments. Additionally the programmer wants to concentrate on the aspects of parallelization for his algorithm, not on specific mapping issues for a particular execution environment.

A good example of infrastructure-independent programming is the popular MPI [7] library. It enables the programmer to use message passing facilities for parallel program instances, while avoiding dependencies on the concrete hardware infrastructure, e.g. number of processors, interconnections, or the communication technology. Another advantage is an easier development process. A programmer can test its software on a local computer without claiming expensive resources like cluster time, simply by using a one-node enabled, local version of the MPI library.

In the current approach of our Grid-Occam project, we want to achieve a similar infrastructure independence within the concept of a .NET [20] Occam runtime system. As a first step, we divide process-independent parts of the implementation from the application-specific code. The process-independent functionality is similar across all Occam programs and covers mainly the distribution aspects. We call the result a *Occam runtime library* that is being responsible for all distribution-related issues within the execution of the program. In an ideal situation, a programmer can adopt her already existing Occam program by simply exchanging this runtime library without any need for reconfiguration or recompilation.

In an implementation every Occam runtime has to solve several critical issues:

- What is the given infrastructure in terms of virtual processors and their interconnection?
- What is the best possible placement strategy for Occam processes?
- What is the precise instantiation mechanism for a *PAR* block on a virtual processor?
- How could global Occam variables be implemented?
- What is a channel instance on this particular infrastructure?
- How is such a channel being allocated and how does the addressing of an other specific process instance work?
- What are the implementation strategies for rendezvous behavior of a channel?
- Which kind of networking optimization, for example with channel arrays, can be done for the given infrastructure?

As it can be seen, in classical Occam most of these questions were solved by manual work in the configuration file. In contrast, we have to work on best-effort placement algorithms for Occam processes on the one side and on automated detection of infrastructure information on the other side.

4.1 Grid Computing

Grid Computing is defined as the coordinated, transparent and secure usage of shared IT resources, crossing geographical and organizational boundaries [9]. It splits up into the research areas of computational grids, data grids and resource grids [11]. The development of research and commercial usage of grid technologies has increased heavily in the last years. The community established the Global Grid Forum (GGF) as standardization group. Major industrial companies like IBM, Sun or Oracle invest in the development of standardized interfaces to their cluster software. Research groups from all kinds of nature sciences are using collaborative grid resources for the computing-intensive applications.

The actual development shows that there is a large range of possible grid technology users. Most of them are not professional computer scientists, therefore the design and usability of grid interfaces becomes an important factor. Actually most users have the choice between basic command-line or library functions and high-level job submission web interfaces, so-called Grid portals. There are several approaches to make the overall usage more easier, even in the GGF standardization process [13]. In this context we see Occam as a useful solution in the context of scientific computing-intensive grid applications. Occam supports parallelism as first-level language construct, which allows a very natural kind of programming for distributed computation. Due to the nature of .NET it is possible to combine old legacy source code (e.g. written in Fortran) with a new Occam program for the execution.

4.2 Process Placement

In our concept we define a set of possible classes for runtime libraries. They mainly differ in their unit of distribution. We assume in the first step that possible granularity levels could be *threads*, *processes*, *cluster nodes* and *grid nodes*. The granularity can be defined by the ratio of communication and execution costs. In every level of granularity, we have a different meaning for the concept of a virtual processor - a single thread, a single process, a single cluster node or a single grid node. The respective interconnection mechanisms for the different distribution could be shared memory, communication pipes, cluster networking techniques like TCP and Myrinet, and grid networking techniques, for example TCP over multiple hops or ATM.

The LogP Model. For a classification of the described granularity levels we make use of Culler's LogP model [3]. It defines a model of a distributed-memory multiprocessor system using 4 parameters:

- Latency: upper bound for the network data transfer time. This parameter increases linearly for the levels of threads, processes and cluster nodes. Latency for grid environments is substantially higher in most cases.
- Overhead: exclusive time needed by a processor for sending or receiving a data packet. This parameter is usually optimized through hardware and should be small enough in all cases to be ignored.
- Gap: minimal interval between two send or received messages. The gap is fixed for a given type of networking infrastructure and mainly influenced by the node communication hardware. The usage of shared memory and local communication pipes for threads and processes leads to a very small gap. The gap for cluster architectures is typically smaller than for grid environments, reasoned by the usage of specialized networking hardware. Grid infrastructures tend to rely on standard TCP/IP communication mechanisms.
- Processors: number of processors in the system. In the case of threads and processes, the number of virtual processors is limited by the number of physical processors in a SMP system. A cluster system could consists of a large number of machines, up to multiple hundreds. We assume that in most practical cases the number of cluster nodes in a cluster is roughly equal or even higher than the number of grid nodes potentially available to a programmer.

As a concretion of the model we consider the fact that most usual SMP systems work on the scheduling granularity of threads. Since both thread and the process granularity levels are designed for single machines, we leave out the level of processes in our further observations.

Task Graphs. After classifying the possible execution environments we have to think about a mapping of communicating Occam processes to a resource network of a chosen granularity level. We want to represent the Occam program as a data-flow or task graph, which is a common approach in parallel computing programming [25]. Nodes in the graph represent a set of sequential processes, edges the data dependencies between them during parallel execution. A data dependency naturally leads to a communication channel between parallel processes in Occam.

We plan to acquire a best possible structural information during the compilation process. It could be possible that the design of a Occam program prevents a complete static analysis, for example in presence of variable-sized channel arrays. However, for the first implementations we simply ignore such information in our architectural graph.

Mapping a task-graph to a given network of processors is a well-known problem in research. There are several approaches to solve this NP-complete problem heuristically. However, the usual communication model in these scheduling algorithms concentrates only on the latency aspect of the processor connection. Other research uses heuristic approaches for mapping task graphs to LogP-described networks of processors. The MSA LogP scheduling algorithm [1] even considers the bundling of messages.

We can conclude that the existing approaches give us the relevant mechanisms to map a task-graph to a graph representation of the infrastructure. Most algorithms rely on 4 parameters: The set of tasks, their interconnection scheme, the execution cost for a particular task (node weight) and on the amount of data transmitted over an interconnection (edge weight).

The overall set of tasks and their interconnection scheme can be determined by the compiler. A single task (graph node) can be seen as a set of sequential atomic Occam instructions after reading a channel value up to the end of the surrounding SEQ block. The node weight could be simply determined by counting the number of atomic operations following the read operation. In fact several issues (like repeated instructions) must be considered in this case, although it should be possible to get a useful estimation. Another major factor is the edge weight, representing the number of fixed-sized messages transmitted through a particular channel. The compiler can analyze the write operation(s) to the typed channel and the amount of data transmitted through this particular instance. Again it could be possible that we have to consider non-static conditions, like conditional or repeated code blocks. We will investigate whether the compiler can simply leave out such information or if there is need for a restriction of the language [21] to achieve valuable results.

Another important characteristic of the Grid-Occam approach is the nested nature of the different granularity levels. An Occam process for a particular type of virtual processor, for example a cluster node, can itself be executed on a network of higher granularity virtual processors, for example with multiple threads. We combine this model of nested granularities with the representation of Occam programs as unidirectional graph, simply by repartitioning a subset of tasks for a higher granularity level. Due to the nature of the different execution levels, the ratio of computation time to communication effort should become higher with decreasing granularity. It must also be considered that we have a fixed number of virtual processors for the thread level. There is no possibility, like in the grid case, to request more processors for a successful execution. This leads to a need for algorithms that are able to perform a partitioning for a fixed set of processors. This could also be relevant if the number of available cluster processors is not large enough for a particular task sub-graph. Beside classical graph partitioning algorithms [5] there are approaches for cluster computing environments that can consider this restriction.

5 Implementation Strategy

The following section will concentrate on specific techniques for the implementation of our Grid-Occam vision. We will explain our choice for the .NET framework and give details about the implementation strategies for the different runtime libraries.

5.1 The .NET Framework

The implementation of our Occam compiler will generate intermediate language (IL) byte code, executable within the .NET framework. Microsoft has published the .NET framework [20] in 2000. An explicit design goal was the support for multiple languages. Major parts of the runtime specification were submitted to standardization organizations like ECMA and ISO. This allows other software vendors to re-implement .NET for other systems. The Microsoft .NET framework product (in its current version 1.1) is only available on Win32/X86 and Windows CE systems. Additionally Microsoft Research has published the Rotor package for non-commercial purposes, which ports .NET to MacOS X and FreeBSD/X86 [30]. The GNU Mono project [34] allows execution of .NET applications on Linux systems, using various processors: x86, PowerPC, Sparc, IBM S/390, and Intel StrongARM. The upcoming next version of .NET (Whidbey) will have support for 64bit Itanium/Opteron systems.

In the context of Grid-Occam, we see .NET as a useful runtime environment that offers execution on differing platforms and the integration of multiple language libraries. On example could be the integration of legacy FORTRAN code by using the commercial Lahey compiler for .NET [22]. .NET offers, in contrast to other virtual machine implementations, an integrated code-access security concept, which becomes relevant in the context of remote execution on cluster grid nodes. Performance investigations for the .NET runtime [32] showed that .NET can give an sufficient result for high-performance computing. The .NET framework offers an integrated support of current web service technologies, which eases the use of OGSI-based grid infrastructures [19]. There also support classes for the dynamic creation and compilation of new IL code, which becomes important in the context of code generation for a cluster node.

It would have been possible to use a different target platform for the execution of Occam code. Indeed, the historical INMOS implementation targeted at transputer byte code. Today implementations for processor architectures such as Intel X86 and IBM PowerPC are available. Instead of targeting one particular architecture we need to consider the heterogeneous nature of distributed computing environments. Java would have been another obvious choice. However, we hope that .NET allows better integration with existing algorithms and library code.

5.2 Program Execution

The figure 1 gives a general overview of the execution environment in the grid context.

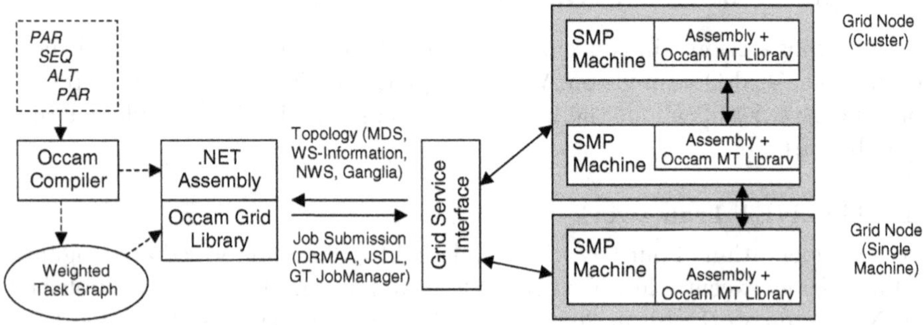

Fig. 1. Overview of the Grid-Occam architecture

In a first step, the Occam compiler generates executable IL code, packaged in an *assembly file*. All instructions relevant to parallel execution, like channel operations or instantiation of *PAR* blocks, are implemented as calls to the Occam runtime library. The compiler will generate C# code in the first version, which can be easily compiled to IL in a post-build step. The compiler also produces a task graph for the different *PAR* blocks and their regarding channels, augmented with an estimation of the node weights (computational load) and edge weights (channel load). This data is used by the respective runtime library to choose a job placement, based on the detected topology of virtual processors. After that the library initiates all planned job submission actions to execute the program. We assume that dynamic changes in the execution environment (e.g. unavailable nodes) are handled by the cluster or grid mechanisms.

5.3 Runtime Libraries

As defined earlier we see 3 possible kinds of runtime libraries, namely for threads, cluster nodes and grid nodes. In figure 1 the resulting .NET executable uses the

Occam grid runtime library. It would also be possible to exchange it with the multi-threaded or the cluster version of the library, which enables the user to test his development on the local computer before submission to a larger resource network.

Multi-threading Runtime Library. The multi-threaded runtime library allows the execution on a single- or multi-processor machine. The number of available physical processors on the machine must be considered in the runtime library. For .NET this information is available through the *System.Diagnostics* namespace.

The realization could be improved with the upcoming new version of the .NET framework (Whidbey). It will be possible to use the popular OpenMP library [2] in .NET, which allows an even more direct mapping of the Occam semantic to .NET code.

The channel communication for parallel processes will be realized by an interlocked shared memory segment. The rendezvous behavior can be achieved by the coordinated usage of multiple semaphore variables, which are available in the .NET environment.

Cluster Runtime Library. The cluster runtime library is intented for usage in a pure cluster environment, without using grid interfaces for the job submission. The cluster runtime needs some kind of topology information to perform a best-effort placement of jobs. The minimal requirements are an identifier for the own node and the list of nodes involved, if we assume that the cluster forms a complete graph. The communication mechanisms, for example an available MPI installation, should be able to address a particular node.

We plan to implement a first prototype based on the Condor [23] system, which offers all the relevant information and coordination services with Condor DAGMan [31]. Therefore it is possible to coordinate the instantiation of parallel jobs on the Condor cluster. Every instance in the cluster has to get informed about its own identification number, usually with a command-line argument. This can be specified in the Condor submit file, which has a notion of the *process id*. The list of involved nodes can be distributed on a shared file system or through the automated file transfer mechanisms. Since all Condor machines get the same executable it must be ensured that a node instance only execute a particular part of the Occam code. The decision for a code part is based on the own identity in the task graph of the Occam program. The assembly itself could also use the multi-threaded runtime library to perform a more fine-granularly execution. This could be the case if one Condor node executes a SEQ block with multiple PAR blocks. Condor offers information services to determine the hardware characteristics of a node. This enables the cluster runtime to choose whether it is appropriate to perform a more granular parallel execution on one node.

Grid Resource Broker. Our Grid-Occam architecture has two possible scenarios for the usage of grid resources.

In the first case the grid acts only as source for computing resources. We use the resource information and job submission services of a grid to utilize a particular cluster resource for execution. Popular examples for information services are the Globus Meta Directory Service (MDS) [8] or the upcoming WS-Information services in WSRF [10] architectures.

The identification of an appropriate resource is followed by a job submission to the chosen grid resource. Globus offers the job manager functionalities for this, but there are also concurrent implementations from other projects [24]. We plan to consider ongoing standardization efforts from the GGF for this problem. There are promising developments in the DRMAA [27] and the JSDL [29] working group for a standardized job submission interface. With the availability of actual implementations we will support such interfaces in addition to existing Globus mechanisms.

Another interesting issue is the availability of input and output files for a job. In the cluster case we can expect a common file system like NFS, or even a transport mechanisms from the cluster software. Similar to the INMOS *hostio* library it should be possible to read and write files in jobs send to a grid node. Most grid environments allow a specification of files to be transfered before and after job execution, in this case standardized mechanisms like GridFTP [8] are used.

Grid Execution Environment. The ongoing development in Grid Computing focuses more and more on an improved support for widely distributed grid applications, called "managed shared virtual system" [26]. In this context we see Grid-Occam as a useful approach for the development of widely-distributed applications. From the investigation in the section 4.2 we know that inter-node communication for grids can have unpredictable and slow behavior. Therefore it must be ensured that the placement algorithm considers this fact carefully. Monitoring services like NWS [33] offering their information through grid interfaces, which allows the collection of all relevant data for the task of process placement.

The implementation of channels is another interesting issue for grid execution. Globus 2 introduced the MPICH-G2 library [8] for cross-node communication facilities, the latest development is Globus XIO [12]. In a service oriented grid it could be possible to implement a channel service, both reader and writer perform there operation against an instance of this service. The service implementation is responsible for rendezvous behavior of the channel, for example through notification [15] of the client. More sophisticated approaches [16] use the tuple-space approach for the implementation of a rendezvous communication model. This could also be realized with an OGSI conforming service as front-end.

6 Conclusion

In this paper we presented our vision of an Occam implementation, capable of being used in modern cluster and grid environments. The availability of distribution as first-level language concept can ease the usage of complicated cluster and grid infrastructures, which is one of the active topics in grid computing research. Occam has a long history in distributed programming and is widely accepted in its suitability for such environments.

We plan to automate the process placement, as far as possible, through infrastructure information services available in modern cluster and grid environments. We will rely on latest developments in this area, including the standardization efforts in the GGF.

We are actually developing an Occam compiler for .NET / Rotor in the context of a lecture. The first version will include prototypes for all presented types of runtime environment and will act as foundation for our further research.

Acknowledgments

This work is partially sponsored by Microsoft Research Cambridge (grant number 2004-425).

References

1. Cristina Boeres and Vinod E. F. Rebello. A versatile cost modeling approach for multicomputer task scheduling. *Parallel Computing*, 25(1):63–86, 1999.
2. Rohit Chandra, Ramesh Menon, Leo Dagum, David Kohr, Dror Maydan, and Jeff McDonald. *Parallel Programming in OpenMP*. Morgan Kaufmann, October 2000.
3. David E. Culler, Richard M. Karp, David A. Patterson, Abhijit Sahay, Klaus E. Schauser, Eunice Santos, Ramesh Subramonian, and Thorsten von Eicken. Logp: Towards a realistic model of parallel computation. In *Principles Practice of Parallel Programming*, pages 1–12, 1993.
4. M. Debbage, M.B. Hill, and D.A. Nicole. Towards a distributed implementation of occam. In *Proceedings of the 13th Occam Users Group*. IOS Press, 1990.
5. Per-Olof Fjällström. Algorithms for graph partitioning: A survey. *Linköping Electronic Articles in Computer and Information Science*, 3(10), 1998.
6. M.J. Flynn. Some computer organizations and their effectiveness. *IEEE Transactions on Computers*, 21:948–960, 1972.
7. MPI Forum. MPI-2: Extensions to the Message-Passing Interface. Technical report, University of Tennessee, Knoxville, Tennessee, July 1997.
8. I. Foster and C. Kesselman. Globus: A Metacomputing Infrastructure Toolkit. *The International Journal of Supercomputer Applications and High Performance Computing*, 11(2):115–128, Summer 1997.
9. Ian Foster. The anatomy of the Grid: Enabling scalable virtual organizations. *Lecture Notes in Computer Science*, 2150, 2001.
10. Ian Foster, Jeffrey Frey, Steve Graham, Steve Tuecke, Karl Czajkowski, Don Ferguson, Frank Leymann, Martin Nally, Igor Sedukhin, David Snelling, Tony Storey, William Vambenepe, and Sanjiva Weerawarana. Modeling stateful resources with web services. *IBM DeveloperWorks Whitepaper*, March 2004.
11. Ian Foster and Carl Kesselman. *The Grid: Blueprint for a New Computing Infrastructure*. Morgan Kaufmann Publishers, Inc., 1999.
12. The Globus Alliance. *Globus XIO*, 2004.

13. Tom Goodale, Keith Jackson, and Stephen Pickles. Simple API for Grid Applications (SAGA) Working Group. http://forge.ggf.org/projects/gapi-wg/.
14. Ian Graham and Tim King. *The Transputer Handbook.* Prentice Hall, January 1991.
15. Steve Graham, Peter Niblett, Dave Chappell, Amy Lewis, Nataraj Nagaratnam, Jay Parikh, Sanjay Patil, Shivajee Samdarshi, Igor Sedukhin, David Snelling, Steve Tuecke, William Vambenepe, and Bill Weihl. Publish-subscribe notification for web services. *IBM DeveloperWorks Whitepaper*, March 2004.
16. K.A. Hawick, H.A. James, and L.H. Pritchard. Tuple-space based middleware for distributed computing. Technical Report 128, Distributed and High-Performance Computing Group, University of Adelaide, Adelaide, Australia, October 2002.
17. C.A.R. Hoare. *Occam 2 Reference Manual: Inmos Limited.* Prentice-Hall, 1988.
18. C.A.R. Hoare. *Communicating Sequential Processes.* C.A.R. Hoare, 2004.
19. Marty Humphrey. From Legion to Legion-G to OGSI.NET: Object-Based Computing for Grids. In *Proceedings of the 17th International Parallel and Distributed Processing Symposium (IPDPS 2003).* IEEE Computer Society, April 2003.
20. Jeffrey Richter. *Applied Microsoft .NET Framework Programming.* Microsoft Press, 2002.
21. U. Kastens, F. Meyer auf der Heide, A. Wachsmann, and F. Wichmann. Occamlight: A language combining shared memory and message passing (a first report). In *Proc. 3rd PASA Workshop, PARS Mitteilungen*, pages 50–55, 1993.
22. Lahey Computer Systems Inc. LF Fortran Manual. http://www.lahey.com/.
23. M.J. Litzkow, M. Livny, and M.W. Mutka. Condor - A Hunter of Idle Workstations. In *Proceedings of the Eighth International Conference on Distributed Computing Systems*, pages 104–111, 1988.
24. Stephen McGough. A Common Job Description Markup Language written in XML. http://www.lesc.doc.ic.ac.uk/projects/jdml.pdf.
25. H.E. Motteler. Occam and dataflow. Technical report, UMBC Technical Report, September 1989.
26. Jarek Nabrzyski, Jennifer M. Schopf, and Jab Weglarz. *Grid Resource Management.* Kluwer Academic Publishers, 2004.
27. Hrabri Rajic, Roger Brobst, Waiman Chan, Fritz Ferstl, Jeff Gardiner, Andreas Haas, Bill Nitzberg, and John Tollefsrud. Distributed Resource Management Application API Specification 1.0. http://forge.ggf.org/projects/drmaa-wg/, 2004.
28. Ram Meenakshisundaram. Transputer Information Home Page. http://www.classiccmp.org/transputer/.
29. Andreas Savva, Ali Anjomshoaa, Fred Brisard, R Lee Cook, Donal K. Fellows, An Ly, Stephen McGough, and Darren Pulsipher. Job Submission Description Language (JSDL) Specification Version 0.2. http://forge.ggf.org/projects/jsdl-wg/, 2004.
30. David Stutz, Ted Neward, Geoff Shilling, Ted Neward, David Stutz, and Geoff Shilling. *Shared Source CLI Essentials.* O'Reilly, December 2002.
31. Condor Team. *Condor Manual.* University of Wisconsin-Madison, 2004.
32. Werner Vogels. HPC.NET - are CLI-based Virtual Machines Suitable for High Performance Computing? In *SC'03*, Phoenix, Arizona, USA, November 2003.
33. Rich Wolski, Neil T. Spring, and Jim Hayes. The network weather service: a distributed resource performance forecasting service for metacomputing. *Future Generation Computer Systems*, 15(5–6):757–768, 1999.
34. Ximian Inc. Mono Framework. http://www.go-mono.org, 2004.

Author Index

Lecture Notes in Computer Science

For information about Vols. 1–3156

please contact your bookseller or Springer

Vol. 3274: R. Guerraoui (Ed.), Distributed Computing. XIII, 465 pages. 2004.

Vol. 3273: T. Baar, A. Strohmeier, A. Moreira, S.J. Mellor (Eds.), <<UML>> 2004 - The Unified Modelling Language. XIII, 449 pages. 2004.

Vol. 3271: J. Vicente, D. Hutchison (Eds.), Management of Multimedia Networks and Services. XIII, 335 pages. 2004.

Vol. 3270: M. Jeckle, R. Kowalczyk, P. Braun (Eds.), Grid Services Engineering and Management. X, 165 pages. 2004.

Vol. 3266: J. Solé-Pareta, M. Smirnov, P.V. Mieghem, J. Domingo-Pascual, E. Monteiro, P. Reichl, B. Stiller, R.J. Gibbens (Eds.), Quality of Service in the Emerging Networking Panorama. XVI, 390 pages. 2004.

Vol. 3263: M. Weske, P. Liggesmeyer (Eds.), Object-Oriented and Internet-Based Technologies. XII, 239 pages. 2004.

Vol. 3260: I. Niemegeers, S.H. de Groot (Eds.), Personal Wireless Communications. XIV, 478 pages. 2004.

Vol. 3258: M. Wallace (Ed.), Principles and Practice of Constraint Programming – CP 2004. XVII, 822 pages. 2004.

Vol. 3256: H. Ehrig, G. Engels, F. Parisi-Presicce (Eds.), Graph Transformations. XII, 451 pages. 2004.

Vol. 3255: A. Benczúr, J. Demetrovics, G. Gottlob (Eds.), Advances in Databases and Information Systems. XI, 423 pages. 2004.

Vol. 3254: E. Macii, V. Paliouras, O. Koufopavlou (Eds.), Integrated Circuit and System Design. XVI, 910 pages. 2004.

Vol. 3253: Y. Lakhnech, S. Yovine (Eds.), Formal Techniques, Modelling and Analysis of Timed and Fault-Tolerant Systems. X, 397 pages. 2004.

Vol. 3250: L.-J. (LJ) Zhang, M. Jeckle (Eds.), Web Services. X, 300 pages. 2004.

Vol. 3249: B. Buchberger, J.A. Campbell (Eds.), Artificial Intelligence and Symbolic Computation. X, 285 pages. 2004. (Subseries LNAI).

Vol. 3246: A. Apostolico, M. Melucci (Eds.), String Processing and Information Retrieval. XIV, 332 pages. 2004.

Vol. 3245: E. Suzuki, S. Arikawa (Eds.), Discovery Science. XIV, 430 pages. 2004. (Subseries LNAI).

Vol. 3244: S. Ben-David, J. Case, A. Maruoka (Eds.), Algorithmic Learning Theory. XIV, 505 pages. 2004. (Subseries LNAI).

Vol. 3242: X. Yao, E. Burke, J.A. Lozano, J. Smith, J.J. Merelo-Guervós, J.A. Bullinaria, J. Rowe, P. Tiňo, A. Kabán, H.-P. Schwefel (Eds.), Parallel Problem Solving from Nature - PPSN VIII. XX, 1185 pages. 2004.

Vol. 3241: D. Kranzlmüller, P. Kacsuk, J.J. Dongarra (Eds.), Recent Advances in Parallel Virtual Machine and Message Passing Interface. XIII, 452 pages. 2004.

Vol. 3240: I. Jonassen, J. Kim (Eds.), Algorithms in Bioinformatics. IX, 476 pages. 2004. (Subseries LNBI).

Vol. 3239: G. Nicosia, V. Cutello, P.J. Bentley, J. Timmis (Eds.), Artificial Immune Systems. XII, 444 pages. 2004.

Vol. 3238: S. Biundo, T. Frühwirth, G. Palm (Eds.), KI 2004: Advances in Artificial Intelligence. XI, 467 pages. 2004. (Subseries LNAI).

Vol. 3232: R. Heery, L. Lyon (Eds.), Research and Advanced Technology for Digital Libraries. XV, 528 pages. 2004.

Vol. 3229: J.J. Alferes, J. Leite (Eds.), Logics in Artificial Intelligence. XIV, 744 pages. 2004. (Subseries LNAI).

Vol. 3225: K. Zhang, Y. Zheng (Eds.), Information Security. XII, 442 pages. 2004.

Vol. 3224: E. Jonsson, A. Valdes, M. Almgren (Eds.), Recent Advances in Intrusion Detection. XII, 315 pages. 2004.

Vol. 3223: K. Slind, A. Bunker, G. Gopalakrishnan (Eds.), Theorem Proving in Higher Order Logics. VIII, 337 pages. 2004.

Vol. 3221: S. Albers, T. Radzik (Eds.), Algorithms – ESA 2004. XVIII, 836 pages. 2004.

Vol. 3220: J.C. Lester, R.M. Vicari, F. Paraguaçu (Eds.), Intelligent Tutoring Systems. XXI, 920 pages. 2004.

Vol. 3219: M. Heisel, P. Liggesmeyer, S. Wittmann (Eds.), Computer Safety, Reliability, and Security. XI, 339 pages. 2004.

Vol. 3217: C. Barillot, D.R. Haynor, P. Hellier (Eds.), Medical Image Computing and Computer-Assisted Intervention – MICCAI 2004. XXXVIII, 1114 pages. 2004.

Vol. 3216: C. Barillot, D.R. Haynor, P. Hellier (Eds.), Medical Image Computing and Computer-Assisted Intervention – MICCAI 2004. XXXVIII, 930 pages. 2004.

Vol. 3215: M.G. Negoita, R.J. Howlett, L. Jain (Eds.), Knowledge-Based Intelligent Information and Engineering Systems. LVII, 906 pages. 2004. (Subseries LNAI).

Vol. 3214: M.G. Negoita, R.J. Howlett, L. Jain (Eds.), Knowledge-Based Intelligent Information and Engineering Systems. LVIII, 1302 pages. 2004. (Subseries LNAI).

Vol. 3213: M.G. Negoita, R.J. Howlett, L. Jain (Eds.), Knowledge-Based Intelligent Information and Engineering Systems. LVIII, 1280 pages. 2004. (Subseries LNAI).

Vol. 3212: A. Campilho, M. Kamel (Eds.), Image Analysis and Recognition. XXIX, 862 pages. 2004.

Vol. 3211: A. Campilho, M. Kamel (Eds.), Image Analysis and Recognition. XXIX, 880 pages. 2004.

Vol. 3210: J. Marcinkowski, A. Tarlecki (Eds.), Computer Science Logic. XI, 520 pages. 2004.

Vol. 3209: B. Berendt, A. Hotho, D. Mladenic, M. van Someren, M. Spiliopoulou, G. Stumme (Eds.), Web Mining: From Web to Semantic Web. IX, 201 pages. 2004. (Subseries LNAI).

Vol. 3208: H.J. Ohlbach, S. Schaffert (Eds.), Principles and Practice of Semantic Web Reasoning. VII, 165 pages. 2004.

Vol. 3207: L.T. Yang, M. Guo, G.R. Gao, N.K. Jha (Eds.), Embedded and Ubiquitous Computing. XX, 1116 pages. 2004.

Vol. 3206: P. Sojka, I. Kopecek, K. Pala (Eds.), Text, Speech and Dialogue. XIII, 667 pages. 2004. (Subseries LNAI).

Vol. 3205: N. Davies, E. Mynatt, I. Siio (Eds.), UbiComp 2004: Ubiquitous Computing. XVI, 452 pages. 2004.

Vol. 3203: J. Becker, M. Platzner, S. Vernalde (Eds.), Field Programmable Logic and Application. XXX, 1198 pages. 2004.

Vol. 3202: J.-F. Boulicaut, F. Esposito, F. Giannotti, D. Pedreschi (Eds.), Knowledge Discovery in Databases: PKDD 2004. XIX, 560 pages. 2004. (Subseries LNAI).

Vol. 3201: J.-F. Boulicaut, F. Esposito, F. Giannotti, D. Pedreschi (Eds.), Machine Learning: ECML 2004. XVIII, 580 pages. 2004. (Subseries LNAI).

Vol. 3199: H. Schepers (Ed.), Software and Compilers for Embedded Systems. X, 259 pages. 2004.

Vol. 3198: G.-J. de Vreede, L.A. Guerrero, G. Marín Raventós (Eds.), Groupware: Design, Implementation and Use. XI, 378 pages. 2004.

Vol. 3195: C.G. Puntonet, A. Prieto (Eds.), Independent Component Analysis and Blind Signal Separation. XXIII, 1266 pages. 2004.

Vol. 3194: R. Camacho, R. King, A. Srinivasan (Eds.), Inductive Logic Programming. XI, 361 pages. 2004. (Subseries LNAI).

Vol. 3193: P. Samarati, P. Ryan, D. Gollmann, R. Molva (Eds.), Computer Security – ESORICS 2004. X, 457 pages. 2004.

Vol. 3192: C. Bussler, D. Fensel (Eds.), Artificial Intelligence: Methodology, Systems, and Applications. XIII, 522 pages. 2004. (Subseries LNAI).

Vol. 3191: M. Klusch, S. Ossowski, V. Kashyap, R. Unland (Eds.), Cooperative Information Agents VIII. XI, 303 pages. 2004. (Subseries LNAI).

Vol. 3190: Y. Luo (Ed.), Cooperative Design, Visualization, and Engineering. IX, 248 pages. 2004.

Vol. 3189: P.-C. Yew, J. Xue (Eds.), Advances in Computer Systems Architecture. XVII, 598 pages. 2004.

Vol. 3188: F.S. de Boer, M.M. Bonsangue, S. Graf, W.-P. de Roever (Eds.), Formal Methods for Components and Objects. VIII, 373 pages. 2004.

Vol. 3187: G. Lindemann, J. Denzinger, I.J. Timm, R. Unland (Eds.), Multiagent System Technologies. XIII, 341 pages. 2004. (Subseries LNAI).

Vol. 3186: Z. Bellahsène, T. Milo, M. Rys, D. Suciu, R. Unland (Eds.), Database and XML Technologies. X, 235 pages. 2004.

Vol. 3185: M. Bernardo, F. Corradini (Eds.), Formal Methods for the Design of Real-Time Systems. VII, 295 pages. 2004.

Vol. 3184: S. Katsikas, J. Lopez, G. Pernul (Eds.), Trust and Privacy in Digital Business. XI, 299 pages. 2004.

Vol. 3183: R. Traunmüller (Ed.), Electronic Government. XIX, 583 pages. 2004.

Vol. 3182: K. Bauknecht, M. Bichler, B. Pröll (Eds.), E-Commerce and Web Technologies. XI, 370 pages. 2004.

Vol. 3181: Y. Kambayashi, M. Mohania, W. Wöß (Eds.), Data Warehousing and Knowledge Discovery. XIV, 412 pages. 2004.

Vol. 3180: F. Galindo, M. Takizawa, R. Traunmüller (Eds.), Database and Expert Systems Applications. XXI, 972 pages. 2004.

Vol. 3179: F.J. Perales, B.A. Draper (Eds.), Articulated Motion and Deformable Objects. XI, 270 pages. 2004.

Vol. 3178: W. Jonker, M. Petkovic (Eds.), Secure Data Management. VIII, 219 pages. 2004.

Vol. 3177: Z.R. Yang, H. Yin, R. Everson (Eds.), Intelligent Data Engineering and Automated Learning – IDEAL 2004. XVIII, 852 pages. 2004.

Vol. 3176: O. Bousquet, U. von Luxburg, G. Rätsch (Eds.), Advanced Lectures on Machine Learning. IX, 241 pages. 2004. (Subseries LNAI).

Vol. 3175: C.E. Rasmussen, H.H. Bülthoff, B. Schölkopf, M.A. Giese (Eds.), Pattern Recognition. XVIII, 581 pages. 2004.

Vol. 3174: F. Yin, J. Wang, C. Guo (Eds.), Advances in Neural Networks - ISNN 2004. XXXV, 1021 pages. 2004.

Vol. 3173: F. Yin, J. Wang, C. Guo (Eds.), Advances in Neural Networks – ISNN 2004. XXXV, 1041 pages. 2004.

Vol. 3172: M. Dorigo, M. Birattari, C. Blum, L. M. Gambardella, F. Mondada, T. Stützle (Eds.), Ant Colony, Optimization and Swarm Intelligence. XII, 434 pages. 2004.

Vol. 3171: A.L.C. Bazzan, S. Labidi (Eds.), Advances in Artificial Intelligence – SBIA 2004. XVII, 548 pages. 2004. (Subseries LNAI).

Vol. 3170: P. Gardner, N. Yoshida (Eds.), CONCUR 2004 - Concurrency Theory. XIII, 529 pages. 2004.

Vol. 3166: M. Rauterberg (Ed.), Entertainment Computing – ICEC 2004. XXIII, 617 pages. 2004.

Vol. 3163: S. Marinai, A. Dengel (Eds.), Document Analysis Systems VI. XI, 564 pages. 2004.

Vol. 3162: R. Downey, M. Fellows, F. Dehne (Eds.), Parameterized and Exact Computation. X, 293 pages. 2004.

Vol. 3160: S. Brewster, M. Dunlop (Eds.), Mobile Human-Computer Interaction – MobileHCI 2004. XVII, 541 pages. 2004.

Vol. 3159: U. Visser, Intelligent Information Integration for the Semantic Web. XIV, 150 pages. 2004. (Subseries LNAI).

Vol. 3158: I. Nikolaidis, M. Barbeau, E. Kranakis (Eds.), Ad-Hoc, Mobile, and Wireless Networks. IX, 344 pages. 2004.

Vol. 3157: C. Zhang, H. W. Guesgen, W.K. Yeap (Eds.), PRICAI 2004: Trends in Artificial Intelligence. XX, 1023 pages. 2004. (Subseries LNAI).